A Concise History of Buddhism

A Concise History of Buddhism

Andrew Skilton

Barnes & Noble Books
New York

This edition is reprinted by Barnes & Noble, Inc.,
by arrangement with Windhorse Publications, Birmingham UK.

2000 Barnes & Noble Books

ISBN 0-7607-2178-5

Printed and bound in the United States of America

00 01 02 03 MC 9 8 7 6 5 4 3 2 1

BVG

Contents

About the Author

Born in 1957 in Croydon, Surrey, Andrew Skilton began to develop an interest in Buddhism for a number of years before he was ordained as a member of the Western Buddhist Order in 1979, and given the Buddhist name Sthiramati. He worked for several years in the development of a Buddhist centre in Croydon, England, before moving to Bristol and initiating the activities of the Bristol Buddhist Centre in 1980. Increasingly drawn to the study of Buddhist doctrine and history, he studied for his first degree in Theology and Religious Studies, which he was awarded in 1988, at the University of Bristol. Having begun a study of the Sanskrit and Pāli languages there, he spent three years studying privately, translating and writing, before moving to Oxford in 1991 to start research for a doctoral thesis on the *Samādhirāja Sūtra*. He is currently a junior research Fellow at Wolfson College, Oxford, and a Fellow of the Royal Asiatic Society. In collaboration with Kate Crosby, he has recently completed a translation and study of Śāntideva's *Bodhicaryāvatāra*, published by Oxford University Press in 1996 in their World's Classics series. Amongst other projects, he is currently working on a biography of the Buddha and a compilation of early Buddhist scriptures.

The Pronunciation of Sanskrit

In this book, technical terms are usually quoted in Sanskrit in preference to Pāli, unless direct reference is being made to a Pāli source. All references to the Pāli Canon are to the editions of the Pāli Text Society. Where reference is made to a complete sutta, the number of the sutta only is given. Where reference is made to a passage from a sutta, volume and page numbers are given for the Pāli text (as is the standard practice). In the English translations published by the Pāli Text Society, these numbers are usually to be found at the head of the page, on the inner margin.

The use of Sanskrit and Pāli terms in this book has been unavoidable. They have been printed with the standard diacritical marks used for transcribing the forty-eight letters of the Sanskrit alphabet into the twenty-five of the Roman alphabet. Readers without any knowledge of Sanskrit or Pāli may find this daunting, but the guide below offers approximate equivalents for those sounds that differ from standard southern British English pronunciation. The 'short' vowels, i.e. a, i, and u, are voiced more briefly than the others which are known as 'long' vowels. Stress is usually placed on the penultimate syllable of a word, unless that syllable contains a short vowel followed by a single consonant, in which case the stress is displaced back towards the beginning of the word on to a syllable without those characteristics. For example, the stress is placed on the first syllable in the word *śāsana*. Where possible compound terms have been hyphenated to ease pronunciation.

A guide to pronunciation is given overleaf.

The vowels are pronounced as in the following words:

a *as in* cut ā *as in* cart i *as in* kick
ī *as in* keep u *as in* soot ū *as in* suit
e *as in* hay ai *as in* high o *as in* oat
au *as in* out

The pronunciation of the semi-vowel ṛ is similar to the 'r' sound in words like 'trip' or 'pretty', but with some rolling of the sound.

The consonants correspond to their English equivalents, with the following qualifications:

g *as in* god c *as in* church j *as in* jay
ṭ and ḍ as English t and d, but with the tongue tip curled up and backwards against the roof of the mouth.
t and d as English t and d, but with the tongue tip against the back of the upper front teeth.
ś and ṣ *as in* sh

The nasal sounds, i.e. ṅ, ñ, ṇ, n, and m:

Before a consonant they make the natural spontaneous nasal sound associated with that consonant:

ṅk *as in* trunk ṅg *as in* sang
ñc *as in* crunch ñj *as in* binge
ṇṭ *or* nt, *as in* tent, but with the above distinctions.
ṇḍ *or* nd, *as in* bend, but with the above distinctions.
mp *as in* pimp mb *as in* bimbo
The *anusvarā*, ṁ, is a pure nasal and can replace any of the above sounds.

Before vowels:

ṅ (does not occur) ñ *as in* banyan
ṇ and n *as in* nit, but with the same distinction made between ṭ and ḍ and t and d. m *as in* mope

The aspirated consonants are those which are shown followed immediately by the letter h, e.g. gh, ch, th, ṭh, etc., and should be pronounced as indicated, but with an audible out-breath. Note that 'th' is *not* pronounced as in 'there' or 'thick', and 'ph' *not* as in 'pheasant'.

Doubled consonants are pronounced as such:

sadda as in sled-dog The combination kṣ *as in* duck-shoot.

PREFACE

BUDDHISM DESCRIBES ITSELF IN MANY WAYS. Amongst a number of roughly synonymous terms, *āgama* is one that I find particularly evocative. It is used to denote the textual heritage, particularly the collections of the Buddha's discourses, which were themselves called *āgama* in those schools of Indian Buddhism that used Sanskrit as their scriptural language. More literally, the term means 'that which comes' in the sense of something being handed down into the present by an existing tradition, and so, to me, it implies not just a body of texts, but also the received methods for interpreting, understanding, and applying those texts – which in their turn inform and are informed by the institutions of Buddhism. It is in these broader implications that I find the term the most suggestive, for it emphasizes that Buddhism is something handed down, something transmitted, for the last twenty-five centuries, by successive generations of Buddhists.

Despite this continuity, the Buddhist tradition is bewilderingly diverse, and this is one of the main reasons for my interest in writing a book of this kind. Since my first meaningful contact with Buddhism, some eighteen years ago, I have been surprised, amazed, frustrated, and perplexed by this diversity – I will not try to measure the proportion of each. Primarily it has been a source of inspiration to try to realize its central ideals, but also of delight, of refreshment, and at times of disbelief at some of the apparent or real contradictions. In the longer run, it has provoked a great curiosity.

I am not the first to feel this curiosity, for the tradition has had its historians in many ages prior to our own. Nor am I alone in the present century, which has witnessed the production of so many attempts to unravel the knots of local traditions and weave a single cloth of Buddhist history. I have always wanted to ask questions about the Buddhist tradition, questions to which its own answers sometimes seemed incomplete or beside the point to my sceptical mind. I have no doubt that this work reflects that urge, but I also know that scepticism is a widespread feature of our modern society. We have been born in a sceptical age and a sceptical culture, but I remain convinced that to be sceptical is not to be irreligious, nor is it to lack faith. However, it does bring with it its own dangers, particularly the twin poisons of superiority and cynicism, and I hope that I have avoided both in this treatment of the Buddhist tradition.

My ambitions for this 'history' were multiple. It began life at the request of Dharmacāri Lokamitra, as a response to the needs of the study programme run by the Trailokya Bauddha Mahāsaṅgha Sahayak Gaṇa (the Indian wing of the Friends of the Western Buddhist Order). However, it was also written with a wider audience in mind, in the hope that, despite its fairly specific brief, this short work might also be of interest and use to anybody who would like to gain a picture of the historical development of Buddhism as a whole.

I hope that this book will provide a compact overview of the history of Buddhism as a basis for further study, be it of doctrine or of history. In part I have wanted to counterbalance the common weakness of more traditional histories of Buddhism, devised by Buddhists themselves, to present a historical account of the 'internal' history of Buddhism, by which I mean the development of doctrines and schools. What I would see as the 'external' history, the history of external events and institutions, located within a chronological structure, is of course no less important, and I have tried to link these two 'histories' together. In particular I have tried to 'locate' features of the Buddhist tradition within a chronological and developmental structure. I have imagined that it would therefore be of interest both to students of Buddhism and to Buddhists themselves, both of whom might have some knowledge of the subject but who wish to get an overview – either as a prelude to more intensive or specialized study, or as a means of contextualizing their own experience of the Dharma.

I am aware that I have given most space to the history of Indian Buddhism. Since Buddhism as a major religious institution effectively died out in India roughly seven centuries ago, is this not perverse? My own view is that to understand the Buddhist tradition as a continuous 'coming down' into the present, one has to have a sound grasp of the developments the tradition underwent within India, its homeland, which in their turn stimulated, or at least provided a starting point for, the tradition when transferred to new countries and cultures. In this sense the book falls into two parts – a more detailed treatment of Buddhism in India, followed by a briefer treatment of Buddhism in the rest of Asia. Without doubt, the history of Buddhism within each country or region outside India deserves its own lengthy book, and many of them already have several. To master the complexity of Buddhist history throughout Asia is beyond the competence of any single author, and this natural limitation is reflected in the proportionate treatment of the two areas. Even so, I hope that my purpose here, which has been to provide the reader with a starting point from which to understand those non-Indian developments, has been fulfilled.

Many accounts of Buddhist history set about writing a history of those schools that are represented in the modern world. One result of this approach is the tendency to emphasize these modern schools out of their due historical importance. This is especially the case with the Theravāda, since this school is also the inheritor of the sole complete recension of the early canon to have survived in its original language, i.e. Pāli. Like the fabric of much early history, that of Buddhism consists more of gaps than narrative, so that the Pāli Canon stands as the greatest single resource of historical data that we possess for Buddhist and Indian history of this period. In the past, introductory books have all too easily slipped into the anachronism of taking the modern Theravāda, or its canon (which undoubtedly shows some degree of sectarian editing), as representative of the original teaching of the Buddha and that of the early schools in their entirety. The Pāli texts could be used with more care and discrimination when discussing the nature of the teaching in the early centuries.

My narrative extends only as far as the 19th century. The description of modern Buddhism is beyond the scope of the task originally set me, and I have been happy to observe that limitation. Nevertheless, I hope this work will help the reader towards a balanced view of the present-day make-up of the Buddhist world, and to achieve an understanding of the roots of present-day forms of Buddhism that are to be met 'on the high street'. Recent centuries of Buddhist history do not always make inspiring reading, and I suspect that the history of more remote centuries often does so only because of the lack of real historical data for the period concerned. I remain convinced that royal patronage and material wealth are not necessarily markers of spiritual health. The idea of a previous golden age contrasted with the present corrupt one is common in religious traditions, no less in Buddhism, probably from the start. On occasion the Buddha himself rued the passing of a more spiritually able following, and predictions of the demise of Buddhism abounded within the tradition itself.[1] I suspect that corruption of one sort or another has been present in the Buddhist tradition from the time of the Buddha, be it the corruption of the mere nominal membership of the Saṅgha, or that of a more vicious character. The acknowledgement and understanding of this fact in the history of the tradition is one of the major tools for the protection of that tradition in the present day, and for securing its future. Some Buddhists scoff at the relevance of the history of Buddhism, apparently seeing it as a kind of sparkling but dispensable ornament to the real business of mastering doctrine and practice. While I agree that the Dharma is essentially ahistorical, in that it speaks of universal truths and addresses the universal human situation, its history reveals to us the attempts of our predecessors to implement those doctrines and practices in society, and to grapple with the biggest obstacle to achieving that goal – namely, human nature. As modern Buddhists we ignore the lessons of our own history at our peril.

ACKNOWLEDGEMENTS

There is something of a time lapse between the discoveries of researchers and the gradual transmission of their results, by a kind of intellectual osmosis, through to popular works available from the bookshops. Several decades can pass, it seems, without new information and perspectives making any public impact. It has therefore been a further intention of mine to integrate the results of recent scholarship into the broader picture of Indian Buddhism, and thereby revise some out dated 'facts' (whether scholarly or traditional). In this respect, it is also an attempt to bring together the worlds of the Buddhist practitioner and of the modern academic. As such it is only a minor contribution to a process of integration that has been under way for some while but which still has some distance to go. The small size of the work has, of course, meant that discussion of such research has not been possible, beyond a few instances. The factual core of the book is the work of many other people, and I do not claim any originality even for observations which are my own. I hope that some of the few annotations will help substantiate some of the less widely-known statements, while the bibliography will help direct readers towards more technical or detailed accounts. My broad brush-strokes of history are painted on a canvas woven by an international community of scholarship which gradually reveals to us the lineaments, if not always the spirit, of our heritage of Buddhist history. I take pleasure in singling out two scholars whose work has greatly helped my own perception of Buddhist history and doctrine, not least because I have been a student of both – Dr P.M. Williams of the University of Bristol and Prof. R.F. Gombrich of the University of Oxford. Underlying this all, however, is the work and inspiration of my Buddhist teacher, Sangharakshita.

Finally, I must offer thanks. I will begin with Lokamitra, who acted as *upanissaya-paccaya* for this book and whose work in India has often inspired me to make an effort. I also thank Dharmacāris Nāgabodhi, Tejananda, and Dharmapriya, and Elizabeth English, each of whom read the first draft of the book and offered much useful comment and encouragement. I also wish to thank Kate Crosby, of St Peter's College, Oxford, who gave the book a close reading, and whose suggestions prompted me to clarify and fill out my narrative and greatly improved the final product. I would also like to thank my mother, Gwen, who has wanted to help my work and has supported me financially to that end; my sister, Jennifer, at whose house I wrote the first draft in 1990; and Wolfson College, Oxford, in whose library I have revised that draft. Last but not least, thanks must go to Dharmacāri Śāntavīra of Windhorse Publications who has proof-read the text, patiently incorporated endless revisions, and fully exemplified the qualities expressed in his name.

Andrew Skilton
(Dharmacāri Sthiramati)
Wolfson College
Oxford
October 1994

Part 1

Buddhism in India

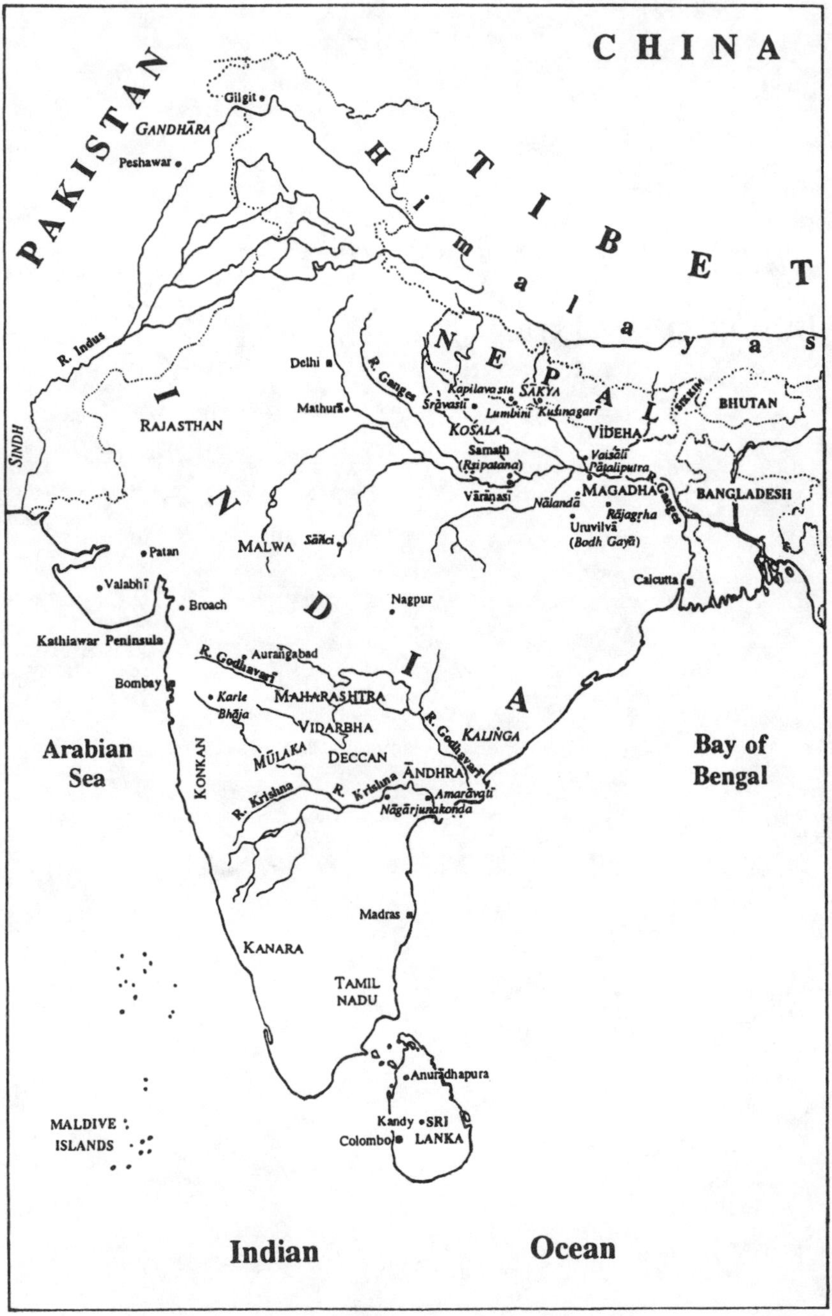

These maps are provided to offer general geographical orientation only. Countries are described by their modern political boundaries; ancient states and sites are given in italics.

1

The Ancient Indian Context: Buddhist Pre-history

Any account of the history of Buddhism must begin with the story of its founder, Siddhārtha Gautama, the historical Buddha. Yet, for us properly to appreciate this story, we need also to know a little of early Indian history, of the context within which Siddhārtha Gautama began his spiritual quest. The story of India's history is a long one, reaching back a millennium prior to the time of Siddhārtha Gautama, and for our purposes it is best to start with the first significant remains of civilization to have survived the ravages of time.

Like much history, that of early India was dominated by certain geographical features. To the north of the subcontinent runs the Himalayan mountain range, standing as a formidable physical barrier to contact with cultures to the north and east. The only break in this barrier is to be found in the mountain passes of Afghanistan, to the north-west of the subcontinent. There are also the two great river basins, that of the Indus in the north-west and the Ganges in the north-east of the subcontinent, each of which formed a fruitful and protective environment that could support a complex civilization.

The Indus Valley Civilization

The first of the two river basins to play a part in this story was that of the River Indus. Here, established some time during the third millennium BCE on the basis of the indigenous neolithic culture, there grew up a city-based civilization, once known as the 'Indus Valley Culture', supported by the wealth derived from agriculture, overseas trade, and fishing. The two greatest city settlements were at Mohenjo Daro and Harappa, for which reason this has also been termed the 'Harappan Culture'.

This society appears to have been highly organized, centralized, and very conservative, showing little change over many centuries. Attempts to reconstruct its mores and beliefs are largely speculative, though it is clear that some form of sophisticated ritual bathing was involved, implying a preoccupation with purity. The most suggestive items that have been discovered are numerous seals, used in extensive trading and especially common at coastal sites. These show a form of writing (as yet undeciphered) and tiny, strikingly beautiful pictures, some evidently of a ritual nature. One famous seal shows a masked human figure in a yogic posture, thought by some to be performing a primitive form of yoga or meditation.

A slow decline of this civilization began c.1200BCE, possibly as a result of environmental changes, most probably a change of direction in the flow of the River Indus, though there are also signs of warfare. However, this last evidence is not likely to have been linked with the coincidental appearance of invading tribes from the north-west. In all probability these newcomers found a culture in its death throes.

Vedic Culture

The exact nature of this invasion is disputed and more recent authors have suggested a model of cultural osmosis rather than military incursion.[2] However, the still dominant picture given of these newcomers is of successive waves of migrating nomadic tribes, pushed out from their homeland which originally stretched from central Europe to Central Asia, making their way south and east in search of new lands to occupy. These are now known as our own Indo-European ancestors, tribes of horse-riding warriors, who utilized the horse-drawn chariot as a weapon of war. Breaching the various passes through the Himalayas to the north-west of present-day India's frontiers, they began a long, slow, but inexorable sweep eastwards across the entire subcontinent, which was to occupy the next several centuries.

They brought with them their own characteristic culture, which included their own pantheon of gods such as Indra, Varuṇa, Rudra, the Vāyus, and so on, which were in many ways parallel to the ancient Greek pantheon, e.g. Dyaus Pitṛ, the Father Sky god, is undoubtedly cognate with the Greek Zeus Pater and the Roman Ju-piter. They also brought their own characteristic threefold division of society into priests, warriors, and cultivators. The first of these were special families of professional reciters of hymns and performers of ritual, the predecessors of the later *brāhmaṇa* class; these last two eventually becoming the familiar *kṣatriya* and *vaiṣya* classes.

They also brought some mysterious substance called *soma*, possibly alcohol or an hallucinogenic mushroom, which seems to have induced ecstatic trances. Whatever it may have been, it seems to have inspired many of the hymns and poems that have survived from this period and go to make up what are called the *Vedas*. The rituals performed by these specialists came to take on a special significance, as, by an elaborate system of correspondences, the stages and elements of the ritual were seen as mirroring and eventually controlling aspects of the universe – so that their correct performance ensured the proper continuance of the cosmos itself. Furthermore, just as the cosmos was sustained by the magical naming of objects performed by the priest, some of their number began to speculate that perhaps the universe arose from the 'One' and that to be able to name this 'One' would give human beings control over that which was the basis of the whole universe. In this respect, religious practice at this time could be seen as a search for power.

All this is known because of the survival of the texts produced by these people. It is not the case that they were written down from the beginning, since originally the tradition was (and still is) orally transmitted – kept within the bounds of the priestly brahmin families, and passed from father to son. Three great collections of this material were made, called the *Ṛg*, *Yajur*, and *Sāma Vedas*, and these formed what was regarded as the sacred threefold knowledge. A fourth *Veda* was compiled somewhat later, containing spells for the warding off of evil, and called the *Atharva Veda*. These compilations were in turn followed by two successive stages of composition which produced bodies of literature known as the *Brāhmaṇas* and the *Āraṇyakas*, in which a strong trend towards mystical speculation on the nature of the universe and its control through the magical process of 'naming' becomes increasingly manifest.

Shortly before the time of the Buddha himself, the earliest prose *Upaniṣads* were compiled. These, as their name suggests, deal with a secret teaching, which was to be passed from master to pupil only, for *upa-ni-ṣad* means 'to sit near'. They were regarded as the final stage in the evolution of the *Veda*, and were therefore known as the *Vedānta*, the 'end or culmination of the Veda'. The ritual elements so prevalent in the earlier texts are less important here, and in their place we find a preoccupation with a teaching, at that point secret and evidently shocking, concerning rebirth or transmigration. This concern in turn evidently provided further fuel to the search to find the 'One' which lay behind the cosmos, and through control of which (still by knowing and reciting its name) the disciple could gain control of the cosmos, and hence freedom from the cycle of repeated death.

The approach to this search was twofold – on the one hand people looked for that which was the basis of the external phenomenal world, the underlying essence of all external objects and things, and which came to be termed *brahman*; on the other hand they looked for the ultimately existent thing *within* the individual, that which supports life and consciousness in each of us, and which came to be termed the *ātman*. Perhaps inevitably, there came those with the ultimate secret teaching that identified these two, which said that *ātman* and *brahman* were one and the same. This 'insight' was encapsulated in the *Upaniṣadic* texts by such famous statements as *tat tvam asi*, 'thou art that', and *brahmo'ham*, 'I am brahman,' etc. By meditating upon these sayings, which encapsulated the ultimate insight into the nature of the cosmos of the *Upaniṣads*, the disciple was thought to internalize that insight, and thereby become free from the round of rebirth and death.

This then is a general, simplified picture of the religious background to the Buddha, but we should also make some mention of more general social changes that were significant at the time. Particularly we should note the spread of Iron Age technology through this same period, beginning c.800BCE, which allowed the clearing of vast tracts of virgin forest ready for cultivation – such that the entire Ganges basin had been colonized by c.600BCE – and which also facilitated a new type of warfare with its own military specialist, the *kṣatriya*, or warrior. New methods of agriculture, especially the iron plough, allowed for improved production and even a surplus of produce, which in turn could be used to support larger governmental and religious institutions.

There was extensive social upheaval as rival kings strove to establish ever larger kingdoms, gradually absorbing the earlier family- and tribe-oriented social structures of the Vedic period. By the time of the Buddha's birth only sixteen city-states existed in the central and north-eastern areas of India occupied by the Āryan invaders. Just as the development of the brahmaṇical religion had kept pace with the gradual movement of the Āryan tribes across the north of the subcontinent, so too the religion of the *Vedas* and *Brāhmaṇas* became increasingly associated with social orthodoxy, and with the growing centralized governments of the day.

One very important effect of this was the production of a new class of religious practitioner who rejected the older traditions of the brahmins and rejected their claim to a privileged knowledge of revealed wisdom (the *Vedas*) hereditary to their class. This was the *parivrājaka* or wanderer. The *parivrājaka* was a person who, dissatisfied with the restrictions of this developing society and with the ritualism of established religion, left their home and their role in society in order to wander at will in the world, supported by alms and seeking spiritual liberation. The Buddha himself was to join this class of religious wanderers at the beginning of his own quest for liberation.

We have substantial evidence of three approaches adopted by these *parivrājakas* to realize their quest.[3] There were those who emphasized transcendence, and who developed various techniques of meditation, in which the mind is calmed and controlled by concentration upon a single object. (Some people identify here a link with indigenous, pre-Āryan practices.) Then there were those who emphasized immanence, and the almost magical power that could be acquired through insight into the nature, not to say even the name, of that ultimate principle that lay behind the universe. (These would seem to have been heirs to the mainstream Vedic tradition.) There was also a third party, more concerned with the purity and pollution of the human body, who used various forms of asceticism to purify their soul so that it might, thus lightened of the burden of impurities, rise to the top of the spiritual universe. (These clearly had some connection with the tradition later known as Jainism, but at the time of the Buddha they were known as the Nirgrānthas, and headed by Mahāvīra.) The teachers of these heterodox schools were known as *śramaṇas* (Pāli *samaṇas*), which means literally 'one who is making an effort' or alternatively 'one fatigued [by the world?]'.

There were still other groups of wanderers with different philosophical views. Amongst these were the Ājīvakas – determinists, who were preoccupied with exact analysis of the present, and who held that all beings will progress towards perfection regardless of their own efforts;

the Lokāyatas – materialists, rather hedonistic in outlook, as they denied causality and said that one should act just as one pleases; there were the 'sceptics' – usually scorned as *amarāvikkhepikas* ('eel-wrigglers') in the Buddhist texts – who neither affirmed nor denied any particular doctrine or belief; and, of course, it is very likely that a large number of these wanderers had no spiritual quest at all, just preferring a life of relative freedom and lack of social responsibility. An account of the views of some contemporaries of the Buddha can be found in the *Brahmajāla* and *Sāmaññaphāla Suttas* of the *Dīgha-Nikāya*[4].

2

The Buddha

Having looked at the cultural and religious background to the Buddha's day, what of the Buddha himself? The Buddha was born in a town called Lumbinī, near Kapilavastu, the capital of the region now divided by the Indian and Nepalese border, which was the home of the Śākya clan. For many years and largely through the greater influence of Theravādin orthodoxy upon Western scholarship, the date of his birth has been accepted as 563BCE, based upon the ancient Sri Lankan chronicles; a second tradition, originating from the Indian mainland, places his birth a little over one hundred years later, c.450BCE. Recent research, based upon the *Dīpavaṁsa*, suggests that he was most likely born c.485BCE.[5]

At the time of his birth, among the foothills of the Himalayas, there were still some clan-based republics resisting the growing expansion of the new monarchies of the central Ganges basin. Among these was the republic of the Śākyas, and it was into this, as the son of the presiding ruler, that Siddhārtha Gautama was born. His father was a member of the ruling oligarchy, and also a warrior, and although it is quite likely that at this time the traditional brahmaṇical society described in the previous chapter had not yet made any great impact upon this region bordering the Ganges basin, it is the case that, when the Buddha travelled among brahmaṇical society, he felt that the most appropriate description he could give of his social background was that of the *kṣatriya* class. Later tradition, knowing only the monarchies which usurped the earlier republics, anachronistically dubbed Siddhārtha a 'prince' and his father a 'king'.

The life of the founder of the Buddhist *śāsana*, or dispensation, has from the beginning been of great interest to his followers. Yet the paradoxical result has been that, whilst there are quite a number of biographies of the Buddha, we cannot be sure what can reliably be taken to be fact and what may be the result of later devout and well-intentioned elaboration. Within the canon (as represented by the Pāli tradition) there are several sūtras which offer in a piecemeal fashion primarily biographical detail. The *Āriyapariyesana Sutta*[6] gives us an account of the Buddha-to-be's early career and Enlightenment, described in terms of the 'Noble Quest'; similar ground is covered in the *Bhayabherava*, *Dvedāvittaka*, and the *Mahāsaccaka Suttas*.[7] The *Mahāparinibbāna Sutta*[8] gives an account of the last months of the Enlightened One's life. The intervening years, during which, after his Enlightenment, the Buddha toured the countryside corresponding to the modern states of Bihar and eastern Uttar Pradesh, are the subject-matter of the bulk of the Buddha's discourses, or sūtras, as preserved in the Sūtra Piṭaka of the canon. These are not arranged with any biographical intent, and the reader must piece together a picture of the Buddha's teaching life from general reading amongst these texts.

It seems that biography proper was not necessarily the concern of the first generation of the Buddha's disciples, and furthermore that when it *was* undertaken it was accompanied by a tendency towards elaborating the basic story, a trait discernible even in the earliest 'biographies'. An important aspect of this elaboration was the recounting of numerous previous lives in which the Buddha-to-be, known as the Bodhisattva, performed countless meritorious deeds in preparation for the life in which he was to achieve Awakening. Among these biographies we can include the *Mahāvastu* of the Mahāsaṅghika School (c.2nd century BCE), the *Buddhacarita* written by the poet Aśvaghoṣa (1st century CE), the *Lalitavistara* of the Sarvāstivādin School (c.1st century BCE), the *Nidānakathā*, the Theravādin commentary to the *Jātakas* (4th century CE), and the *Abhiniṣkramaṇa Sūtra*, probably belonging to the Dharmaguptakas.

However, from all of these sources there is a central core of detail that remains consistent, and which we can assume reflects the true events of the Buddha's life, at least as perceived by his disciples. This 'core' biography has functioned as the archetypal model for the Buddhist over the centuries, and we can offer a summary account of the details here.

Siddhārtha Gautama was born to a life of privilege; his father, Śuddhodana, a man of wealth and power, his mother, Māyādevī, a woman of leisure and refinement. At his birth, a seer, Asita, predicted that the young boy was destined for either political or spiritual empire, and doubtless his parents felt this augury appropriate for their son. Perhaps for this reason they chose his personal name; variously, Sarvārthasiddha, 'one who has accomplished every goal', or Siddhārtha, 'one who has accomplished his goal'. His mother died shortly after his birth, and in his earliest years he was nursed and nurtured by his aunt, Mahāprajāpatī. Whilst preoccupied with the training appropriate to a young man of his position, his early life was characterized by luxury, for his father wished that his handsome son should be firmly attached to the advantages of wealth and power, and thereby choose the life of political empire. By his sixteenth year he had been provided with a young wife, Yaśodharā.

His father's plans were not to be successful, however, for around this time the young man began a physical and intellectual exploration of his environment that was to have far-reaching consequences. This period in his development is captured or symbolized by the story of the 'four sights', four formative experiences that befell the young man while he was travelling abroad in his carriage. Beginning with the appearance by the roadside of an old man, the first time Siddhārtha had ever truly understood the fact of inevitable old age, and followed by similar confrontations with disease and death, these shattering 'insights' into the human condition upset his complacency with his life of privilege and forced him to acknowledge that such painful and undignified conditions awaited him and his pretty wife, as surely as they awaited all other creatures. The fourth sight, a meeting with a wanderer, a *parivrājaka*, sowed a seed in his mind that, as he pondered his situation in the following months, was to grow into a conviction that there was an alternative to the passive acceptance of suffering and decay, but that this quest was one that required radical and even painful action.

The final event which seems to have tipped the balance of decision towards his yearning for the freedom to explore the 'Noble Quest', which was to lead to the spiritual empire predicted by Asita, was the birth to Yaśodharā of a boy. In frustration, he saw the birth of his son as the birth of a fetter.

His response to this event was to be decisive. Without the approval, or even the knowledge, of his parents, he stole away from his home, leaving behind wife and child, family and social status, pleasure and privilege. At the age of twenty-nine he cut his hair, donned the rag robes of a wanderer, and began his search for truth and liberation.

His first thought was to find a teacher, and he travelled south, towards Rājagṛha, where he met the king of Magadha, Bimbisāra – a period movingly described in the early poem, the *Pabbajjā Sutta* of the *Sutta Nipāta*.[9] He found his first teacher, one Ālāra Kālāma, who taught him a form of meditation that led to an exalted state of absorption, known technically as *ākiṁcanyāyatana*, the 'sphere or state of no-thingness'. However, whilst he eventually equalled his teacher in attainment, Siddhārtha recognized that such a state, lacking a moral and cognitive dimension,[10] had made no radical difference to his human condition, that he was still subject to old age, sickness, and death, and that his quest was not over. Though Ālāra Kālāma offered him co-leadership of his other pupils, Siddhārtha left in search of further guidance. A similar pattern unfolded with his next teacher, Udraka Rāmaputra, who schooled him in the attainment of a meditative absorption termed *naivasaṁjñānāsaṁjñāyatana*, the 'state or sphere of neither perception nor non-perception', and who eventually offered him sole leadership of his following. Again, this was not what Siddhārtha was looking for, and he now devoted himself to the cause of asceticism in the hope that this might reveal a resolution to his quest. For some five to six years he lived at Uruvilvā, on the Nairañjanā River, with five fellow ascetics, at first companions, and then followers. He carried self-torture to unprecedented extremes, holding his breath for long periods, and at a later point reducing his intake of food. The story of this phase of his search is told in the *Mahāsaccaka Sutta*.[11]

Having endangered his life by his wilful pursuit of asceticism, Siddhārtha again rejected his attainment, this time as dangerous and ultimately wasteful. He took food in reasonable quantities again, and was therefore rejected by his ascetic pupils who left him, and set out for the deer park at Ṛṣipatana, near present-day Benares. In a mood of profound resolution he sat beneath a tree on the banks of the Nairañjanā, where he recalled a natural and unforced experience of *dhyāna*, or meditative absorption, that had occurred to him in his youth as he was sitting beneath a rose-apple tree, and, taking this as indicative of a more balanced and harmonious approach to his quest, during the course of the night, through contemplating the mystery of death and rebirth, he eventually gained a new and profound insight into the nature of our condition, into the way things really are. This was his Enlightenment, his 'waking up' to the way things really are (*yathābhūta*), for which reason he came to be called Buddha, the 'one who has awoken'. This was in his thirty-fifth year.

It remains for me to give some account of the remainder of his life, of the career which lasted for another forty-five years and which took him back and forth across the countries of northern India, to the cities and towns of the central Ganges basin. Immediately after his Enlightenment he spent several weeks in the vicinity of the Bodhi Tree (a place later known as Bodh Gayā), absorbing and assimilating the impact of his transforming insight.[12] He experienced some doubts as to the value of trying to communicate this to others, but was entreated by the *brahmā*, or high deity, called Sahaṁpati, to do so for the benefit of those who might be able to understand his message. He thought first of his earlier teachers, Ālāra Kālāma and Udraka Rāmaputra, but realizing that they were by then dead, he remembered his ascetic companions who had left him in disgust, and to whom he now went at Ṛṣipatana (present day Sarnath). There he taught in the deer park, about six miles north of the main city, and by a slow process, prolonged because of their initial reluctance to receive teaching from him, he brought these five to the same insight that he himself had achieved at Bodh Gayā.

After this hard-won attainment, his teaching was rewarded by the successful instruction of a further fifty-five young men, whereupon he exhorted this initial group of sixty to wander, each on their own, the roads and by-ways of the land, teaching this same insight into the way things are, for the benefit of the many (*bahujanahitāya*). The Buddha continued to teach for a period of forty-five years. His Saṅgha, the community of his followers, grew quickly, and whilst he evidently enjoyed the pleasures of solitude,[13] the evidence of the sūtras suggests that he spent much of his time in urban centres, such as Rājagṛha, Vaiśālī, and Śrāvastī, where he would have the opportunity to contact the greatest number of people. Indeed, it appears that he spent the last twenty to twenty-five rainy seasons of his life in Śrāvastī,[14] the capital of Kośala, a large and wealthy city at the junction of two major trading routes, where an important lay follower called Anāthapiṇḍada had donated a pleasant park or glade for the use of the Buddha and his disciples.

At the age of eighty the Buddha grew seriously ill at Vaiśālī, and decided that he was to die, or enter his parinirvāṇa, three months hence. The immediate cause of death was a meal (of pork or truffles, we cannot be sure) received from a metal-worker called Cunda, which led to dysentery. He passed away among a grove of sal trees at Kuśinagara. His final words were *vayadhammā saṁkhārā, appamādena sampādetha,* 'All compounded things are liable to decay; strive with mindfulness.'[15]

Seven days later his remains were cremated, and the relics from this cremation distributed among the local rulers for incarceration in ten stūpas or memorial mounds.

3

The Buddha's Teaching

The Buddha was Enlightened at the age of thirty-five. He spent the rest of his life trying to communicate that experience to others, and he encouraged his disciples to do the same. The Buddha had 'awoken' to a liberating insight into the nature of the human condition. By his achieving this insight it is understood that the very nature of Siddhārtha Gautama had been radically changed. It had been changed so radically that he was no longer subject to continued death and rebirth in this world, which is the lot of the unenlightened being and in traditional terminology called *saṁsāra*. It is this insight, this radically transforming awareness of the world and of people, that forms the content of wisdom, or *prajñā*, in the Buddhist tradition.

Levels of Understanding

What can we say about the Buddha's Enlightenment? Can anything be said about it? From a certain point of view the answer to this last question would be an emphatic 'No!'; yet the evidence of the Buddha's own life is that the attempt was worth the trying. One would answer 'no' if one was reflecting upon the nature of the Buddha's insight, attained on that night, for it has always been understood that this insight was something that transcended the rational mind, that went beyond the workings of mere intellect, and it was for this reason that it had such a transforming effect, both upon the Buddha and those of his disciples who attained to that same vision. Therefore, transcending intellect and the vehicle of the intellect, namely words, the essence of the Buddha's insight is something which is beyond description. There are many accounts and formulas which describe the nature of Buddhist insight, yet ultimately they fall short of the experience itself – otherwise one could become Enlightened merely by reading a book, or listening to an exposition of the Dharma.

This distinction between levels of understanding, between levels of wisdom, is fully acknowledged in the Buddhist tradition, and is worked out as a graded ascent through three distinct levels of wisdom, or *prajñā*. Firstly, there is *śrutamayī prajñā*. This is wisdom which is merely 'heard', *śruta*. This refers to the sort of understanding which one has after something has been explained verbally, or read in a book. It is, if you like, the most superficial form of understanding that we can have. It is the stage in understanding at which one takes things on trust, on the word of another person.

At the second level, there is *cintamayī prajñā*. This is the wisdom or understanding which is developed through thinking, *cintā*, the kind of wisdom that one develops for oneself, through one's own sustained thinking upon a particular subject. It is important to remember that the three *prajñās* form a series of graded levels of wisdom, which means that the Buddhist tradition regards understanding through thinking as superior to that which has merely been heard from another. (This suggests that 'faith', in the sense of a passive belief of received – or revealed – dogma, is alien to the Buddhist outlook, and that when we come upon references to 'faith' in a Buddhist context, as we frequently do, it must carry some meaning other than that familiar to those with a theistic background.)

Thirdly, there is *bhāvanāmayī prajñā*, which is wisdom or understanding that is developed through *bhāvanā* – literally 'causing to become'. This level of understanding refers to the complete assimilation of a set of ideas into the depths of one's being. It refers to the deepest form of understanding that there is – an understanding in which one has not merely heard that something is the case, nor even thought of it for oneself; but, rather, that one has taken the matter totally to heart, and can no longer think, act, or perceive without that thinking, acting, or perceiving being permeated by one's new understanding. Furthermore, this wisdom, the highest level of understanding that is possible, is only attainable through an active practising of meditation.

THE BUDDHA'S INSIGHT

The insight which occurred on the night of the Buddha's Enlightenment is recounted in a number of sūtras, several different descriptions being used in different places. It is described in terms of the arising of the three *abhijñā*, the 'higher knowledges' (a name which is a clear rebuff to the Vedic threefold knowledge, i.e. the first three *Vedas*), which are the divine eye, remembrance of former existences, and the extinction of the biases (of unenlightenment). In other places it is described in terms of the Buddha's understanding of *pratītya-samutpāda* (or universal conditionality); in others still, in terms of the *skandhas* (the ultimate constituents of conditioned existence); whilst the *Āriyapariyesana Sutta*[16] has a description unique to itself. All this confirms the innate difficulty in the use of words to give an account of the Buddha's insight. Perhaps, therefore, it may be easier if we look instead at the first teachings, according to tradition, ever given by the Buddha, to the five ascetic disciples at Vārāṇasī. These are to be found in two sūtras, known as the *Dhammacakkappavattana Sutta*[17] and the *Anattalakkhaṇa Sutta.*[18] I shall deal with them as a single whole.

(a) THE CONDITIONED WORLD: THE THREE *LAKṢAṆAS*

We might begin with a phrase, already used several times as a shorthand description for the Buddha's insight – 'seeing things as they really are'. This is a reference to *yathā-bhūta-jñāna-darśana,* 'knowing and seeing things as they really are', a phrase that appears in many sūtras.

The sense of the expression is that the nature of the Buddha's insight was such that he saw the universe and the human situation as it really is, implicitly stating at the same time that unenlightened mankind does not, indeed cannot, see it so.

How then did the Buddha see the world? The tradition tells us that he saw the world, and everything in it (including the deities of other religions, as well as human experience) as being characterized by three *lakṣaṇas,* three qualities or marks. These are *anitya, duḥkha,* and *anātman,* or, in English, the 'transitory' or 'impermanent', the 'painful' or 'unsatisfactory', and 'that devoid of a self' or 'essence'.

i. Anitya: *Impermanence*

The first, the *lakṣaṇa* or mark of impermanence or *anitya* (Pāli *anicca*), says that all conditioned things are transitory, or passing. Everything within the universe was seen by the Buddha as having both a beginning and therefore necessarily an end to its existence. This was the insight he gained through the first and second of the *abhijñā*, that all beings arise and pass away, life upon life. This is reflected in the cosmology of Buddhism, which depicts a universe of infinite space and time in which innumerable universes arise and then disappear; as also it is reflected in the microcosmic world of the smallest perceptible particles, which are conceived not as static atoms (a concept rejected by modern physicists too), but as ever-changing patterns of interacting energy. Moreover, the universe is not made up of regions occupied by the eternally damned or saved, but is formed by objectified mental states. In other words, subjective states of mind are experienced as perceptible worlds which, though they may last for aeons, are bound to a dissolution upon the exhaustion of the mental impulses that created them. The individual person, too, is born and dies, and throughout a fleeting life changes from day to day, from moment to moment. Nothing remains unchanged.

ii. Duḥkha, *and the Four Truths of the Noble Ones*

This brings us to the second mark of conditioned existence, that of *duḥkha* (Pāli *dukkha*), suffering or unsatisfactoriness. Not only is *duḥkha* the second of the three *lakṣaṇas*, it is also the subject of one of the most famous teachings of Buddhism, the doctrine of the Four Truths of the Noble Ones, the *catvāri āryasatyāni*. This famous teaching follows an ancient medical formula, in which one first states the nature of an illness, then the conditions which have given rise to its existence, next whether the condition can be cured, and finally the means for bringing about that cessation. There are various other instances in which other states or conditions are analysed in this way by the Buddha and his disciples, and it would be wrong to think that it was only suffering, only *duḥkha*, that was accorded this kind of treatment.[19] The first of the Four Truths is the truth of *duḥkha*. This was the Buddha's diagnosis of the sickness of humankind.

Having discussed the first *lakṣaṇa*, we can understand the basis for the suggestion that conditioned existence is a source of suffering. The point is not that life is solely painful, nor that pain is more real than pleasure, but rather that the pleasant and the painful in life are interconnected. At the simplest level this amounts to realizing that some pleasures bring with them a reflex experience of regret or remorse. The consumption of a cream cake, a glass of beer, or a cigarette might indeed be pleasurable now, but each carries with it the potential for suffering – be it obesity, heart disease, or just a hangover or bad breath. But it also refers to the fact that the experience of any pleasure, however innocent, will induce some suffering when the pleasant experience finishes. Here we can at last begin to see the connection between this *lakṣaṇa* and the previous one, for it is an undeniable psychological fact that we always wish the pleasurable and enjoyable to continue, and are frustrated, if not bereft, when the object of our delight, be it gross or subtle, be it possessions or a treasured companion, are taken away from us, or we cease to enjoy them. The problem for mankind, said the Buddha, is that these things will always be taken away, for, as was stated by the first *lakṣaṇa*, all conditioned things, all objects, all people, all mental states, all worlds, are transitory. Because all these things pass away, they are all *duḥkha*, all unsatisfactory.

Does this make Buddhism pessimistic? Historically, this accusation has a certain irony, for, rather than at the Buddha, we must look to the contemporary systems of the Ājīvakas and even the Brahmaṇical orthodoxy to find the truly pessimistic approach to man's condition. For it is there that we find total resignation to one's lot in life, a fatalism that culminates in the teaching of the *Bhagavad Gītā*, that each of us is to perform our allotted duty in life without any thought for the human consequences of those actions. But if we look at the Buddha's first discourse, which contains his full teaching upon the subject of *duḥkha*, we can see that he propounds Four Truths, not just one. Whilst he identifies the problem of suffering in the first of these four Truths, and the cause of suffering in the second (this being the greed and hatred that result from our profound spiritual delusion), the third Truth is a firm statement that it is possible for us to transcend the suffering that characterizes our conditioned existence. Moreover, the fourth Truth sets out to describe the means by which we can each achieve this transformation. This means is the *āryāṣṭāṅgikamārga*, the Eightfold Path of the Āryas, or Noble Ones, the path of practice that leads from the world of dissatisfaction to an experience of freedom and bliss.

iii. Anātman: *The Absence of Selfhood; and* Pratītya-Samutpāda: *Dependent Origination*

To understand the third *lakṣaṇa, anātman,* we must remind ourselves that it was axiomatic to the brahmaṇical religion of the 5th century BCE that each living creature possessed a self, *ātman,* which was pure, subtle, eternal, and which passed from one life to the next. Needless to say, in the light of the first of these *lakṣaṇas,* this theory was not allowed to stand unquestioned. Indeed, it only requires a rigorous following through of the implications of the first *lakṣaṇa* to arrive at the third, *anātman,* or not-self. For, just as all aspects of the external world are seen to be impermanent, continually changing, so too is the individual person seen not as containing some everlasting essence or soul, temporarily embodied on this earth, but as an uninterrupted flow of mental states and events which arise upon conditions and in their turn set up further mental states.

But this *lakṣaṇa* is not to be taken only literally. In another sense it stands as a warning against the false perception of the world that arises from our mental habit of naming things, of habitually assigning the objects of our world to arbitrary conceptual categories which do not really match experience. This is well illustrated by the example of the leaf, which in the autumn turns from green to red. We naturally assume that there is a thing called a leaf, which has undergone a change of attribute – in this case of colour. But the Buddhist says that this is not really so. The leaf is not a thing, it has no essence or *ātman* that exists aside from the collection of its attributes. Could we seriously consider the existence of the leaf without any colour? The very existence of the leaf as an entity is inseparably tied up with its colour and its other attributes. What the Buddhist tradition says is that the leaf, in reality, is the sum total of its conditioning factors and various parts. In our example, the red leaf arises, neither entirely different nor wholly the same, in dependence upon the former green leaf. Thus, whilst the first *lakṣaṇa* states that everything changes, the third points out that there is in fact no universe of fixed, static things that can change. To abstract fixed entities from the continuous flux of changing events around us, and to say that change is something that happens to these 'fixed entities', is delusion.

This example also illustrates the meaning of another teaching in the Buddha's first discourse, the Middle Way. This had a dual sense, for the

Buddha referred to a path between sensual indulgence and self-destructive asceticism (both of which he had already explored in his own life prior to his Awakening), and to one between the metaphysical extremes of eternalism and nihilism. He taught that things neither exist permanently, nor have absolutely no existence. Like the leaf, where a red leaf arises in dependence upon a green leaf, neither entirely different from its cause, nor wholly the same, so all other conditioned things arise in dependence upon other factors, neither entirely different nor wholly the same. The most important sphere in which this principle operates is the moral or ethical sphere, for it was here that the Buddha demonstrated that all intentional actions, *karman*, have consequences.[20] The general principle he termed *pratītya-samutpāda*, the principle of 'dependent origination'. In order to explain this principle as it operated on the ethical level, at later points in his teaching career he analysed the human condition, showing the various stages by which past actions condition future mental states. Through this analysis it becomes possible for people to break out of habitual negative actions, and to transform their lives in conformity with the Enlightened mind of the Buddha. The most elaborate example of this analysis is one which numbers twelve *nidānas* or links in the cycle of conditioning in which we are grasped.[21] We can also see that the Four Truths are simply a practical application of this same principle, illustrating the conditions for the arising and the cessation of *duḥkha*.

iv. Conclusion

The three *lakṣaṇas* characterize the whole of conditioned existence, of saṁsāra. In a sense they can be seen as a refutation of the *Upaniṣadic* teaching that Reality was *saccidānanda*, 'existent, conscious, and blissful'.[22] The Buddha realized that what the *Upaniṣads* described as *sat*, existence, was *anitya*, impermanent; what was *cit*, mind, was really *anātman*, lacking selfhood; and what was thought to be *ānanda*, bliss, was really *duḥkha*, unsatisfactory. One could say that the essence of the Buddha's insight, the core of his wisdom, was the understanding, assimilated to the depths of his being, that all conditioned things change. If we then ask why *duḥkha* and not *anitya* was the subject of his first discourse, we can only surmise that his interest was in speaking to people and to their experience of the world. Very often the Buddha is likened to a doctor, and it is in this role that he wished to address himself to the immediate problems of the world.

(b) NIRVĀṆA: THE UNCONDITIONED

In the last pages we have discussed the Buddha's insight into the nature of conditioned existence, of saṁsāra. Can anything be said about nirvāṇa, the state the Buddha achieved upon his Enlightenment? Again the answer should be no, for, being unconditioned, the state of nirvāṇa is totally outside the conditioned world, the world that we know in our unenlightened state. But we can devise a provisional description by looking again at the *lakṣaṇas*. In so far as the *lakṣaṇas* were applied to conditioned things, we can assume that the unconditioned is characterized by the opposite of the *lakṣaṇas* of the conditioned. Thus, when it says in the *Dhammapada*: '"All conditioned things are impermanent." When with understanding one sees this one becomes weary of suffering. This is the Way to Purity,' we can perhaps understand that the unconditioned is something that is permanent and lasting; when it says: '"All conditioned things are painful." When with understanding one sees this one becomes weary of suffering. This is the Way to Purity,' we can understand that the unconditioned is satisfying, even blissful; but of the third *lakṣaṇa* it says: '"All things (whatsoever) are devoid of unchanging selfhood." When with understanding one sees this one becomes weary of suffering. This is the Way to Purity.'[23] Here we must understand that even the unconditioned cannot be characterized by *ātman*, by selfhood. In terms of human qualities it is clear from the sūtras that Buddhahood is a state of profound wisdom, extensive compassion, and upwelling energy.

> *And is it possible to consider in this way what is perishable, painful, and liable to change: 'This is mine. I am this. This is my self'?*
> *'Blessed One, That is not possible.'*[24]

4

The Path to Awakening

Did the Buddha offer only a vision, an insight into our condition, or did he also teach his disciples a means of effecting change? The answer, of course, is that he did teach a path leading to liberation, and the sūtras record many accounts of practices that help one towards Awakening. The most famous of these is that of the Eightfold Path of the Noble Ones, the *āryāṣṭāṅgikamārga*, the subject of the Buddha's fourth Truth. In essence this consists of eight *aṅgas*, or 'factors', the perfection of which lead to liberation, or Awakening: the first two are Right Understanding and Right Resolve – the cognitive and volitional aspects of wisdom, which correspond to the deepening understanding and integration in the individual of the insight of the Buddha, as described in the previous chapter. Right Speech, Action, and Livelihood, the third to fifth factors of the path, are essentially ethical in character, and seek to guide the practitioner in the proper conduct of body and speech, as do the first two for the mind. Right Effort, Mindfulness, and Concentration are concerned with the cultivation of mind and heart through meditation. Thus we can see that the Eightfold Path falls into three divisions: *śīla* (ethics), *samādhi* (meditation), and *prajñā* (wisdom), a threefold division of the path that became almost ubiquitous. In the same way as the Eightfold Path begins with Right Understanding and Right Resolve, we have already begun our account of the path with our discussion of wisdom in the previous chapter. It remains to give a general account of *śīla* and *samādhi*.

Śīla

Being neither the edicts of an irrational deity, nor merely the rules of membership of a sect, the ethical principles upheld by the Buddha were described as 'principles of training' or precepts, *śikṣāpada*, of which there are lists of various lengths, including five, eight, and ten items. The most comprehensive formula of ten ethical precepts is the *daśakuśalakarmapatha*, the path of ten skilful actions, which consists of the following undertakings: to avoid all taking of life and to cultivate loving kindness; to avoid taking what is not given and to cultivate generosity; to abstain from all sexual misconduct and to cultivate physical contentment; to abstain from telling lies, from harsh speech and slander, and from frivolous and senseless speech, and to cultivate in their stead speech that is truthful, kindly and gracious, helpful and harmonious; to avoid covetousness and to cultivate tranquillity of mind; to abandon malevolence and to cultivate compassion; and, finally, to abandon false views and to cultivate wisdom – all ten catering for the full person by encompassing the activities of body, speech, and mind.[25]

The more widely known set of five precepts, *pañcaśīla*, includes the first four of the above ten, and concludes with the undertaking to abstain from all mind-clouding intoxicants, cultivating mindfulness in their place. Overall, these two sets of precepts describe the natural, spontaneous behaviour of an Enlightened person, and through their practice the Buddhist helps his own behaviour to conform with that of the Buddha.

Not to be confused with the *daśakuśalakarmapatha* are the ten precepts binding upon all novices and monks, which comprise the *pañcaśīla* plus abstention from eating after midday; from dancing, singing, music, and shows; from garlands, scent, cosmetics, and adornments; from luxurious beds; and from accepting gold and silver (i.e. money). In South-east Asia eight precepts are observed by devout lay men and women, *upāsakas* and *upāsikās*, on full and new moon days. These are the same as the ten precepts of the novice and the monk, except that the seventh and eighth are merged as one, and the last, prohibiting gold and silver, is dropped.

Samādhi

Meditation is seen as the most direct method for the transformation of consciousness from its unenlightened to its Enlightened state. Numerous meditation techniques were taught by the Buddha to his various disciples, who often chose one rather than another according to the temperament of the person concerned. On occasion, each meditation technique is shown leading to full Enlightenment. These techniques include practices involving the recollection of the six *smṛti* (Pāli *sati*), or remembrances (of the Buddha, the Dharma, the Sangha, of the rewards of ethical conduct, of *dāna* or generosity, and of the happy state of the gods); or of the body, including the stages of its decomposition; the reflection upon death; the analysis of the elements; concentration upon a coloured object or device (*kasina*); and even the contemplation of the loathsomeness of food. But foremost among the techniques recommended by the Buddha must be two: the mindfulness of the breath, and the immeasurable (*apramāṇa*) contemplations – the latter consisting of the development of loving kindness (*maitrī*), compassion (*karuṇā*), sympathetic joy (*muditā*), and equanimity (*upekṣā*). The states to which the practice of these techniques lead are described in at least two ways: either in a series of superconscious states termed *dhyāna*, characterized by an ever-simplified state of absorption or concentration; or in terms of the entry into what are called the *brahma-vihāras*, or the Abodes of Brahmā, these being associated exclusively with the immeasurable contemplations. Whilst later Theravādin orthodoxy relegated these latter to a secondary role, the sūtras record incidents in which the *brahma-vihāras* are used in the cultivation of liberating insight.[26] Meditations leading to these tranquil states are known as *śamatha* meditations, and are contrasted to *vipaśyanā* or insight meditations, usually involving the practice of mindfulness, which inculcate the cognitive transformation by which the practitioner comes to see 'the way things really are'.[27]

The *Bodhyaṅgas*

In contrast to the Eightfold Path, it is of interest to examine briefly a formulation of the Path that reflects its cumulative character. The *bodhyaṅgas*, the 'factors of *bodhi* (Awakening)', are a series of seven stages or factors, each arising in dependence upon the full realization of the preceding factor.

(a) They begin with *smṛti*, or awareness, usually understood as awareness of the body, feelings, the mind and its thoughts, and finally of *dharmas* – these to be understood either as the objects of mind, or as the Dharma (Teaching) and the Reality it represents.

(b) From general awareness one moves to awareness of one's mental states in particular, through the investigation of mental factors, *dharma-vicaya*, and the identification of those mental states which are positive and conducive to the spiritual life.

(c) The third factor is *vīrya*, energy, both in the sense of the effort required to cultivate the positive mental states identified in the previous stage and the energy released by the resultant state of increasing clarity upon which one has entered.

(d) The release and application of energy result in strong feelings of rapture (*prīti*), a delight and ecstasy which encompasses the entire psycho-physical organism.

(e) The grosser elements of *prīti* subsiding, one experiences the more refined, purely mental *praśrabdhi*, a state of spiritual happiness in which awareness of one's physical surroundings is minimized and one is absorbed in bliss.

(f) The tendency towards absorption innate in the previous stage impels one naturally towards the superconscious states denoted by the term *samādhi*. These are the *dhyānas*, and represent states of total, unforced, and harmonious psychic integration.

(g) The culmination of the Path is the state of *upekṣā*, equanimity. One is poised, free from wavering between psychological or spiritual opposites. It is a state of profound tranquillity and insight, and is synonymous with Enlightenment itself.

The Goal

The realization of the impermanence, suffering, and insubstantiality of mundane existence occurs by degrees, and involves the breaking of a succession of fetters (*saṁyojana*), ten in number: (a) belief in separate selfhood (*satkāya-dṛṣṭi*), (b) sceptical doubt (*vicikitsā*), (c) attachment to rules and rituals for their own sake (*śīlavrata-parāmarśa*), (d) sexual desire (*kāma-rāga*), (e) ill will (*vyāpāda*), (f) desire for existence in the world of form (*rūpa-rāga*), (g) desire for existence in the formless world (*arūpa-rāga*), (h) conceit (*māna*), (i) restlessness (*auddhatya*), and (j) ignorance (*avidyā*). The stages of development of insight are marked by the eradication or weakening of various groups of these fetters. Those who attain these stages are identified according to the resultant degree of liberation achieved and are said to have entered upon the 'Supermundane Path', *lokottaramārga*, in contrast to the 'mundane path' pursued prior to attaining insight. The first stage is known as that of the 'stream-entrant', or *śrotāpanna*, who has eradicated the first three fetters, and has only a further seven rebirths in the human or divine realms before full emancipation. The 'once-returner', or *sakṛdāgamin*, has weakened the fourth and fifth fetters, and will be reborn once more, in which lifetime he will be Enlightened. The 'non-returner', *anāgamin*, has broken all the first five fetters, and is reborn in a divine realm from where he gains Enlightenment. Finally, the *arhat*, the 'worthy one', has broken all ten fetters, and by doing so has won Enlightenment in this life. These four stages of realization represent the goal of individual spiritual practice, and together define the members of what came to be called the Ārya-Saṅgha. The Ārya-Saṅgha formally constitutes the Saṅgha Jewel for the early schools of Buddhism.

5

THE EARLY SAṄGHA

For one who goes for refuge to the Enlightened One, to the Truth, and to the Spiritual Community, who sees with perfect wisdom the four ariyan truths, namely, suffering, the origin of suffering, the passing beyond suffering, and the Eightfold Path leading to the pacification of suffering, this is a safe refuge, this is the best refuge. Going to such a refuge one is released from all suffering.[28]

THOSE WHO WISHED became followers of the Buddha by going to him for refuge. Often they spontaneously declared their desire so to do in direct response to the impact of the Buddha's teaching or even just his personality. The act of Going for Refuge expressed a wholehearted but radical reorientation of their being in sympathy with the living example of the Buddha himself, and the Dharma that he preached. There is evidence that this was first done by a simple twofold formula referring to the Buddha and his Dharma,[29] but this was soon replaced by the familiar threefold formula, as the Saṅgha itself grew in importance.[30] The first sixty disciples all had a direct and personal contact with the Buddha, but once they had begun to wander abroad they brought back an increasing number of others who wished to become the Buddha's disciples. To circumvent the inconvenience of this arrangement the Buddha instituted a criterion by which his disciples could themselves receive newcomers into the Saṅgha. This was by their taking of the threefold refuge in what have been known from the earliest times as the Three Jewels: the Buddha, as spiritual exemplar, the Dharma, his teaching, and the Saṅgha, the spiritual community: in Pāli, *buddhaṁ saraṇaṁ gacchāmi, dhammaṁ saraṇaṁ gacchāmi, saṅghaṁ saraṇaṁ gacchāmi* – 'I go for refuge to the Buddha, I go for refuge to the Dharma, I go for refuge to the Saṅgha.' This simple formula, thrice repeated, but deeply felt, was the essential criterion by which spiritual aspirants made a public commitment to the practice of the path of the Buddha. The practical working out of that commitment was and still is expressed by the observance of the precepts.

We have already seen how the Buddha sent his first sixty disciples to wander abroad among the villages and towns teaching his Dharma: 'Go now, monks, and wander, for the gain of many people, for the welfare of many people, out of compassion for the world, for the good, the gain, and the welfare of gods and men.'[31] From this we can gather that the Saṅgha, the spiritual community of the Buddha's disciples, was originally peripatetic, that it consisted of a loose organization of homeless wanderers, *parivrājakas*, who had no fixed abode but during the dry season would sleep in the open and beg for their food. For this reason they came to be called *bhikṣus* (Pāli *bhikkhus*), because they wished to share or partake (*bhikṣ*) in the food of the community.

During the rainy season they would stay together in a single place, perhaps a grove provided by a sympathetic householder, or maybe some clearing in the forest which still covered large parts of the Ganges basin. Some early sūtras provide a glimpse of their harmonious way of life, begging for their food, practising meditation, helping and supporting each other, and teaching newcomers as and when the opportunity arose.[32]

These early wanderers would meet periodically to renew their shared commitment and ideals. At first, the senior monk would recite the rules and individuals could then declare if they had broken any. Later, possibly under the pressure of embarrassment, there was a communal recitation of rules, after which monks confessed privately in pairs.[33] What they recited was probably in origin a simple statement of their shared ideals. This formed an early *prātimokṣa*, understood as either a 'purgative'[34] or as a 'bond',[35] and which some have identified in a passage attributed in the texts to a previous Buddha, Vipassī:

> *Patient endurance is the highest form of asceticism. 'Nirvāṇa is the highest,' say the Enlightened Ones. No true 'goer forth' is he who injures another, nor is he a samaṇa who causes harm to others.*
>
> *Not to do evil, undertaking the good, purifying one's mind: this is the dispensation of the Buddhas.*

> *Not to speak evil, not to injure, restraint according to the 'bond'* (pātimokkhe)*, restraint in food, secluded dwelling, the pursuit of higher mental states: this is the dispensation of the Buddhas.*[36]

During the life of the Buddha the Saṅgha was unified through the direct sense of refuge that each disciple had with him. After his death such formal recitation and confession helped the community cohere, especially as the Buddha had specifically stated that no individual was to succeed him as head of the order.[37] After the Buddha's death his followers were to take his teaching and the 'rule' (*vinaya*) of the spiritual community as their guides.[38] Though externally the Saṅgha was bound by the laws of the monarchist state (e.g. slaves and royal servants were not permitted to join the Saṅgha), internally its constitution reflected the ancient republican institutions of the clans among which the Buddha himself had been born.[39]

There seems to have been some flexibility in the early Vinaya, or Monastic Code, which was apparently defined to some degree, but not fully codified, by the time of the Buddha's death. He seems to have been willing to adapt the rules of conduct to the specific conditions and attainments of individuals. There are a number of references which show the Buddha stating a preference for mental discipline over bodily discipline,[40] and in one instance he explains to a *parivrājaka* called Udāyin that the other disciples admire the Buddha not for his observance of the *prātimokṣa* rules (only five are mentioned, and maybe these were all that were established at that time), but for his practice of *śīla*, *samādhi*, and *prajñā*, i.e. morality, meditation, and wisdom.[41]

In the first years the Saṅgha was undoubtedly most strongly established in the countries in which the Buddha himself had travelled and taught, i.e. Magadha and Kośala, though there were also significant numbers of followers in the more easterly regions of the Videhas, Koliyas, and Licchavis. Whilst there seems to have been less impact on the regions to the north and west, there is evidence from the oldest stratum of literature that more distant and isolated contacts were made there. The *Sutta Nipāta* records the interest shown in the Buddha by a teacher living in Mūlaka on the Godhavarī, in modern day Maharashtra, who sent sixteen of his disciples to question the Buddha.[42] Elsewhere it is recorded that some of these pupils, among them a certain Piṅgiya, converted by the Buddha, returned to the Auraṅgabad region and founded one of the first Buddhist communities there. The

Theragāthā mentions three *theras*, 'elders', who came from Maharashtra: Puñña, who came from Sopara and, converted by the Buddha at Śrāvastī, returned later to his place of birth and founded a community there. He was also responsible for the conversion of one Isidinna, from southern Konkan, and there was a third, Vaḍḍha, who was again converted by the Buddha, and came from Broach. All three, it appears, were merchants, this reflecting the strong support given to the Buddha by the merchant communities of his day. This picture of early isolated contacts in western India, outside of the Buddhist 'heartlands', doubtless holds true for other outlying regions.

During his lifetime the Buddha trained a succession of illustrious disciples whose characters are depicted in the sūtras. There was Kauṇḍinya, the first of the five ascetics to realize Awakening; Śāriputra, the expert on doctrine, and his friend, possessor of supernatural powers, Maudgalyāyana; Ānanda, the Buddha's cousin and companion for almost thirty years, and witness to much of the Buddha's teaching over that time; Upāli, the expert upon matters of the Saṅgha's 'rule', and Aṅgulimāla, the reformed tantric practitioner.[43] There were female disciples too, starting with the Buddha's aunt and foster-mother, Mahāprajāpatī, who had had to beg the Buddha and enlist the help of Ānanda before the Buddha would allow her to enter the community of wanderers.[44] Members of the Buddha's family followed him into the Saṅgha, including his son Rāhula, and both he and the Buddha's father, Śuddhodana, became arhats. In general, the evidence of early texts, particularly the *Thera-* and *Therī-gāthās*, seems to suggest that the greater proportion of the ordained Saṅgha was drawn from the *brāhmaṇa* and *kṣatriya* classes, though it is very clear that membership was open to all, and that the Buddha specifically denied the spiritual validity of class distinctions, maintaining that true excellence was to be found in wisdom and ethical conduct, and not in birth.[45]

The Buddha also attracted many lay followers, people impressed by his teaching and his person but unable or unwilling to adopt the homeless life. In the sūtras the Buddha is often depicted instructing such people (who included his father) e.g. the *Sigālovāda Sutta*,[46] and many, such as the merchant Anāthapiṇḍada, became generous patrons of the Saṅgha, giving parks and monasteries for their use.[47] Lay followers were usually encouraged to give material support to the monastic community, if they could not join it themselves, and there is evidence that the full teaching was not disclosed to them,[48] but there were some lay followers, such as Ugra (Pāli Ugga), who, without joining the monastic order, lived a life of full commitment to the Three Jewels – Going for Refuge, observing the precepts, and teaching the Dharma.[49]

Episodes such as the Buddha's visit to a disciple called Soṇa demonstrate the affectionate and considerate interest the Buddha showed in his disciples, and also reveals that, even in his own day, individuals memorized small sections of teaching. At the Buddha's request, Soṇa recited the section of 'eights', now the fourth book of the *Sutta Nipāta*.[50] Even when separated from their teacher, the disciples responded to him with deep faith, as witnessed by the elderly Piṅgiya.

With mind I see him as by eye,
In earnest, brahman, day and night;
I brighten night in praising him;
Hence not as absence deem I that.
With faith and joy and heart alert
Naught turneth me from his behest:
Unto what realm the quickening sage
Doth move, to that then I am drawn.
Since I am frail and worn with age
Thither my body goeth not,
But with strong purpose e'er I move
And so my heart is linked with him.[51]

6

The Councils

Whilst the early Saṅgha soon established a regular rhythm of fortnightly *upavasatha* (Pāli *uposatha*) meetings, which helped unify and regulate the life of the community, there also occurred, during the first four to five hundred years of its life, several larger meetings, or Councils, in which matters of greater importance were discussed and clarified. Traditions vary as to the number of these, and much modern thinking upon them has been (perhaps unduly) influenced by the picture presented in the accounts preserved, and sometimes written, by the conservative Theravādin School.

The First Council

The first of these Councils is said to have taken place immediately after the Buddha's parinirvāṇa, as follows: After the Buddha's death, his disciples slowly began to gather, among them Kāśyapa. The Enlightened disciples understood that all things are impermanent, while the unenlightened grieved at the loss of the Bhagavan, the Blessed One. However, one monk, named Subhadra, was pleased because he thought that now he and the others need no longer be restrained by the Buddha's instructions. In response to this attitude, it was suggested by Kāśyapa that they hold a recitation of the Buddha's teaching and discipline, his Dharma-Vinaya. Agreement was reached, and Rājagṛha chosen as the venue. Kāśyapa was also elected to choose the participants, and he arrived at a list of 499 arhats. Some pleaded that Ānanda, as the Buddha's long-time companion, should be included though not yet an arhat, and this was allowed. The Council was held during the rainy season retreat, and it proceeded on the basis of Kāśyapa questioning two of the gathering, Upāli and Ānanda, about the Buddha's rules of conduct and discourses respectively. Upāli, as an ex-barber, had an extensive knowledge of the rules of ordination and the *prātimokṣa,* since he was supposed to have shaved the heads of the ordinands prior to ordination. Having shared the company of the Buddha for a period of thirty years, Ānanda had a natural authority to determine what should be accepted as the word of the Buddha. Though Ānanda reminded the gathering that the Buddha had said the minor rules could be rescinded, no one felt sure which rules could be regarded as minor, and so they were all accepted as part of the rules of conduct for the ordained Saṅgha. Among some other interesting details, it is also recorded that Purāṇa, the teacher of some five hundred disciples, arrived late for the gathering just as it was finishing, but when asked to join and endorse the work of the Council, he refused, maintaining that he could remember the Buddha's teaching well enough for himself.[52]

This First Council is important, for it shows the early Saṅgha trying to organize itself, and establish its own identity and continuity, with a definitive body of discourses and regulations, its own Dharma and Vinaya. (For a discussion of the contents of these, see Chapter 9.) In particular the incident with Subhadra suggests there was some need to unify the Saṅgha on a basis other than the charismatic figure of the Buddha. It also suggests that Rājagṛha was a major centre for the early Saṅgha, where there was a sufficient concentration of the Buddha's disciples and sufficient support in terms of food and shelter for such a meeting to take place. However, there remains considerable doubt as to whether such a meeting as described, a rather grand and imposing affair, could have taken place within the time and distances involved – after all, Rājagṛha was some 500 kilometres distant from Kuśinagarī. Moreover, it is quite clear that parts of the collections of discourses and monastic regulations (Sūtra and Vinaya Piṭakas), as we have them, date from a much later period than this. What seems very likely is that a number of the Buddha's disciples came together, and made some attempt to pool their recollection of his various discourses, perhaps arranged according to their style and content, and recited together some form of *prātimokṣa*, possibly as described in the previous chapter. Finally, it is clear from the incident involving Purāṇa that there were those who chose not to participate in these regularizing activities, and did not accept them. That Purāṇa was not, so far as we know, censured in any way, shows that his stance was regarded as a legitimate one.

THE SECOND COUNCIL

Traditions regarding the Second Council are confusing and ambiguous. It seems, in fact, as though there were two meetings, separated by a period of roughly forty years, and though it is agreed that the overall result was the first schism in the Saṅgha, between the Sthaviravāda and the Mahāsaṅgha, it is not fully clear what the cause of the split was.

According to the Theravāda tradition, the first of these meetings, or Councils, took place at Vaiśālī, about a hundred years after the Buddha's parinirvāṇa. It is now clear that the figure of a hundred years was a convenient round number used to denote a lengthy period of time, and it seems more likely that this Council took place about sixty years after the parinirvāṇa, i.e. c.345BCE. It concerned the allegation that certain bhikṣus at Vaiśālī permitted ten unlawful practices amongst their number, amounting to minor infringements of the Vinaya, or Rules of Conduct, such as handling money, eating after midday, and not observing certain rules regarding the boundaries of *nikāyas*. The Council was convened, the elder Sarvagāmin (a pupil of Ānanda) was asked for an authoritative verdict on the ten points, which were condemned by him, after which the Council was closed.

The second meeting of this period, though not recorded as such in the Theravādin accounts, apparently took place some thirty-seven years later at Pāṭaliputra, and concerned the teachings of a bhikṣu called Mahādeva, who maintained five theses concerning the arhat, viz. that the arhat could be subject to temptation, might have a residue of ignorance, have doubts, gain knowledge through another's help, and enter upon the Supramundane Path by means of an exclamation such as 'Duḥkha!' or possibly even fall away from the Path.[53] This was regarded as deprecation of the status of the arhat by some, who gathered in opposition. The king of Magadha, Mahāpadma Nanda, was asked to convene a council in order to clarify the position, but since he had no spiritual expertise or authority he decided to adjudicate by measuring the size of the respective parties. He found the greater number to be in favour of Mahādeva's points. This party dubbed itself the Mahāsaṅgha, the 'greater community', while the other party referred to themselves as the Sthaviras, the 'elders', so as to identify themselves with the 'original' teaching of the Buddha, which they claimed the others were distorting.

Whilst the sources which record the Pāṭaliputra Council clearly identify it as the basis of the first schism within the community, it is also clear that *saṅghabheda*, i.e. schism as such, took place on the basis of differences only over Vinaya, or the Rules of Conduct, and not over matters of doctrine. For this reason, among others, scholars have suggested that the Vaiśālī meeting, which debated matters of Vinaya, was the real basis for the schism, as the points at issue in the Pāṭaliputra meeting are really doctrinal. However, accounts of the Vaiśālī meeting record no schism as taking place at that point, but rather that the 'lax' bhikṣus held their own council afterwards, at which they established themselves as the breakaway Mahāsaṅghika sect.

The problems posed by these contradictory accounts may be solved by a Mahāsaṅghika text, preserved in Chinese translation, called the *Śāriputraparipṛcchā*. It is the earliest surviving account of the schism to have been compiled, and describes this Council in a rather different light. This text is concerned with a debate over matters of Vinaya, and explains that the schism resulted from the greater party (later to become the Mahāsaṅgha) refusing to accept the addition of rules to the Vinaya by the smaller party (later to become the Sthaviras). It describes 'an old bhikṣu avid for glory and prone to disputing. He copied and arranged our vinaya, developing and increasing what Kāśyapa had codified and which is called "The Vinaya of the Great Assembly" (*mahāsaṅgha-vinaya*). He collected from outside some material which had been neglected [until then], with the aim of deceiving beginners.'[54] No mention of Mahādeva is made in connection with this schism, which takes place at Pāṭaliputra, but he appears in an account of a later split which occurred within the Mahāsaṅgha itself, between two parties who disagreed over the status of the arhat.

It could be objected that this is only another partisan account of the first schism, but at least we can see that the Theravāda and the Mahāsaṅgha are both agreed that there was a dispute concerning the observance of the Vinaya, the only basis technically possible for *saṅghabheda*. Its story is supported by the fact that the Vinayas affiliated to the Sthaviras do contain more rules than the Mahāsaṅghika Vinaya, and it is generally agreed that the Mahāsaṅghika Vinaya is the oldest.

This second, Mahāsaṅghika, version therefore affirms that the first schism that occurred in the Saṅgha took place over a matter of monastic discipline, and had nothing to do with Mahādeva. Furthermore it underlines the difficulty the Saṅgha experienced in interpreting the Buddha's injunction that the minor Vinaya rules could be ignored, since it appears that the Sthaviras wished to institute or revive certain minor monastic regulations that had been discounted. Far from representing the falling away from original discipline and purity by 'lax' Mahāsaṅghika monks, it really involved the attempted addition of rules to the Vinaya by a minority group numbered at only a hundred or so, who were preoccupied by the letter rather than the spirit of the Buddha's injunctions. The majority party were those who wished to live by the old, original Vinaya rule, while the breakaway group are described as exclusively 'senior members' i.e. *sthaviras*, for which reason their party was given that name. ('Elder', *sthavira*, is a title given to monks automatically after ten years of full ordination.) Finally, there is some unclarity concerning the date of this Council and schism. One tradition places it at the time of Mahāpadma Nanda, 362–334BCE, but if one follows the shorter chronology concerning the dates of the Buddha, then it would have occurred during the reign of Aśoka, as is circumstantially confirmed by the account in the *Śāriputraparipṛcchā*.

FURTHER COUNCILS

There are records of two further Councils held during the next couple of centuries, but as they were far less important for the history of the Saṅgha as a whole, they will be dealt with in the context of their respective patrons, the kings Aśoka and Kaniṣka.

7

Developments in the Saṅgha: Up to the First Century CE

Organization of the Saṅgha

In Chapter 5 the ordained Saṅgha was described in terms of a body of *parivrājakas*, or wanderers, who toured the hills and towns of Magadha, Kośala, and beyond, coming together in larger numbers for the annual rainy season retreat, the season when travel was not possible. Gradually, in the succeeding centuries, this picture began to change. Under the dual impact of these regular retreats, and numerous endowments of land and buildings to the Saṅgha by wealthy lay supporters, the community became increasingly static. An intermediate stage was reached at which most bhikṣus wandered during spring and summer but returned to the same abode for each rainy season. Eventually, many ceased to wander at all, settling instead at a single dwelling place. Doubtless many individuals continued the practice of wandering, but it seems probable that by the end of the first century after the Buddha, the average life of a bhikṣu was not peripatetic but residential. One could say that it was from this time that it becomes accurate to describe the life-style of the ordained Saṅgha as 'monastic'. It was also from this time that the Vinaya, as a compendium of rules and regulations, began to evolve. Another reason for an increasing emphasis being paid to the new monastic community was that it represented the main mechanism for the preservation, by oral recitation, of the Buddha's teachings (later to become the Sūtra Piṭaka). The lay followers had no such corporate mechanism for the preservation of the Dharma. Whereas in the past the bhikṣus, touring the countryside, had come to them and imparted the teaching, this now meant that increasingly, in order to hear the Buddha's teachings at all, lay followers had to go to a monastery where a bhikṣu would be able to recite it for them.

This new stasis led, among other things, to the arising of geographically distinct Saṅghas. The essential principle behind this development was that ideally all the Saṅgha's actions should be carried out in unity. However, there were inevitably cases of dispute, and since the minimum size of an effective Saṅgha was four bhikṣus, once four or more agreed with each other in a dispute they could separate, form their own Saṅgha, and become legally, or administratively, separate. In turn this meant that they would hold their own separate *upavasatha* meetings. Once this separation had occurred, they no longer co-operated for the purposes of ordination, with the result that distinct ordination lineages arose. These new local Saṅghas, termed *nikāyas*, became an extremely important feature of the monastic community, and much attention was given to the boundary, or *sīmā*, that defined individual *nikāyas*, for this determined, among other things, who would and who would not recognize each other's ordination, and who could or could not use a particular residence. A monk from one *nikāya* could not use the facilities of another. Not all such divisions would have arisen as a result of disagreements since, after a certain point in time, geographical separation inevitably made regular meetings impossible, or at least highly difficult, and this was probably the major factor promoting the growth of new *nikāyas*. (See Chapter 8 for further discussion of the divisions based upon observance of the Vinaya.)

Apart from the increasing complexity of the Vinaya code, as it grew to encompass the many new details of settled monastic life, these first centuries saw the introduction of a new ordination procedure, whereby the old practice of accepting someone upon their public declaration of the Threefold Refuge was replaced by a new ritual which involved a threefold request for entry into the Order, accompanied by detailed questioning to make sure that the entrant was free from all impediments, including illness or being in service.[55] This period also saw the development of the *upavasatha* ceremony as a ritual recitation of the *prātimokṣa* rules,[56] preceded by a formal confession in place of the more personal and practical institution of the Buddha's day.[57] Great emphasis also came to be placed on the *kaṭhina*, or robe ceremony, at the end of the rainy season retreat, at which lay followers were expected to present the bhikṣus with gifts, especially fresh material for the manufacture of new robes. Lay practice became increasingly restricted to the making of merit, largely through *dāna*, or giving, to the monks.

RESIDENCES FOR THE SAṄGHA

This period also saw considerable development in the nature of the residences for the bhikṣus. Generally there was an increase in size, both of the *āvāsas* (built by monks for themselves, for which topic there is a long section of rules in *Vinaya* iii), and *ārāmas*, built for the Saṅgha by lay followers, which were situated close to towns and villages for ease of collecting alms. Inside the *āvāsa* or *ārāma* a dwelling hut would be built, called a *vihāra*, though later this term was used for the whole establishment. One of the first *ārāmas* was built near Rājagṛha, in Jīvaka's mango grove, a park recorded in the Pāli Canon as donated at the time of the Buddha. Archaeological investigation has revealed the remains of living quarters, an assembly hall (for teaching and recitation of the *prātimokṣa*) and a walkway. There is no evidence of a shrine-room or hall in the earliest examples. Later designs, from about the 2nd century BCE, included chapels built to house a stylized *caitya* or stūpa of stone or brick, surrounded by a walkway for circumambulation. These appear to have been the standard form of shrine-room or hall.

An area into which there was considerable Buddhist expansion during this time was western India, where there was extensive traffic along trade routes, and where Buddhism was propagated and supported by merchant lay followers. By 200BCE numerous communities were established in Maharashtra, and between the 2nd century BCE and the 2nd century CE, some forty-five rock-cut cave dwellings (*leṇa*) had been excavated in the Western Ghats.[58] The earliest cave is at Bhāja, pre-200BCE, and the largest at Karle. By 300BCE Buddhism had spread to central India and the Deccan, Nagpur being the site of an important early community of the period.

DEVELOPMENTS IN PRACTICE

This period also saw the growth of the worship of the Buddha's relics, housed in stūpas, or funerary mounds, at all major sites associated with events in his life – the Lumbinī Grove at Kapilavastu, marking the place of his birth; the Bodhi Tree at Gayā, marking his Enlightenment; the Deer Park at Ṛṣipatana, near Vārāṇasī, where he gave the first teaching;

and the grove near Kuśinagarī, where he died. All became sites of pilgrimage. Such sites often housed monasteries, from which the resident bhikṣus often undertook the care of the stūpa. Nor was stūpa worship restricted to the laity – the Vinayas of all schools, apart from the Theravāda, contain rules governing the worship at stūpas by monks.[59] Such worship included the decoration and circumambulation of the site, and the donation of gifts for its upkeep.

There is also evidence of flower offerings made to the Buddha, and, as part of a ritual invocation of his presence and worship of him, the construction, sometimes with flowers, of *kuṭīs*, or huts, in imitation of the Buddha's *gandhakuṭī*, the hut in which he resided at Śrāvastī.[60] In later usage the term *gandhakuṭī* came to refer to the hall or room in a *vihāra* which held the Buddha image. The recitation and communal singing of hymns in praise of the Buddha was another significant feature of practice in this period, and has clear links with the practice of *buddhānusmṛti*, or recollection of the Buddha, and may well be reflected in the devotional hymns of praise by Mātṛceṭa (2nd century CE).

Political Influences – Royal Patronage and Persecution

Though Buddhism received the patronage of kings, at the time of the Buddha and afterwards, from figures such as Bimbisāra and Mahāpadma Nanda, the spread of the Dharma made only modest headway during the first century after the Buddha's parinirvāṇa, and its spread was still largely provincial until the second half of the 4th century BCE. The gradual rise in power and extent of the monarchies of the Ganges basin had culminated in the almost complete supremacy of the kingdom of Magadha in the region. This kingdom then formed the core territory of an imperial dynasty which was initiated under the sovereignty of Candragupta Maurya, c.322BCE. The third emperor of this lineage, Aśoka (269–232BCE), though initially an aggressively expansionist monarch, was converted to Buddhism after witnessing the horrors of his own campaign for the conquest of Kaliṅga. Thereafter he embarked on a campaign of 'conquest by the Dharma' which renounced all use of force, adopted a policy of complete religious tolerance, and set about trying to improve the lot of his people – a people that stretched across much of the Indian subcontinent.

This remarkable story is told by his edicts, which are carved on rock-faces and pillars at public places throughout his empire, and recovered and deciphered only since the 19th century. His importance to the Buddhist tradition is reflected in the large number of stories about him in most of the canonical languages of Buddhism, only the most notable among these being the *Aśokāvadāna*, and the Chronicles, or *vaṁsa*, of Sri Lanka. Aśoka was associated with several other historical developments of major significance to the history of Buddhism. He sent Buddhist missions to a number of foreign countries as an aspect of his conquest by Dharma. The most famous of these, headed by his son Mahinda, went to Sri Lanka, but others were sent to northern Kanara, Karṇaṭaka, Kashmir, the Himalayan region, and Burma. Hitherto exclusively regional in its character, Buddhism now became an international religion, and, though it appears that several of these missions came to nothing, a boost was given to its expansion which had lasting and far-reaching effects. Some missions were sent to the Greek kingdoms of Bactria (the legacy of Alexander's conquests of 327–325BCE, which now forms part of Afghanistan), and it was from this milieu that the famous *Milindapañha*, the 'Questions of King Milinda', arose, recording the dialogues between a Greek king, Menander, who ruled during the middle of the 2nd century BCE, and a Buddhist teacher, Nāgasena. The composition probably dates from the turn of the millennium.

Aśoka is also credited with the construction of 84,000 stūpas, and whilst this is clearly an exaggeration, he undoubtedly gave great impetus to the construction of these monuments at places associated with real or mythical events in the life of the Buddha and those of past Buddhas. Finally, he is also associated with the Third Buddhist Council, held in Pāṭaliputra, c.250BCE. The immediate motive for this Council was the undermining of the Saṅgha in Pāṭaliputra by the entry of non-Buddhists into the Order. Aśoka therefore undertook the purification of that Saṅgha, and invited a *thera*, Moggaliputta Tissa, to convene a council. One thousand monks gathered, refuting and expelling the offending parties. The refutation of views was recorded, and formed the core of what was later named the *Kathāvatthu*, 'Points of Controversy', and is now found in the Theravādin Abhidhamma. Whilst later Theravādins claimed that this was a pan-Indian gathering in which the Theravāda refuted all opposing Buddhist views, and that they also received the direct support of Aśoka, this was clearly not the case. From the accounts given by Aśoka in his own edicts, historians have concluded that the Council was convened to solve a regional problem, involving the local Saṅgha at Pāṭaliputra, and that Aśoka was concerned not to give his support to one school against others but simply to sort out a situation which was bringing the Saṅgha as a whole into disrepute.[61] The situation is also remarkable for the precedent which it set for the interference of the secular state in the affairs of the Saṅgha, a precedent which had serious repercussions in the history of Buddhism in Sri Lanka. The *Aśokāvadāna* story records that in his last days, while suffering a fatal illness, Aśoka gave to the Saṅgha much of the wealth of the state and of his personal fortune. Fearing economic disaster, his ministers apparently denied him access to the treasury and took away his power. Left with only half a myrobalan fruit in his possession, he gave that too.

With the collapse of the Mauryan empire after the death of Aśoka, Buddhism underwent a period of persecution under Puṣyamitra Śuṅga, though the Śuṅga period as a whole (185–75BCE) also saw the efflorescence of schools of Buddhist sculpture at Sāñci, Amarāvatī, Bodh Gayā, and other places, in connection with the stūpas there. For the last century or so it has been argued that in the earliest period the physical form of the Buddha was not depicted, his presence instead indicated by symbols, such as a *dharma-cakra*, or wheel of the Dharma, a throne, a parasol, or a footprint. Recent argument suggests that such images should be seen to be only what they explicitly are, and that this prevailing aniconic interpretation (for which there is no doctrinal basis) contravenes and has led to the suppression of contradictory evidence.[62] The favoured subjects of sculpture were stories from the *Jātakas*, the tales of the Buddha's former lives.

A second royal patron of note was Kaniṣka (1st to 2nd century CE). Kaniṣka was the third in succession as king of the Central Asian horsemen who had invaded north-west India in the early part of the 1st century CE. He ruled a modest empire that encompassed a large section of northern and north-west India, including Sindh, Rajasthan, Malwa, the Kathiawar peninsula, and Mathurā, and which boasted a rich and cosmopolitan court. Though clearly well disposed towards Buddhism, he never adopted a policy of non-violence, and perpetrated a number of terrible massacres, for which he was most unpopular. Nevertheless he also built the great monastery at Peshawar and gave great wealth to other establishments, and is celebrated among the

Buddhist traditions of northern India as a great patron of the Dharma. The Fourth Council took place in Kashmir under his auspices. At this Council a gathering of 499 Sarvāstivādin monks compiled a new canon, and codified the doctrines of their school in a huge commentary called the *Mahāvibhāṣa*. The poet Aśvaghoṣa, author of the *Buddhacarita*, a verse biography of the Buddha, the *Saundarananda*, an account in verse of the conversion of the Buddha's half-brother Nanda, and at least one drama, was said to have been at Kaniṣka's court. (The works of Aśvaghoṣa are the earliest Sanskrit *kāvya* poetry to have survived.) The teacher Saṅgharakṣa, author of a work called the *Yogācārabhūmi*, which reflects the practices of new meditation schools growing at this period in Kashmir and Central Asia, also attended Kaniṣka's court. If the aniconic theory of early Buddhist art is true, then the new style of representation of the Buddha as a human figure, appearing at Gandhāra and 'Mathurā almost simultaneously, seems to have begun during his reign, and it may be that he was responsible for the construction of the first tall 'pagoda' type of stūpa at the Peshawar monastery.

Finally, mention must also be made of the Śātavāhana dynasty, which established itself as the dominant power in the Deccan after the collapse of the Mauryan empire. Its original homeland appears to have lain in Āndhra, between the Krishna and Godhavarī rivers in southern India, although it expanded dramatically westwards and northwards, before a period of contraction and its final demise in the mid-3rd century CE. It is noted for its royal patronage of a flourishing Buddhist community seen at its best in the remains of Amarāvatī and Nāgārjunakoṇḍa. Hsüan-tsang counted twenty monasteries there, housing 3,000 monks. The region is also famous as the home of Nāgārjuna, whose letter of advice to a contemporary Śātavāhana king, the *Suhṛllekhā*, still survives. Āndhra is also known to have had important links with Burma and to have been one source for Burmese Buddhism.

8

The Buddhist Schools

The last chapter explored the origin of the first split in the Buddhist Saṅgha, between the Sthaviravādin and Mahāsaṅghika Schools. This was to be the first of a number of splits that occurred, and by which were created a number of different schools. Buddhist tradition mentions eighteen non-Mahāyāna schools, although over thirty different names have come down to us, and once again the real picture is not at all clear. Part of this unclarity concerns our understanding of the nature of these different schools. In fact there were three quite distinct types of Buddhist school, which can be differentiated on the basis of their function. These were: the *nikāyas*, based on variations in Vinaya, such as that between the Sthaviravādin and the Mahāsaṅghika Schools; the different -vādas, based on variations in doctrine; and, thirdly, what have been described as the 'philosophical schools', although there is no particular traditional term used for these, and they are essentially a development of the doctrinal schools.[63]

Background to the Formation of the Buddhist Schools

Variations in the Vinaya

In order to understand how the formation of the schools came about we need to look at a number of related issues. We must remember that Indian culture as a whole emphasized what is called 'orthopraxy' rather than 'orthodoxy'. Hence the identity and continuity of religious institutions in India has tended to be established through continuity of practice and behaviour, rather than through the conformity of ideas.

This general position is reflected in Buddhism too, for *saṅghabheda*, or schism, has always been the product of the adoption of different codes of behaviour, of different Vinayas, rather than of different interpretations of dogma. We have seen how provision had been made in the Vinaya for a more peaceful splitting of the Saṅgha into different *nikāyas*, or ordination lineages of monks using the same Vinaya, but it is also clear that more radical splits, i.e. *saṅghabheda*, occurred involving variations in the monastic code itself. A *nikāya* produced by such a split consisted of a community of monks (and presumably nuns) that recognized the validity of their own ordination lineage, and used the same distinctive version of the Vinaya which varied in some respects from the Vinayas of other communities.

Causing such a split was regarded as one of the six heinous crimes. These include harming a Buddha and murdering a parent, which demonstrates the degree of concern that was felt within the Saṅgha to preserve itself from acrimonious division and possible collapse. However, it is not necessarily the case that all such splits were intentional or adversarial in origin, and it seems likely that geographical isolation, possibly resulting from the missionary activities during the time of Aśoka, may have played its part in generating differences in the *prātimokṣas* recited by various gatherings.[64] The results of all these factors are seen in the seven different recensions of the Vinaya that have survived to the present day. There being a universal adherence to the five or ten precepts, those differences which did appear in various Vinayas, thereby giving rise to *saṅghabheda*, were largely insignificant. It is small changes of this sort which, for example, accounted for the difference in the colour of the robes worn by Theravādin, Tibetan, and Zen monks, or for the precise manner in which the robe was to be worn. The area of greatest difference lies in the rules of etiquette governing things like posture, dress, consumption of food, and the manner of address.[65] It is also important to point out that differences in sectarian allegiance only concerned the bhikṣu and bhikṣuṇī, because they revolved around differences of Vinaya and therefore had no relevance for the laity.

Variations in Doctrine

The concept of schism elaborated above needs to be clearly distinguished from the matter of doctrinal divergence. It appears that differences in the interpretation of doctrine were largely personal matters, which explains how it came to be that monks of different doctrinal schools lived quite happily together in the same monasteries, observing the same Vinaya, as is recorded by medieval Chinese pilgrim monks who travelled through India in the 5th and 7th centuries. An example of this is provided by the Sautrāntikas, who necessarily lived with monks of other schools because they had no Vinaya of their own. The rule by which they lived would be determined by the affiliation of the *nikāya* into which they had been ordained. As Sautrāntika doctrine evolved in reaction to the Vaibhāṣika Sarvāstivādin School (see below), it is probable that Sautrāntika monks observed the Sarvāstivādin Vinaya. In this they contrast with the Mūla-Sarvāstivādins, who appear to have held the same doctrinal position as the Sarvāstivādins, but had their own separate Vinaya, and therefore formed a distinct *nikāya*. This meant that they therefore could not live together as a single community with the Sarvāstivādins whose doctrinal views they shared.

This doctrinal diversity was doubtless encouraged by a number of factors. We have already observed that the Buddha refused to appoint any successor as head of the Saṅgha. Furthermore the Saṅgha itself had a non-centralized structure. The Buddha specifically advised his disciples to remain as islands to themselves. 'So, Ānanda, whether now or after my decease, whoever you are, you must remain as islands to yourselves, as defences to yourselves with the Dharma as your island and the Dharma as your defence, remaining unconcerned with other islands and other defences.'[66] We have already seen the example of Purāṇa at the First Council, and it is quite possible that whole groupings of disciples followed his example, again allowing for the growth of doctrinal and disciplinary diversity. It is also probable that once monks had begun to settle in particular places, the possibility for them to develop distinct interpretations of the teaching must have increased.

Due to the geographical spread of the teaching, different recensions of the Buddha's discourses and Vinaya began to appear recording accounts of the Buddha's teaching in the various local dialects and languages. This situation was in a sense encouraged by the Buddha himself, in that he refused to allow his teaching to be standardized into any particular dialect or format.[67] Without a lingua franca in which the Dharma could be transmitted, the resulting variety of languages may have contributed to mutual misunderstanding, and more certainly to differing interpretations of doctrinal issues.

The undoubted lack of system, plus instances of ambiguity, even in the Buddha's own teaching, delivered as it was to different individuals over the course of forty-five years of teaching, must inevitably have encouraged interpretation by later Buddhists. For instance, in any given discourse one might question whether the Buddha's language should be understood as colloquial or literal, traditional or reinterpretative. This sort of debate is clearly seen in relation to the Pudgala controversy (see below), or his use of terms such as *brahman*, i.e. to refer to the brahmanical deity of that name, as a synonym for nirvāṇa, or simply to mean 'the best', its literal meaning.

Then again it appears that individual monks specialized in the recitation of particular sūtras or groups of sūtras, or in the Vinaya – eventually in the Abhidharma texts, too. It seems possible that the Sautrāntikas were sūtra specialists, as is reflected in their name – *sautra* being derived from *sūtra*. We even find terms used in Pāli sources to denote various types of bhikṣu that seem to suggest this kind of specialization. For example, there are references to: *suttantikas* – masters of sutta, *vinayadharas* – those versed in the rules of discipline, *mātikādharas* – those versed in *mātṛkās* (lists), *dhammakathikas* – preachers of doctrine, and *Dīgha-* and *Majjhima-bhāṇakas* – reciters of the *Dīgha-* and *Majjhima-Nikāyas* respectively.

Finally, it appears that monks grouped themselves around individual teachers who were themselves specialists in some aspect of the Dharma-Vinaya. We find references to a school known as the Dharmaguptaka, who probably originated amongst the circle of a teacher called Dharmagupta; similarly, the Vātsīputrīya School around Vatsīputra. Even the Buddha's own disciples showed some specialization in this way. Śāriputra could be seen as a philosophical analyst (and is traditionally associated with the origins of the Abhidharma), Upāli, the monk who traditionally recited the whole of the monastic code, was obviously a Vinaya specialist, whilst Ānanda would have been regarded as a *suttantika*, a master of the discourses. Indeed, the Sautrāntika regarded Ānanda as the Patriarch of its school. The Buddha himself suggested that, in accordance with their particular psychological leanings, certain new disciples should learn from particular expert teachers – another source of partisan affiliations.

From this survey it should be apparent that diversification is not in itself a bad thing. It allows for the adaptation of the doctrine to the needs of specific hearers, and fits well with the identification of the

Buddha as a doctor, giving the appropriate medicine to cure different sicknesses. Moreover, before looking at individual schools, it is important to point out that many doctrinal divergences were largely theoretical, and that it is possible to over-emphasize the differences between the Buddhist schools. For instance, one can safely say that all schools upheld the doctrinal principles and practices discussed in Chapters 3 and 4. However, there were clearly a number of doctrinal areas that provoked considerable speculation and debate. These included the nature and functioning of *karma-vipāka* (intentional action and its consequences), the status of the arhat, the nature of nirvāṇa and of space, whether there was an intermediate existence after death, whether insight occurs instantaneously or gradually, whether the mind is inherently pure and contaminated only by adventitious defilements, and so on. The polemical treatises of the doctrinal schools of Buddhism are filled with discussion of these and other issues.

The Philosophical Schools

Later tradition, both Buddhist and non-Buddhist, usually lists four schools of Buddhist thought or philosophy: the Sarvāstivādin, Sautrāntika, Mādhyamika, and Yogācārin Schools. The last two are Mahāyāna schools and will be dealt with in their own chapters, but each of these four developed coherent systems of thought that became the touchstone for debate among later thinkers. In this broader sense these are schools that made a distinct contribution to the common intellectual property of the Indian religious scene. They contrast with doctrinal schools who advocated teachings that made no great impact outside their own circle. An individual Buddhist could therefore espouse the philosophy of any of these four schools, regardless of their ordination lineage, or *nikāya,* or of their affiliation to Hīnayāna or Mahāyāna. This was the only option for members of distinct *nikāyas* who had no particular doctrinal position of their own.

The Non-Mahāyāna Schools

A detailed account of all the schools in a history of this size is not possible, nor would it necessarily give a balanced picture of these developments. The Chinese pilgrims of the medieval period mention most frequently the Mahāsaṅghika, the Sthaviravādin, the Pudgalavādin, and the Sarvāstivādin of the non-Mahāyāna schools, to which we can add the Sautrāntika from the philosophical schools. We will now focus attention on these five schools, and, in terms of their function, how they differed from each another.

The Mahāsaṅghika School

As we have seen, the Mahāsaṅghika School was differentiated from the Sthaviravādin as a result of a council held roughly one hundred years after the parinirvāṇa. Hitherto, under the influence of Theravādin orthodoxy, modern historians have tended to see the Mahāsaṅghikas as a lax, breakaway group which was not prepared to accept the Buddha's teachings to the fullest degree. The result has been that, when trying to uncover the character of the earliest years of the Buddhist Saṅgha, attention has always been focused upon the evidence provided by the Theravādin School as representative of the original or pure teaching of the Buddha. However, the account provided by the Mahāsaṅghika School itself presents a different picture, suggesting that the Sthaviravāda was the breakaway group that was trying to modify the original Vinaya, and it may be that in the long run historians will decide that a study of the Mahāsaṅghika School will contribute to a better picture of the early Dharma-Vinaya than the Theravādin School.

Such a study would, however, be problematic, for the information that we have on the Mahāsaṅghika School is scarce and incomplete, since both the school itself and the bulk of its canon were destroyed by the Muslim invasions of the medieval period. We do know that this school was very strong in Magadha, at Pāṭaliputra in particular, and there is epigraphical evidence of its presence in Mathurā, dating from c.120BCE. It developed its own canon, and gave birth to several subsects. At a later point, it developed a centre in southern India, concentrated in the Guntur district, around Amarāvatī, Jaggayapeṭa, and Nāgārjunakoṇḍa, though its adherents seem to have been distributed to some degree through all the centres of Buddhist population.

Whatever the origin of the schism, a major development of Mahāsaṅghika teaching was the doctrine of the *lokottaravāda*, or 'supermundane' Buddha – *lokottara* meaning literally 'beyond the world'.[68] Before looking at this in detail some comments on the nature of the Buddha are in order. It is important to stress that, despite modern Theravādin teachings to the contrary (often a sop to sceptical Western pupils), he was never seen as being merely human. For instance, he is often described as having the thirty-two major and eighty minor marks or signs of the *mahāpuruṣa*, 'superman'; the Buddha himself denied that he was either a man or a god;[69] and in the *Mahāparinibbāna Sutta* he states that he could live for an aeon were he asked to do so.[70] Besides his human character, which is very strongly evoked in the Pāli Canon, and his role as the focus for the new religious movement that was Buddhism, there is frequent reference to his outstanding magical powers.

Now the new *lokottaravāda*, or doctrine of the supramundane Buddha, appears in Mahāsaṅghika works, e.g. the *Mahāvastu* and the *Lokānuvartana Sūtra*, although statements reminiscent of it can be found in the Pāli Canon, e.g. in the *Āriyapariyesana Sutta* the Buddha describes himself as *sabbesu dhammesu anūpalitto*, 'among all things undefiled'.[71] We should also note the influence of the contemporary development of the *Jātakas*, an extensive and popular literature recounting the previous lives of the Buddha, and describing the immense *puṇya*, or merit, that he had accumulated through ethical action. The natural conclusion from listening to these tales is that, if the Buddha has such vast stocks of merit, then this last life of his could not possibly be that of an ordinary human. Whatever the source, the general idea underlying the *lokottaravāda* was the conclusion that the Buddha was completely devoid of the impurities of the world. The Mahāsaṅghika School therefore depicted him as extra-ordinary.[72] He was in the world but not tainted by it. He was conceived without sexual intercourse, and was born miraculously from his mother's side. Even so he was a real being, but his ordinary human appearance and activities were illusory.

This last is an important point, and needs some clarification. In the early texts generally the term *lokottara* is used to refer to members of the Ārya Saṅgha and to nirvāṇa. It literally means 'beyond the world', and is used in contrast to the term *laukika* – which means 'worldly, or unliberated'. The exact nature of this 'other-worldliness' is clarified by the Mahāsaṅghika view that the Buddha was born miraculously – literally *upapāduka*, which means 'spontaneously'. The *Saṅgīti Sutta*[73] explains that spontaneous birth is one of four kinds of birth that can occur – the others being birth from a womb, an egg, or moisture. In Buddhist cosmology, spontaneous birth is the prerogative of *devas* or gods, the most refined kind of birth that a being can have. But this does not reflect a process of deification in the sense found in the theistic religions, because the gods in Buddhist cosmology are likewise subject to death and rebirth as are we. They are born within the cycle of rebirth, but their birth is of a more refined kind than is ours. Therefore the contrast being made between *lokottara* and *laukika* is not one between illusory and real, but between subtle and coarse. The *lokottaravāda* is not a form of Docetism, despite being represented as such in the Theravādin *Kathāvatthu*.[74] What is unreal is that the Buddha appears to be an ordinary human being.

This elevation of the Buddha's standing could be seen as corresponding to a lowering of the status of the arhat, as possibly represented in Mahādeva's five points; although, looked at objectively, Mahādeva's position is little different from that regarding the arhat in the Pāli Canon. If this is really so, it is possible that Mahādeva's points reflect a response to an over-idealization of the arhat, an idealization which had begun to make the goal of arhatship seem beyond attainment, and which tended to serve the interests of an elite group of monks who saw themselves as arhats. If that is the case, we can understand Mahādeva as seeking to reassert the original status of the arhat in order to compensate for this trend. On the other hand, it could even have been that Mahādeva himself was a follower of the new Mahāyāna ideal of Buddhahood, and therefore saw arhatship as an inferior attainment. Whatever the case, in historical terms the *lokottaravāda* can help us to understand the development of the idea of the archetypal Buddha in the Mahāyāna.

Another innovative and influential doctrine of the Mahāsaṅghika School was the description of the Buddha's career as the Bodhisattva, prior to his last life as Siddhārtha Gautama, in terms of a progression through ten *bhūmis* or 'stages' – and, moreover, as a path that is open for others to follow. These *bhūmis* are elaborated at length in the *Mahāvastu*,[75] and were to be taken up, albeit in modified form, in the Mahāyāna. Finally, some of the Mahāsaṅghika sub-schools upheld a doctrine of *dharmaśūnyatā*, a position which had great significance both for the Abhidharma and for the Mahāyāna.[76]

The Sthaviravādin School

The Sthaviravādin School has had a profound influence on our conception of the early Saṅgha. The sole representative of this school (or of any non-Mahāyāna school) to have survived into the modern period, the Theravādin School of Sri Lanka and South-east Asia, has identified itself exclusively with the party that split from the Mahāsaṅghika School at the Second Council. This is reflected in the name, since the Pāli term *thera* is the equivalent of the Sanskrit term *sthavira*, and this has led early Western historians to assume that the two parties are identical. This is not the case, however, for by the time of Aśoka the Sthaviravādin School had itself split into the Sammitīya, the Sarvāstivādin, and the Vibhajyavādin sub-schools. Later the Vibhajyavādin School also split into two parties, the Mahīśāsika School, which was established in the south-eastern mainland, and the Theravādin School, which was established in Sri Lanka when Aśoka sent his son Mahinda there. A further reason for the prominence of the Theravādin School is that it has preserved the only complete Buddhist canon in its original language, in this case Pāli, although it is not clear if this was the language of the original Sthaviravādin canon.

It is, however, possible, with reservations allowing for the intrusion of later developments, to take the Theravādin School as representative of the Sthaviravāda as a whole. As one might expect, given its origins, the Theravādin School is conservative in its doctrines and practices. It regards the Buddha as having been an ordinary human being (despite indications to the contrary in its own canon). It maintains that there is only one Bodhisattva at present, who is Maitreya. He currently resides in the Tuṣita heaven, from which he will be reborn in the human realm when the Dharma has died out. The arhats are perfect in all respects, incapable of regression, and identical to the Buddha in their attainments. Whilst there are examples of laymen becoming arhats in the Pāli Canon, it regards it as almost impossible for this to happen now, and indeed holds the view that it is impossible for anyone to gain arhatship in the present degenerate age.

More characteristic of the Theravādin School as a sub-sect of the Vibhajyavādin School is its emphasis on theoretical analysis, especially of *dhammas*, for this was apparently a particular preoccupation of its mother school, reflected in its name – *vibhajya* meaning 'dividing, analysing'. The Theravādin School developed a rather austere orthodoxy, epitomized in the works of the 5th century scholastic Buddhaghosa, especially in his *Visuddhi-magga*, which on a theoretical level tends to exclude doctrines and practices incompatible with its preferred preoccupations. An example of this exclusion might be the meditational practices called the *brahma-vihāras*, which in its Abhidhamma and commentarial literature are relegated to an ancillary function only, whereas its own canon records instances which substantially refute this role. Canonical passages frequently contain editorial additions 'demoting' the *brahma-vihāras* but, where parallel texts survive from the Mahāsaṅghika canon, it is interesting to note that the latter did not feel any need to qualify such practices in that way.[77] This typifies a tendency in the Theravādin School to promote a view of the path which favours the cultivation of a 'dry' insight achieved by purely analytical meditations.

The Pudgalavādin School

Pudgalavādin is one name given to a school which upheld a special doctrine concerning the *pudgala*, or 'person'. It was formed on the basis of a doctrinal division within the Sthaviravādin School in the 3rd century BCE, and survived until the 9th or 10th centuries CE. Originally called Vātsīputrīya, after its teacher, Vatsīputra, it was later named the Sammitīya, and gave rise to several sub-sects of its own. Though its doctrine concerning the *pudgala* was considered by its opponents to be completely un-Buddhist, it had in fact a very strong following, and the Chinese pilgrims visiting India in the 7th century estimated that the majority of all the non-Mahāyāna monks were Pudgalavādin. Unfortunately it is not easy to gain a balanced picture of its doctrine since all its literature has been lost, with the exception of four authentic Abhidharma-type works surviving in Chinese translation. These indicate that there were a total of sixteen special theses by which the Pudgalavādin School differentiated itself from other schools.[78]

The teaching that caused such a violent reaction on the part of its opponents was that, whilst the *anātman* doctrine of the Buddha was entirely true in a conventional sense, there was still a *pudgala*, or person. This 'person' is an ultimately real thing, the substratum which allows for continuity between rebirths, for memory, and for the future ripening of intentional actions (*karman*) which are performed in the present or the past. If there was no person at all, as its opponents claimed, then Buddhism would be open to the charge of nihilism and immorality, for there would be nobody who could undertake moral actions. It insisted that the *pudgala* was indeterminate in relation to the *skandhas*, neither outside them nor within them; neither identical with them, nor different from them. In fact this *pudgala* was only perceptible to the Buddhas. In support of its position it frequently quoted sayings of the Buddha such as 'Monks, there is a single person born into the world for the welfare of many people, for the happiness of many people, out of compassion for the world, for the benefit, welfare, and happiness of gods and men. Who is that single person? He is the Tathāgata, the

Worthy One, the Fully and Perfectly Awakened One.'[79] In response the critics of the Pudgalavāda claimed that such language was purely conventional, and not to be taken literally.

In a historical context, it seems as though this doctrine was in part a reaction to the depersonalizing effect of the Abhidharma, but one could also say that the Pudgalavāda represents a persistent, if hotly disputed, trend in Buddhist thinking which sought to give a positive account of what is real. One might see later versions of this sort of position reflected in the *Tathāgatagarbha* doctrines of the Mahāyāna, the Ch'an and T'ien t'ai Schools of China, and the rNying-ma and Jo-nang Orders of Tibet.

The Sarvāstivādin School

The Sarvāstivādin School was formed from another schism, in the sense of *saṅghabheda*, within the Sthaviravādin School at some time in the 3rd century BCE. (The remaining section of the Sthaviravādin School took the name of Vibhajyavādin.) Some obscurity clouds its precise origins, and it is not clear whether the momentum for its formation came as a result of the Third Council, or from one of the missions of Aśoka to the region of Gandhāra.[80] What is clear is that it became firmly established in north-west India at an early date. At the Fourth Council, held under the patronage of Kaniṣka, five hundred Sarvāstivādin monks gathered, established a canon, and compiled several commentarial works called *Vibhāṣas*. From this time on it was to dominate northern and north-west India for at least another ten centuries, and since it also spread through to Kashmir and Central Asia, it was Sarvāstivādin doctrines that were to find their way to China. Furthermore, it was the Sarvāstivādin Abhidharma which was to be taken as definitive by the later Mahāyāna schools. The most widely known and easily accessible work conveying its doctrines is the *Abhidharmakośa*.

The Sarvāstivādin School developed a number of distinctive doctrines. Like the Mahāsaṅghika School it questioned the absolute status of the arhat, even maintaining the possibility of his regression. Its chief claim to distinction, however, was the doctrine after which it was named. *Sarvāstivāda* is supposedly derived from the phrase *sarvam asti*, 'all exists', and, as with the Pudgalavāda, refers to a teaching concerned with the mechanism for memory and *karman*, the universal Buddhist teaching that the ethical nature of actions determines future experiences for the agent. Its proposition was that, while *dharmas*,[81] the irreducible elements of existence, might be momentary, they also exist in the past and the future. In fact the three times – past, present, and future – are to be seen as 'modes', and the passing of time as the moving of individual *dharmas* between these three modes, under the stimulus of appropriate conditions. This was both consistent with the doctrine of impermanence and explained how a past action could have some fruit in the future: because the *dharmas* constituting that past action still existed, albeit in the past 'mode', and were thereby capable of exerting an influence at a later time. Memory too was explained by this doctrine, for it is nothing more than the consciousness of an object, and since it is axiomatic in Buddhism that one cannot have consciousness without an object, to say that past *dharmas* still existed allowed memory its necessary object.

The Sarvāstivādin School is also to be noted for its teachings concerning the Buddha Jewel. It saw a problem in Going for Refuge to the Buddha Jewel once the Buddha as a historical personality was dead, reasoning that his physical body was hardly a proper object of refuge. It was not satisfied with the explanation that the Buddha was to be identified with the *dharmakāya*, in the sense of the body of the doctrine, because this then made the Buddha Jewel much the same as the Dharma Jewel. It maintained that the Buddha Jewel consisted of all the pure *dharmas* that made up the Buddha as an Enlightened being – his knowledges and his *skandhas*. In doing this it established an important precedent for the later Mahāyāna doctrines concerning the Buddha.[82] It also developed a scheme of the path which involved the practice of six perfections – generosity, morality, patience, energy, meditation, and wisdom – again, a doctrine that was to have profound repercussions in the Mahāyāna concept of the Bodhisattva.[83] Finally, it was also the originator of the famous 'Wheel of Life', depicting the six realms of existence and the twelve *nidānas*, or links, of the *pratītya-samutpāda*, which its followers painted inside the gateways to their monasteries, a practice taken over from them and preserved by the Tibetan traditions until the 20th century.[84]

Its most famous offshoots were the Vaibhāṣika and the Sautrāntika Schools. The Vaibhāṣika School gave pride of place to the increasingly comprehensive and bulky *vibhāṣas*, or commentaries, produced within the Sarvāstivādin circle in the 2nd century CE. Its stronghold was in Kashmir, though it had a very considerable influence upon other

Buddhists and came to epitomize early Buddhist scholasticism through its emphasis upon the Abhidharma.

The Sautrāntika School

The Sautrāntika School arose as a reaction to the commentarial and *abhidharmic* trend of the Vaibhāṣikas, denying the authority of the complex manuals and treatises that it produced. As implied by its name, which means 'ending with the sūtra' and indicates that as its concept of what was canonical ended with the Sūtra Piṭaka, the second of the canonical collections, it did not regard such treatises as the word of the Buddha. Its views are best known from the *Abhidharmakośabhāṣya*, and this, with its open rejection of the Abhidharma, is dealt with in Chapter 10.

There were a number of other points on which the Sautrāntika School differed from the Sarvāstivādin. In particular it opposed the Sarvāstivādin concept of *dharmas* existing in the three modes of time, asserting that all *dharmas* had only a momentary, or *kṣaṇika*, existence.[85] This doctrine in its turn led to the position that direct perception of an object is not possible (a position maintained and developed by later Mahāyāna thinkers, including the Logicians). One perceives mental images which are produced by the senses (themselves momentary in their functioning) when they are in contact with momentary objects, but these mental images necessarily lag behind the momentary existence of the object and senses themselves. This is because the mental image is produced by the contact, and must therefore follow it in time. If it was exactly simultaneous with it, then it could not be said to be dependent upon it.

In order to deal with the problems of *karman* that the Sarvāstivāda had sought to resolve through the idea of *dharmas* persisting through all three times, the Sautrāntika School proposed that actions 'perfumed' one's mental continuum in such a way as to determine particular results. Difficulties with this model led them to develop the idea of *bījas* or 'seeds' which were 'planted' by an action with a particular ethical character, only to 'sprout' at a later point, when conditions allowed, and give rise to a 'fruit' appropriate to the original action.[86]

9

THE TRIPIṬAKA: THE MAINSTREAM BUDDHIST CANON

THE MAINSTREAM BUDDHIST CANON, accepted by Mahāyāna and non-Mahāyāna traditions alike, is composed, as we know it, of three major divisions. Each of these is called a *piṭaka*, which is usually understood to mean 'basket' and hence 'collection'. However, it is also likely that the term is derived from the word for 'father', *pitṛ*, and originally meant 'that which belongs to the Father', in the sense of that which has been handed down from the Father, i.e. the Buddha. This would parallel the same metaphor by which monks called themselves *śākyaputra*, 'sons of the Śākyan', i.e. the Buddha, who came from the Śākya clan. Whatever the origin of the term, the entire canon is known as the Tripiṭaka, the threefold collection. These three divisions are known respectively as: the Vinaya Piṭaka, this being the portion of the canon that is concerned with regulating the life of Buddhist monks and nuns; the Sūtra Piṭaka, the collection of sūtras, i.e. of discourses given by the Buddha; and thirdly, the Abhidharma Piṭaka, which is concerned with the systematic explanation and ordering of key teachings and analyses, i.e. teachings and analyses that are to be found in the Sūtra Piṭaka. It seems that the term *piṭaka* itself only came into use in the 2nd century BCE.[87]

Although tradition has it that these Piṭakas were created at the First Council from the recitations of Upāli and Ānanda, each of whom held in their memory the entire corpus of Vinaya rules and discourses that now constitute the first two Piṭakas, this story seems very unlikely. Whilst there was undoubtedly a highly sophisticated culture of oral recitation at the time, which was capable of retaining in memory large quantities of material, there are several factors which suggest that the

Piṭakas we know today were not formed at that time. Firstly, some of the texts contained in the Piṭakas clearly date from some period after the death of the Buddha. In some instances, we can tell this because they relate events that occurred after that Council, in others, because they contain doctrines or specific formulations of doctrines that only developed some time after the Buddha. The entire Abhidharma Piṭaka is a good example of the latter, and is confirmed as such by the fact that the earliest references to the canon as a whole speak of a Dharma-Vinaya only. Since the Abhidharma is connected with a major development within Buddhist practice, it will be considered on its own in the following chapter.

It appears that different schools had their own canons, their own recensions of the Buddhavacana, 'word of the Buddha'. Some schools also had more than three Piṭakas. The Mahāsaṅghika apparently had a Dhāraṇī Piṭaka and a Kṣudraka Piṭaka in addition to the above three.[88] We have already seen how differences in Vinayas came into existence, and the significance of this for the early community. The collections of discourses did not have the same corporate significance as the Vinayas, and whilst they all undoubtedly drew upon a common reservoir of traditions and memories of the Buddha, each collection probably reflected the particular concerns and practices of the community that retained them. Only one complete version of a set of Vinaya, Sūtra, and Abhidharma Piṭakas has survived, that in the Pāli language, preserved by the Theravādin School. Consequently this has been regarded as the sole authoritative account of the Buddhavacana in Sri Lanka, Burma, Thailand, Laos, and Cambodia, the home of the Theravādin School.

Associated with the Vinaya and Sūtra Piṭakas was a parallel body of commentarial literature, explaining the details of the sūtras in each division. Again, it may be that there were separate commentarial traditions for each of the schools, but only that associated with the Theravāda has survived in an Indic language. The bulk of this was said to be derived from Indian originals, which were summarized and translated into Pāli by Buddhaghosa in the 4th or 5th century. Some of the Pāli commentaries were written by Dhammapāla, in the 5th or 6th century.

As the Vinaya and Sūtra Piṭakas are quite distinct in their content and purpose, they will be discussed separately.

THE VINAYA PIṬAKA

There are several reasons why one should start with the Vinaya Piṭaka. According to tradition, the composition of the Buddhist canon began with the Vinaya, for it was Upāli who was the first to be questioned at the Council. This makes some sense, for it is very likely that the first concern of those who gathered at that Council was to define the Buddhist Saṅgha, to define the nature of their own community, after the death of their founder. Furthermore, the monastic traditions do not see any dichotomy between the Buddha's teachings and the monastic regulations, both of which have always been transmitted by monks. As far as they are concerned the very rules by which their lives are governed, and which are recorded in the Vinaya, were devised by the Buddha himself, and enjoined upon the monastic Saṅgha in specific circumstances, the majority of which the Vinaya purports to record, even down to the very words that the Buddha used at the time. In fact, it is clear that the Vinaya was the product of many years of development, and its present form could only have been devised at least one hundred years after the death of the Buddha.[89]

A total of seven different Vinayas have survived to the present day. Most well known is that of the Theravāda, preserved in Pāli, but recently those of the Mahāsaṅghika, the Sarvāstivāda, and the Mūla-Sarvāstivāda have been found in Sanskrit, and those of the Mahīśāsika, the Kāśyapīya, and the Dharmaguptaka have survived in Chinese translations. The Vinayas are of great importance for the history of Buddhism, for they were not restricted just to the use of the non-Mahāyāna schools, but were adopted and used by the later Mahāyāna and Vajrayāna schools, both inside and outside India.

The Vinaya literature has a paradoxical nature, since those parts that are most frequently used by the monastic community are not included within the canon, i.e. within the Vinaya Piṭaka. These are the *Prātimokṣa* and the *Karmavācā*. They are both essentially functional in character. The *Prātimokṣa* is, in its fully developed form, an inventory of rules which must be observed by the monks and nuns. It is, in theory, chanted regularly at each *upavasatha* day by the various *nikāyas*, i.e. local monastic communities. Though termed a sūtra, and thereby purporting to be the word of the Buddha, it is clearly a later compilation. This is reflected by the fact that the *Prātimokṣas* of different schools list differing numbers of rules. The variations involve only the most trivial rules, the *śaikṣya-dharmas*, concerning etiquette. The *Karmavācā* are ritual texts, or liturgies, used in the various duties and obligations of the collective Saṅgha, such as ordination.

The canonical Vinaya literature, i.e. that found within the Vinaya Piṭaka, falls into two, sometimes three, sections: the *Sūtravibhaṅga*, the *Skandhaka*, and the *Appendices*. The *Appendices*, in the Pāli Canon called the *Parivāra*, are a summary of the previous two divisions in the form of a kind of catechism, and are specific to individual schools.

THE SŪTRAVIBHAṄGA

The first of these sections, the *Sūtravibhaṅga*, literally the 'analysis of the sūtra', is a detailed analysis of the rules presented in the *Prātimokṣa Sūtra*. Following the layout of the *Prātimokṣa*, the offences are organized into categories, arranged according to their gravity. For those who fail to keep them, it also prescribes the appropriate punishment. The *Sūtravibhaṅga* attempts to explain in detail the nature, origin, and intention of each of the rules which came to govern the monastic community. As part of this explanation, individual rules are set in the context of a story which reveals the reasons for which the Buddha supposedly set the rule.

There are a total of 227 rules in the Theravādin *Vinaya*, governing the life of the monk (there are additional rules for nuns), and these are concerned with eight classes of offence distinguished by the punishment they incur. The first and most serious class contains four rules, known as the *pārājika dharmas*, and involves expulsion from the Saṅgha. These four rules prohibit sexual intercourse (the monk and nun were required to be completely celibate), theft, the taking of life, and boasting of supernormal attainments. Expulsion for these offences was irrevocable (although we should note that people could otherwise freely leave and re-enter the Order up to seven times.) Other offences involve lighter punishments, such as temporary expulsion from the Order, expiation, and/or confession. There are also numerous rules governing etiquette – such as how food should be placed in the mouth, what sort of noises should not be made while eating, and how the robes of the monk or nun should be worn.

THE SKANDHAKA

We have already seen how the *Prātimokṣa* originated in the peripatetic life-style which developed during the Buddha's lifetime, and therefore reflects the rules that were needed to regulate the lives of wandering monks and nuns in the towns, villages, and forests of north-eastern India. However this sort of life-style came to be replaced by a more stable coenobitical life, conducted in *ārāmas* and *vihāras* – the latter donated by wealthy lay followers, as Buddhism itself became more popular and widely respected. Not surprisingly, therefore, a new body of rules grew up, which was concerned to help regulate the life of the broader community. This is the concern of the second division of the Vinaya, the *Skandhaka* (Pāli *Khandhaka*). Just as the *Prātimokṣa*, analysed in the *Sūtravibhaṅga*, regulates the life of the individual monk, so the *Karmavācā*, elaborated in a similar way in the *Skandhaka*, regulates the life of the whole monastic community.

There are twenty sections to the *Skandhaka*, and in the Pāli Vinaya they are divided between two books, the *Mahāvagga* and the *Cūlavagga*, i.e. between the 'Greater' and 'Lesser Divisions'. These are essentially concerned with explaining the origin of all aspects of the organization of the Saṅgha, and cover such things as admission to the Order, the ritual of confession, i.e. the recitation of the *Prātimokṣa* – the rules of personal training, the rainy season retreats, food and medicine, proper dwellings, permissible clothing, the proper resolution of disputes between monks, the nature of schism in the Saṅgha, along with a host of other things. As in the *Sūtravibhaṅga*, each rule is introduced in the context of an anecdote which explains how that rule came to be formulated. All the rules were supposedly devised by the Buddha himself.

It is the *Skandhaka* that shows how the punishments for infringements of the rules decreed in the *Prātimokṣa* are to be administered, for such punishment was the responsibility of the Saṅgha as a whole, and not of individuals. It is important to note that the most severe punishment possible was the exclusion of a person from the dealings and activities of the Saṅgha. This reveals that the nature and dealings of the life of the Saṅgha are essentially concerned with functioning in what one might call the 'love mode'.

This term is best understood through what might in contrast be called the 'power mode'. This governs any action towards another being that is committed against their will or better interest, and for the benefit of the actor. Obviously, it includes all forms of violence and coercion, but it also includes more subtle actions such as manipulation and the use of psychological pressures to obtain one's will over and against that of another. The love mode, in essence the implementation of the first precept, is the complete abnegation of this attitude in every detail, and its replacement with an over-riding concern for the welfare of the individual with whom one is dealing.

This means that in the context of the spiritual community there is, ideally, no possibility whatsoever of so-called 'punishments' involving violence or coercion, because this would be against the very spirit of the Buddha's teaching. It is for this reason that even the highest 'punishment' is merely that of expulsion from the circle of the Saṅgha – which is why an offence for which expulsion is decreed is termed a *pārājika*, 'defeat'. Clearly what is understood here is that a person who has joined the monastic order, yet who is still capable, for example, of intentionally taking life, is so fundamentally flawed that true (rather than nominal) membership of the Saṅgha is not possible, and that their quest for Awakening is fundamentally 'defeated'.

Care should be taken to avoid confusing the rules of the Vinaya with the purely ethical principles of conduct that lie at the heart of the Buddhist Path, something which is all too frequently done by writers upon Buddhism. The Vinaya Piṭaka is essentially a legal code concerned with rules of conduct for the monks and nuns, but not with the systematic exposition of Buddhist morality. The latter is encapsulated in various lists of precepts, found in numerous places within the Sūtra Piṭaka, that Buddhists chant regularly as an expression of their commitment to the Path, and try to observe in their lives.

This is not to suggest that there is no relationship at all between the Vinaya rules and the ethical life of the monks and nuns. All these rules (or most of them) were devised as means whereby the monk or nun could all the more easily, given the conditions prevailing in the India of their day, realize in themselves each one of the precepts as a living, active state of mind. In other words, rules were, at least originally, subservient to the states of mind that the practising Buddhist wished to engender and which are encapsulated in the precepts. Whilst in later centuries the monks tended to reduce the recitation of the *Prātimokṣa* to the chanting of a liturgy, in origin it was an opportunity to search their hearts for any failings in their practice of the precepts, and to accept admonishment from others if that was due. Something of this original spirit is revealed in a short sutta that shows the Buddha and an assembly of arhats asking for a mutual examination of faults in conduct at the end of the rainy season retreat.[90]

Having given in previous chapters some picture of how the *Prātimokṣa* arose, it is appropriate to give a similar account of the origins of the *Skandhaka*. As it stands at present, the *Skandhaka* contains, at its beginning and conclusion, portions of biographical material concerning the Buddha. Research has suggested that the *Skandhaka* may have been the central portion of a major literary composition which originally included a biography of the Buddha. The rationale for this is not difficult to see. The early monastic community was, not surprisingly, concerned with the validity of its own status and practices, and it sought to demonstrate its own authenticity by setting the rules which governed its behaviour, its 'constitution', in the context of a biography of the founder of that community. In other words, the *Skandhaka*, the central portion of the Vinaya, was originally a part of an extensive biography of the Buddha. As this extended biography became larger and larger, it became unwieldy and, as a consequence, various parts of it 'broke away', i.e. were memorized separately, and became independent texts in their own right, although one could argue that this theory goes against the inclusive and cumulative character of Indian religious literature. That biography, if it existed, is now to be found broken up and scattered amongst various sūtras that are now contained within the Sūtra Piṭaka, and functioned as the basis of all the early biographies of the Buddha. This interpretation also helps to explain why the *Mahāvastu*, describing itself as the introduction to the Mahāsaṅghika Vinaya, is in fact an extensive biography of the Buddha, and contains not a single rule.

This original *Skandhaka* would probably have been compiled about one hundred years after the death of the Buddha – but before the first schism in the Saṅgha. Erich Frauwallner suggests that it was the work of a single author and, as such, though remaining anonymous, it constitutes the 'first great literary work of Buddhism'.[91]

THE SŪTRA PIṬAKA

The Sūtra Piṭaka is the collection of the Buddha's sūtras (Pāli *suttas*), or discourses. The only complete version of the Sūtra Piṭaka survives in

Pāli. It is known, largely through the survival of fragmentary manuscripts from Central Asia, that there were versions in Sanskrit, Prakrit, Gandhārī, and other vernacular languages belonging to various other early schools. Larger portions of these other Sūtra Piṭakas have survived in Chinese translation, though only a small proportion of these have yet been translated into any European languages, and a full comparison between them and the Pāli Sutta Piṭaka is still awaited.[92] In the Pāli version over 5,000 suttas are gathered together, representing the teaching activity of the Buddha over forty-five years. Even so it appears that much was thought to have been lost after only the first thousand years of the transmission. Supposedly recited by Ānanda at the First Council and so personally witnessed and authenticated by him, each sutta begins with the words 'Thus have I heard. At one time ...'. However, as already suggested, many of them post-date this time, and some can be seen to be composite in character, with an early core surrounded by additions. In the Pāli recension some of these additions appear to be editorial in function, seeking to modify teachings in the light of a preferred doctrinal stance. It seems reasonable to suppose that the Sūtra Piṭakas of other schools showed similar modifications, though this has yet to be established.

Each sūtra has an introduction which describes the setting in which the Buddha delivered his discourse, and often names the others who were present. Whether these attributions reflect historical reality we cannot know. Not all the teachings are recorded as given by the Buddha. Some show his most important disciples, such as Śāriputra or Dhammadinnā, or even *devas* and *brahmās* (deities), expounding the Teaching too. Many of the earliest texts are in simple verse, most with no introduction, but some with prose introductions from a later period. The style of the sūtras is highly repetitious, because for the first four to five centuries they were preserved exclusively by oral recitation – a tradition taken over from the brahmaṇical Vedic transmission. The Pāli Sutta Piṭaka was only written down for the first time at the end of the 1st century BCE, in Sri Lanka, at a time when it seemed possible, through the scarcity of monks who held it in memory, that the whole Tipiṭaka might be lost.

THE STRUCTURE OF THE SŪTRA PIṬAKA

There is evidence to suggest that the first arrangement of the Buddha's discourses was based on literary principles, for it seems that originally the Saṅgha decided to compile collections of the discourses under twelve factors, or *aṅgas*, representing that number of types of composition.[93] Whether this was the arrangement chosen at the First Council we cannot be sure. These literary styles are: *sūtra* (the *Prātimokṣa*), *geya* (mixed prose and verse), *vyākaraṇa* (explanation, analysis), *gāthā* (verse), *udāna* (inspired speech), *ityukta* (beginning with 'Thus has the Bhagavan said'), *jātaka* (story of former birth), *adbhūtadharma* (concerning wonders and miraculous events), *vaipulya* (either 'extended discourses' or 'those giving joy'), *nidāna* (in which teachings are set within their circumstances of origin), *avadāna* (tales of exploits), and *upadeśa* (defined and considered instructions). This division is mentioned by all the non-Mahāyāna schools in their collections of sūtras (except for the Theravāda which does not mention the last three), and was continued by the Mahāyāna.

Be that as it may, a later system of division superseded that of the *aṅgas* among the non-Mahāyāna schools, involving the distribution of the Buddha's discourses between four or five categories. The divisions were known as *Āgamas* in Sanskrit, literally, 'that which has come [down]', or more interpretatively, the 'tradition'. The Pāli tradition chose instead to use the term *Nikāya* (not to be confused with *nikāya* as a designation for local monastic communities and ordination lineages). This time the principles of the distribution were a combination of length for the first two collections, and of content for the second two.

The first division was that of the *Dīrghāgama* (Pāli *Dīgha-Nikāya*) in which the longest of the discourses were gathered together – *dīrgha* meaning 'long'. The Pāli version contains 34 texts, which are divided into three sections. The longest among them is the *Mahāparinibbāna Sutta*, with a total of 95 pages, though this is exceptional, the rest averaging some 30 pages or so. The *Dīrghāgama* of the Dharmaguptaka School, containing 30 sūtras, survives in Chinese translation.

The second division contained all the remaining sūtras of any length and so was called the *Madhyamāgama* (Pāli *Majjhima-Nikāya*) – the 'middle length collection'. The Pāli version contains 152 suttas. A Sarvāstivādin *Madhyamāgama*, containing 222 sūtras, survives in Chinese translation.[94]

The next two collections, into which the remaining and shortest sūtras were placed, were compiled on a basis of content. In the *Saṁyuktāgama* (Pāli *Saṁyutta-Nikāya*) those sūtras with common themes, settings, interlocutors, etc. were collected together – *saṁyukta* meaning 'grouped'. The Pāli version holds over 2,800 suttas. A version of the *Saṁyuktāgama* belonging to the Sarvāstivādin School, containing only 1,300 sūtras, survives in Chinese.

In the *Ekottarāgama* (Pāli *Aṅguttara-Nikāya*) sūtras were grouped on the basis of the number of items of doctrine (ranging from one to eleven) expounded within them. These groups were arranged in order of ascending number – hence the name *ekottara*, meaning 'plus one'. This division contains over 2,300 suttas in the Pāli. There is a recension of the *Ekottarāgama* in Chinese translation which is thought to have belonged to the Mahāsaṅghika canon.[95]

Finally, some schools also compiled a *Kṣudrakāgama* (Pāli *Khuddaka-Nikāya*), the 'smaller' or 'inferior' collection. Clearly this division was adopted as an appropriate place for items that did not fit easily into the other four divisions, and it therefore has something of a miscellaneous character. The Pāli Sutta Piṭaka happens to be one that did contain such a division, which, in this case, is composed of fifteen different texts. They are very diverse in character, some very late, such as the *Buddhavaṁsa* and *Cariyāpiṭaka*, but others are very early and of great interest for giving a glimpse of the early character of the Buddha's teaching and activity, at a stage before it had become extensively formulated. Among these early texts one can include the famous *Dhammapada*, the *Sutta Nipāta*, the *Itivuttaka* and the *Udāna*. The *Khuddaka-Nikāya* also contains the *Thera-* and *Therī-gāthā*, 'Verses of the Elder Monks and Nuns' – usually spontaneous verse utterances of the disciples of the Buddha. One of the most popular sections of this *Āgama* is that of the *Jātaka*, the stories of the previous lives of the Buddha. Individual items from this *Āgama* survive in Chinese and Tibetan translations, e.g. there are three versions of the Dhammapada in Chinese. If a school did not have a *Kṣudrakāgama* it did not mean that it rejected these texts, but rather that it placed them in one of the other collections.

As can be seen from the numbers given above, there is not a close relationship between the sizes of the *Āgamas* and the *Nikāyas*, and it seems that these divisions were not only flexible, but were probably introduced after a number of the schools had separated from one another. Often texts associated with one *Nikāya* in Pāli are not to be found in the corresponding *Āgama*, and vice versa. As already indicated, individual monks and lineages of monks specialized in the memorization of a particular *Āgama*, suggesting that single collections may have been seen as complete and adequately authoritative in their own right. It should be stressed that the Sūtra Piṭaka was theoretically defined and closed to further addition at the First Council. However, in response to new materials that continued to appear during the first few centuries (perhaps stray sūtras preserved by a Purāṇa or his like), the community developed criteria to assess them for acceptance into the canon. The Sanskrit version of the *Mahāpadeśa Sūtra* explains that such material had to be 'collated' with the sūtras, 'compared' with the Vinaya, and inspected to see if it 'contradicted the nature of the Dharma'. Only then could it be accepted, and then only by either the Buddha, a legally formed Saṅgha, a group of Elders, or a particularly knowledgeable Elder, and in that order of authority.[96]

The contents of the Sūtra Piṭaka are very diverse, and quite fascinating in the picture that they paint of the Buddha and his disciples. Some discourses are philosophical in character, whilst others are narrative; some are technical, others poetic; some give historical detail, others recount legends. Overall, they offer an account of moving simplicity and grandeur, but they are not without humour. The Buddha clearly had a strong sense of irony, which he often used at the expense of arrogant brahmins, though not exclusively so.[97] Many Buddhists have found the Sūtra Piṭaka of inestimable value, for in reading or hearing the stories it contains they have felt as though they were in the presence of the Buddha himself, hearing the Buddhavacana.

> *Monks, just as the mighty ocean has one taste, the taste of salt, this Dharma too has one taste, monks, the taste of freedom.*[98]

10

The Abhidharma

Definition

The Abhidharma is not a school as such, but rather a body of literature. Not all the early schools had such a body of literature, but when they did they incorporated it into the canon. In essence it is an ordering and explanation of the key terms and categories of analysis that appear in the sūtras. The prefix *abhi-* means 'above' or 'for the sake of, with regard to', so the title is usually understood to mean 'that which is above the Dharma' or 'the higher or special teaching'. However, it could also be construed as meaning 'for the sake of the Dharma' or 'the ancillary to the Dharma'.

The Abhidharma was regarded as special in the sense that it presents the Dharma in a pure, theoretical framework, rather than in a historical context, as do the sūtras – though whether this is an advantage could be disputed. It is regarded as a 'higher' Dharma because it is thought to be offering an explanation of these terms superior to that offered by the sūtras themselves.

Background and Origin

It seems that the Abhidharma proper grew out of, or was built around, *mātṛkā* – i.e. lists of technical concepts, originally serving as mnemonic devices for memorizing teachings.[99] (It is in this sense that Abhidharma could be understood as 'ancillary to the Dharma'.) For example, the ubiquitous list of 37 *bodhipakṣika-dharmas*, or 'teachings that are requisite for Awakening'[100] may have been an early example, given by the

Buddha himself. We have another early example of this tendency in the *Saṅgīti Sutta*[101] where Sāriputta, who is traditionally associated with the origin of the Abhidharma, recites lists of teachings arranged according to number. Overall, the Abhidharma represents the attempt to extract from the Buddha's discourses a coherent and comprehensive statement of teaching.

The majority of the sūtras employ various systems of analysis of the perceived world, of what it is possible for human consciousness to be conscious. The most ubiquitous of these systems is the analysis of experience into the five skandhas: *rūpa*, forms; *vedanā*, feelings; *saṁjñā*, determinate perceptions; *saṁskāra*, volitions; and *vijñāna*, consciousnesses. Other common analytical systems are those of the twelve *āyatana* and the eighteen *dhātu*, which look at experience in terms of the six senses and their respective objects in the former, and these twelve items plus their respective sense fields in the latter. These early analytical lists, under which all other factors might be arranged, were of especial interest to the compilers of the Abhidharma, who could use them to organize the total body of material.

It is in the Abhidharma section of the Tripiṭaka that the greatest divergence between the schools became apparent, since different schools had their own unique Abhidharma collection. Because they were systematic works of exposition and arrangement, the compilers often employed or expounded the characteristic theories which their own school upheld, and moreover in places attempted to refute the competing theories of other schools. The *Kathāvatthu* of the Theravāda, for example, is a manual which seeks to refute 'five hundred heterodox views' upheld by twenty-six non-Theravādin schools.

LITERATURE

The position of the Abhidharma Piṭaka in the Buddhist canon, which is regarded as the word of the Buddha, is paradoxical. The individual volumes that make it up clearly post-date the Buddha's parinirvāṇa by at least a century or so, whereas the accounts of the compilation of the canon at the First Council in the post-canonical chronicles and commentaries state that the Abhidharma Piṭaka was recited then. Canonical texts refer only to the recitation of a *mātṛkā*. The best justification for the Abhidharma being included in this way is that some of the original *mātṛkā* may have been the work of the Buddha himself, and may have been recited at the First Council by way of summarizing the Buddha's teaching. The bulk of the Abhidharma works that survive are the product of the period between Aśoka (3rd century BCE) and Kaniṣka (1st century CE). This is very important, since it means that they are of roughly the same period as the very earliest Mahāyāna sūtras.

Two complete Abhidharma Piṭakas survive to the present day; that of the Theravādin School of South-east Asia, and that of the Sarvāstivādin School of north-west India. Each of these comprises seven treatises, but beyond that there is no similarity between them. Indeed, the Sarvāstivādin School, with the exception of its Vaibhāṣika offshoot in Kashmir, readily acknowledged that its Abhidharma works were the product of separate authors, among whom were included Śāriputra and Maudgalyāyana, the personal disciples of the Buddha. The *Jñānaprasthāna* was the work of the arhat Kātyāyanīputra (c.200BCE), and it was around this text that its followers arranged the remaining six Abhidharma treatises, likening them to the six feet that supported the body that was the *Jñānaprasthāna*.

By contrast the Theravādin School insisted that its Abhidhamma was the work of the Buddha himself – formulated by him during the fourth week of his sojourn by the Bodhi Tree after his Enlightenment, and later expounded by him, first to his mother in the Tāvatiṁsa *devaloka*, and then to his personal disciple most closely associated with wisdom, Śāriputra – who in turn recited it all at the First Council. The only exception to this was the *Kathāvatthu*, which was said to have been elaborated by Moggaliputta Tissa at the Third Council, but even this was really the work of the Buddha, for he had anticipated the future doctrinal divergences that were to occur, and had outlined a *mātṛkā* giving a list of the *Kathāvatthu*'s contents. Moggaliputta Tissa had only to expand these headings to form the treatise as it was included in the Abhidhamma Piṭaka! However, it seems likely that in reality the earliest treatise of the Theravādin collection, the *Dhammasaṅganī*, dates in its earliest part from a century after the Buddha.

That of the Theravāda is the only Abhidharma collection to survive in its entirety in its original Indian language. The Sarvāstivādin Abhidharma, originally composed in Sanskrit, survives only in Chinese and Tibetan translations. A brief analysis of the works of these two collections follows.

THE BOOKS OF THE THERAVĀDIN ABHIDHAMMA PIṬAKA

(a) *Dhammasaṅganī*, the 'classification of things' – listing and defining good, bad, and neutral mental states, and an analysis of material form.
(b) *Vibhaṅga*, 'analysis' – offering a detailed analysis or classification of sixteen major topics of the Dharma, including the skandhas, *nidānas*, the elements, the faculties, mindfulness, *bojjhaṅgas*, *jhānas*, and insight.
(c) *Dhātukathā*, 'discussion of the elements' – based on the *skandha* and *āyatana* analyses, and proceeding by means of questions and answers.
(d) *Puggalapaññati*, 'description of personalities' – the analysis of human character types, by various factors that range in number from one to ten.
(e) *Kathāvatthu*, 'subjects of controversy' – the refutation of the heterodox views of other Buddhist schools.
(f) *Yamaka*, the 'pairs' – concerned with clear definition of terms.
(g) *Paṭṭhāna*, 'causal relations' – a full discussion of *pratītya-samutpāda*.

THE BOOKS OF THE SARVĀSTIVĀDIN ABHIDHARMA PIṬAKA

(a) *Jñānaprasthāna*, the 'setting forth of wisdom', by Kātyāyanīputra – concerned with the definition of terms.
(b) *Prakaraṇapāda*, the 'basis of exposition', by Vasumitra – discusses elements under the skandha analysis and a revision of that analysis under the headings of *rūpa, citta*, and *caitasika dharmas;* also introduces a list of ten positive mental events.
(c) *Vijñānakāya*, the 'collection on consciousness', by Devaśarman – concerned with substantiating the Sarvāstivādin doctrines on the past and future existence of *dharmas*, and *anātman*.
(d) *Dharmaskandha*, the 'heap of elements', by Śāriputra – discussion of the *kleśas, āyatanas*, and *skandhas*, and the practices required to gain arhatship.
(e) *Prajñaptiśāstra*, the 'treatise on designations', by Maudgalyāyana – the arising of mental events, and cosmology.
(f) *Dhātukāya*, the 'collection of elements', by Pūrṇa – discussion of ever-present and negative mental events.
(g) *Saṅgītiparyāya*, the 'way of putting things in the rehearsal', by Mahākauṣṭhila (or Śāriputra) – a commentary on the *Saṅgīti Sūtra*.

Translations of single texts of the Dharmaguptaka, Pudgalavādin, and Mahāsaṅghika Abhidharmas survive in Chinese translation.

THE METHODS OF THE ABHIDHARMA

When the Buddha offered an analysis of the perceived world in the sūtras, he was making a fundamental distinction between things as they appear (how things seem to be to the unenlightened) and what really is the case (how things really are – *yathābhūta*). This distinction issues forth in the Abhidharma as the distinction between the two truths: *saṁvṛti-satya* – conventional truth – the way things appear, and *paramārtha-satya* – the ultimate truth, which is the object of *yathā-bhūta-jñāna-darśana*, 'knowing and seeing things as they really are'. The Abhidharma project was an attempt to systematize and to analyse all that exists, the conventional world, into its building blocks of ultimate existents, or *dharmas*, and thereby reveal the way things really are. The tools of analysis were meditation and clear, analytical thinking. Only those things that resisted analysis with such tools could be regarded as ultimately existent. When such 'elements' were identified they were termed *dharmas* – which results in a rather confusing duplication of terminology (but religious and linguistic development is rarely planned). In this context a *dharma* is something which is real, and it is known to be real because it is irreducible. It is irreducible because it is not made up of parts, either physical or qualitative.

Dharmas are not fixed, permanent objects, but momentary forces that are said to arise in a continual stream. They exist for a very short time, and during that time have a real existence. A mental *dharma* lasts for one-seventeenth of the time of a material *dharma*. For this reason we tend to identify the 'self' with the body, because it seems more permanent than our evanescent mental states. *Dharmas* could be described as those unique, elemental forces which constitute, or underlie, the flow of the conventional world. The Abhidharma developed a concept termed *svabhāva*, by which it indicated that each and every kind of *dharma* was differentiated from every other kind of *dharma* by its possession of unique defining characteristics. Each *dharma* is endowed with its *svabhāva*, 'own being' – that essence by which it could be differentiated from other *dharmas*. This differentiation is functional – each *dharma is* essentially what it *does*. Thus the defining characteristic of a *rūpa dharma* is its action of resistance to our subjective cognition, i.e. its very 'object-ness'. This 'object-ness' has four primary forms: hardness, fluidity, heat, and vibration, denoted by the terms earth, water, fire, and air. The insight of the Abhidharma was that conventional objects in the everyday world, such as pots and stones, do not have *svabhāva* because they are only mental constructs erroneously projected on to the 'real' *dharmas* that underlie the complex, superficial phenomenon.

It was a natural development that these analysts should begin to ask how many of these ultimate existents there are, and in the systems of different schools different numbers are given for the final total. The Theravāda enumerates 82 *dhammas*: 28 *rūpa* or material *dhammas*, 52 *caitasika* or mental *dhammas* (covering *vedanā, saṁjñā*, and *saṁskāra*), one *citta* or consciousness, all conditioned; and one unconditioned *dhamma*, *nibbāna*. The Sarvāstivāda lists 11, 46, and one conditioned *dharmas*, respectively, adding another category of 14 neither mental nor material; and distinguishing 3 unconditioned *dharmas*; space and two kinds of nirvāṇa, making 75 in all. That the majority of such *dharmas* are mental underlines the fact that the Abhidharma analysis is essentially related to meditation and what is perceived by the mind in higher meditative states. It would be misleading to assume that this analysis was in any way pseudo-scientific, and claimed to be analysing the make-up of the physical environment.

A practical example of the application of this method might be as follows: An ordinary, unenlightened person says 'I am pleased with this apple.' The Abhidharmic analysis would restate this by saying 'In association with this momentary series of material *dharmas* (*rūpa*) which constitute an apple, there is a concurrent series of feeling *dharmas* (*vedanā*) of a pleasant kind, of perception *dharmas* (*saṁjñā*) recognizing the object of happiness as an apple, of volitional *dharmas* (*saṁskāra*) both reflecting my past pleasure in apples and affirming a future predisposition to do so, and of consciousness *dharmas* (*vijñāna*), whereby there is awareness.' Clearly, the effect of such an analysis, if applied and sustained over a long period, is to reduce the tendency to identify with a fixed sense of selfhood, and instead to emphasize that experience is made up of a constantly changing flux of conditions.

Linking this in with our broader understanding of spiritual practice, the purpose of this analysis was to enable the monk or nun to develop the ability constantly to analyse experience into such *dharmas*. The main targets of this critical analysis were the ingrained but deluded tendency of a person to experience themselves as a fixed and unchanging entity and the greed and hatred attendant upon this tendency. This tendency is regarded as the prime cause of suffering in the world, and the eradication of that suffering is the chief function of Buddhist spiritual practice. So, when Abhidharma specialists analyse the world that they perceive (including their own person) into these ultimately real existents called *dharmas*, they are confronted by the fact that there is no fixed permanent entity called 'a person'. This *prajñā* or wisdom, the prime goal of the Abhidharma analysis, is termed the *pudgalanairātmya*, the 'absence of selfhood in people'. This in its turn would enable them to see things as they really are, eradicating ignorance, and cutting desire and hatred.

Schools who Rejected the Abhidharma

Not all non-Mahāyāna schools accepted the Abhidharma project. There appear to have been two reasons for such a rejection:

(a) The Sautrāntika School rejected the claim that the Abhidharma was ultimately authoritative. Its name means 'Ending with the Sūtra', implying that its concept of what was canonical ended with the Sūtra Piṭaka, the second Piṭaka. In fact, the origin of the Sautrāntika School lay in the rejection of the ever growing Vibhāṣas, or scholastic summaries, of the Vaibhāṣika-Sarvāstivāda. This conflict grew in intensity until, in the 4th century, the teacher Vasubandhu wrote his famous *Abhidharmakośa*, in which, in the verse portions, he sets out the Vaibhāṣika doctrine as he had learnt it from his teacher, Saṅghabhadra. In the prose commentary to these verses, he criticizes that doctrine from a Sautrāntika viewpoint. It seems that he was so successful in his criticism that the Vaibhāṣika School eventually died out, though its tenets continued to be studied in the monastic schools because of their inherent interest. Thereafter Vasubandhu's work was regarded as a definitive Abhidharma text, expounding both the Sarvāstivāda and Sautrāntika philosophies, and was the main focus of attention in this field for the Mahāyāna schools, and is still so among Tibetan Buddhist schools today. It should also be pointed out that, while some schools undoubtedly rejected the Abhidharma treatises as canonical texts and so had no Abhidharma Piṭaka, they did have their own non-canonical treatises or manuals functioning in much the same way.

(b) There were also schools which, whilst perhaps accepting the *dharma* analysis provisionally, rejected the idea that these *dharmas* were in any sense real, or ultimate. Among these we may include the Pūrvaśaila School (a Mahāsaṅghika sub-sect) which adopted what is called a *dharmaśūnyatā* stance in its *Lokānuvartana Sūtra*.[102] The term *dharmaśūnyatā*, 'emptiness of *dharmas*', is used to indicate that, just as conventional objects in the world are to be seen as *svabhāvaśūnya* (literally, 'empty of selfhood'), so too are the *dharmas* of the Abhidharma analysis. Since this is the case, they cannot be regarded as ultimately existent. *Dharmaśūnyatā* teachings also appear in the Mahāsaṅghika *Satyasiddhi-śāstra* of Harivarman (3rd century).[103]

That there was some disagreement over the value of such an analysis as was conducted by the Abhidharma, and that the theory of 'real *dharmas*' was rejected by some Buddhists, is of major significance for the story of the beginnings of the Mahāyāna.

11

Origins of the Mahāyāna

During the centuries either side of the beginning of the common era, teachings criticizing aspects of the Buddhism of the early schools, and introducing their own new religious preoccupations, began to make an appearance. From the modern perspective it is impossible to know the exact context for these developments, other than that they were embodied in new sūtras not belonging to the Tripiṭaka of the early schools. The new movement came, in the long term, to identify itself as the Mahāyāna, the 'Great Way', by way of a conscious contrast with, and criticism of, the non-Mahāyāna schools, which it dubbed the Hīnayāna, the 'Lesser or Inferior Way'. (The term *yāna* is often understood to mean 'vehicle', which it can do, but in an early Mahāyāna scripture, the *Saddharma-puṇḍarīka Sūtra,* it is clear that the broader sense of 'way' or 'path' is intended. The confusion appears to have arisen in the Chinese translations of the *Saddharma-puṇḍarīka Sūtra.*[104]) The Mahāyāna regards the aspirations and goal of the non-Mahāyāna schools, i.e. individual liberation and arhatship, as selfish and inadequate, and replaces them with a radical emphasis upon total altruism and fullest Awakening, embodied in the Bodhisattva Path, and full and perfect Buddhahood attained for the sake of alleviating the suffering of all beings.

However, it would be wrong to assume that this self-identification as a 'great way' was present from the very beginning. The earliest passages of the *Saddharma-puṇḍarīka* and *Aṣṭasāhasrikā-prajñāpāramitā Sūtras* lack certain key Mahāyāna terms,[105] and those of the *Vajracchedikā* and the *Kāśyapa-parivarta* do not mention the Bodhisattva ideal.[106] The *Ajitasena Sūtra,* thought to be an early or proto-Mahāyāna sūtra,[107] describes both a śrāvaka and an elderly washerwoman who are predicted to full Buddhahood, and throughout the sūtra there is neither any criticism of the spiritual ideals of non-Mahāyāna schools, nor any mention of the very word Mahāyāna. Generally, the textual and epigraphical evidence suggests that the term Mahāyāna may not have become current until as late as the 4th century.[108] But these earliest texts indicate three areas which were characteristic concerns of the early Mahāyānists – the doctrinal position and the practices of the Abhidharma schools, the changing status of the Buddha, and the relevance of lay versus monastic status to spiritual attainment – each of these being responses to trends of development evident among the early schools.

The Perfection of Wisdom sūtras, among the earliest Mahāyāna sūtras, attack the view, attributed to followers of the Abhidharma (and probably a direct reference to the *sarvam asti* doctrine of the Sarvāstivāda[109]), that the *dharmas* identified by the Abhidharma had some sort of ultimate existence, in that they represented the irreducible and permanent elements from which the experienced world was derived. Central to this debate was the concept of *svabhāva*, which, in the Abhidharma, referred to the unique defining characteristics of *dharmas*. The Perfection of Wisdom broadened this terminology of *svabhāva* from meaning 'defining characteristic' to a synonym for 'inherent existence', i.e. ultimate, permanent existence. Understood in this way, *svabhāva* became not just a technical Abhidharma concept, but also an epitome of the conventional views of permanence and selfhood held in the world. This critique proposed that, although the Abhidharma claimed that it had arrived at the ultimate truth by analysing all experience into its component *dharmas*, it had in fact fallen into the same error as the ordinary unenlightened person, because it attributed to these *dharmas* an ultimate, permanent existence. In the same way that the Abhidharma taught the 'lack of self in people', *pudgalanairātmya*, so the Perfection of Wisdom sūtras taught the 'emptiness of *dharmas*', *dharmaśūnyatā*.

Moreover, the Abhidharma appears to have developed (in certain instances) a relatively negative conception of nirvāṇa. This was expressed by a rather narrow and emotionally alienating approach to spiritual practice, which must have reduced the apparent possibility of spiritual progress through personal interaction and devotion[110] – although there is much evidence in the Pāli Canon to suggest that these were originally very important. Furthermore, the later Abhidharma gives the impression that the mere intellectual grasp of the enumeration of elements was equated with spiritual wisdom.[111] The Mahāyāna therefore emphasized the 'perfection' of wisdom, the attainment of a wisdom that altogether transcends that of the Abhidharma wisdom.

It is clear that the nature of the Buddha, and of the Buddha Jewel as Refuge, was a matter of some concern and debate in the non-Mahāyāna schools. Many Mahāyāna sūtras bear witness to the intense wish felt by many Buddhists to see, i.e. to have visionary contact with, Buddhas – be it Śākyamuni or one of the many new Buddhas whose existence was affirmed from this time onwards. This development was clearly connected with the meditation schools of Kashmir and Central Asia, amongst which ideas of archetypal 'meditation' Buddhas and Bodhisattvas may well have originated. The new Mahāyāna sūtras show new forms of spiritual practice oriented around devotion to these new archetypal Buddhas and Bodhisattvas.[112] The historical background to this period of the emergence of the Mahāyāna was one of political disturbance and turmoil in northern India. The persecutions of Buddhism by Puṣyamitra Śuṅga (183–147BCE) were followed by repeated invasions from the north-west, the first that of the Śakas (c.90BCE). The pro-Buddhist king, Kaniṣka, with whose reign several significant developments are associated, was himself a Kuṣāṇa king, who took control of a north-western empire created by a second wave of invasion beginning in the early 1st century CE. It seems likely that the insecurity and uncertainty of the period may have contributed to the emergence of the new religious forms characterized as the Mahāyāna, and it is probably significant that in places the practice of *buddhānusmṛti*, the recollection of the Buddha, is recommended as an antidote to fear.[113]

The Mahāyāna sūtras clearly re-evaluate the relative roles of the monastic and lay practitioner, making it clear that the new movement put less stress upon formal membership of the monastic community as a prerequisite for pursuit of the Bodhisattva Path. This is suggested by the frequency with which lay people, sometimes women, are shown with high attainments, and reaches its apogee in the figure of Vimalakīrti, the layman Bodhisattva who trounces all the śrāvakas and even the archetypal Bodhisattvas. The principle seems to be that spiritual attainment is not defined by, or restricted to those occupying, formal positions and roles within the monastic Saṅgha.

However, this is not to say that the Mahāyāna was started by laymen, as has often been asserted, especially in Japanese scholarship. Such involvement is unlikely because innovation in the Mahāyāna is always associated with monks. The great proponent of the Perfection of Wisdom sūtras was the monk Nāgārjuna, and, even when the authenticity of the new sūtras was questioned, the accusation was never that they were lay creations. Epigraphical evidence implies that there was no extensive lay patronage of a consciously distinct 'Mahāyāna' movement till as late as the 6th century, i.e. 600 years after the compilation of the first Mahāyāna Sūtras, at a time when, according to the conventional chronology, the Mahāyāna was being superseded by the Vajrayāna.[114] There is no evidence that the Mahāyāna attempted to denigrate or eradicate the monastic way of life (as one might expect if the theory of a lay 'rebellion' were the case). If anything it records a more ascetic view of the path, with repeated criticism of those who fall back to lay habits. As in the Tripiṭaka of the non-Mahāyāna schools, the Mahāyāna sūtras include lay and monastic interlocutors, and teachings for the lay and monastic communities (e.g. the *Ugradattaparipṛcchā* and *Upāliparipṛcchā* respectively). The Mahāyāna sūtras were undoubtedly the product of a monastic milieu, especially if the connection with meditation noted above was the case, since intensive meditation is surely the privilege of the specialist who is free from household responsibilities. However, these were clearly monks who had a vision of spiritual development that transcended monastic formalism, and perhaps this should be linked with the trend apparent in some early schools that questioned the status of the arhat.

It should be remembered that by this time (1st century BCE to 1st century CE) Buddhism had become a rather more static phenomenon than the early community at the time of the Buddha. It was a religion of wealthy monastic endowments, and was patronized by kings, especially foreign invaders who wished to find support against the brahmaṇical orthodoxy of Indian society, who regarded foreigners as among the lowest of the low in social and religious terms. The growth of monastic life, and its increasing complexity (evidenced by the development of the full Vinaya) must have resulted in greater separation between the life of the monk and the life of the lay-person.

It is possible that lay people appear in such positive light in the sūtras as an implicit criticism of the conservative and elitist monks against whom members of the Mahāsaṅgha had protested, monks who said that Enlightenment was only for the monk, and who claimed for themselves the prestige of the arhat. Indeed, the very same point may also be made to account for the increased emphasis placed upon Buddhahood rather than arhatship in these sūtras. Whilst in the Buddha's day Enlightenment was seen as a single, undifferentiated attainment, in the sense that the Awakening achieved by the Buddha's disciples was regarded as identical to that of the Buddha, the Mahāyānists may have emphasized the distinction between the two attainments in order to demote the status of supposed arhats in the monasteries, and to reassert the original spiritual values in the Buddha's teaching. On the other hand, the miraculous powers and transformation of laypersons may also have been intended as metaphors for the potency of spiritual ideals promoted in the new scriptures. Be that as it may, as the goal of full Buddhahood came to be seen as superior to that of arhatship, so the layperson as a potential Bodhisattva also gained in importance. In this respect the impact of the *Jātaka* stories, always one of the most popular teaching media, in which the historical Buddha-to-be appears as ordinary people or even as various animals, must have been significant.

Yet the dynamic involved in this development was not one of schism in any technical sense. Whilst the fully evolved Mahāyāna strongly criticized the attitudes of the Hīnayāna, this was done on the basis of individual conscience, and not institutional segregation. There was no such thing as a Mahāyāna Vinaya. All Mahāyānists were ordained within the *nikāyas* of the non-Mahāyāna schools, and observed whichever Vinaya governed their *nikāya*. Mahāyānists lived in the same monasteries as their 'Hīnayānist' brothers, as was observed by the medieval Chinese pilgrims, though this is not to say that they did not supplement the Vinaya code with their own characteristic views on morality. In particular, the new teaching of *upāya*, '[skilful] means' relativized the regulations of the Vinaya by reasserting spiritual expediency in the service of compassion above institutional formalism. Even today, the Buddhists of Tibet, all adherents of the teachings of the Mahāyāna, observe the Vinaya of the Mūla-Sarvāstivādins.

In addition to the worship of new Buddhas and Bodhisattvas, it also seems that the early Mahāyāna involved the worship of the new sūtras themselves. Many early sūtras contain passages where the hearer is encouraged to worship the sūtra, using incense, flags, and bells, much as one would a stūpa – and where stūpa worship itself is denigrated, or at least held to be inferior to praise of the sūtra and of the *dharmabhāṇaka*, the preacher of the sūtra.[115] On an organizational level it seems likely that, in origin, the Mahāyāna was an informal coalition of mutually sympathetic sūtra cults, in which groups of followers recited, studied, and worshipped their own sūtra.

The Mahāyāna sūtras paint a picture of widespread popularity, suggesting that the new movement was singularly successful and quickly won the support of all but the most intransigent and spiritually myopic. Yet the true story may well have been rather different. Mention has already been made of the lack of evidence for lay support prior to the 6th century, and for any self-conscious Mahāyāna identity before the fourth. Each of the Chinese pilgrims who travelled in India between the 5th and mid-7th centuries observed that the majority of monks were followers of the Hīnayāna. Tārānātha, the 17th century Tibetan historian, records that most Indian Buddhists rejected the authenticity of the Mahāyāna sūtras, on the grounds that they were not to be found in the Tripiṭaka, and therefore could not be Buddhavacana.[116]

It may even be that, in the long run, we shall be forced to see the Mahāyāna in India itself as, for many centuries, a largely monastic preoccupation, limited to a relatively small number of peripheral monks – the latter point being deduced from the fact that there is only occasional refutation of Mahāyāna doctrines contained in the treatises of the non-Mahāyāna schools. This contrasts strongly with the position in the Mahāyāna sūtras where there is frequent and sometimes bitter criticism of the so-called Hīnayāna. It may be that this reflects a vigorous polemical position adopted by Mahāyānists as they sought to establish their reforms in competition with the claims to authenticity which the adherents of the Tripiṭaka could make for their own position, but it is also possible to see it as a defensive stance adopted by a minority who felt embattled and insecure. Perhaps there were elements of both. The greatest successes for the Mahāyāna were achieved outside its Indian homeland, as it spread, via Central Asia, to Tibet, China, Korea, and Japan, where it was able totally to supplant the position of the non-Mahāyāna schools.

12

The Mahāyāna Sūtras: New Scriptures

THE MOST CHARACTERISTIC FEATURE KNOWN of the emergence of the Mahāyāna, and of its later development, was the compilation of numerous sūtras teaching new Mahāyāna doctrines, and praising the new Mahāyāna religious ideal, the Bodhisattva. Unlike the sūtras of the Tripiṭaka, which are mostly historical in character, the Mahāyāna sūtras tend either to offer a lengthy and abstract discourse, or to portray a magical world of archetypal figures divorced from historical time and place, and make their greatest appeal to the spiritual Imagination, which they expand and transform through the means of visionary drama.[117] The new scriptures did not form a coherent body of doctrinal exposition; they propounded different and even apparently contradictory teachings. Moreover, many individual sūtras are clearly composite works, compiled over many centuries, such that the final text is formed from layers of material of different ages, and sometimes with different outlooks, so that even individual sūtras do not necessarily present a unitary, coherent teaching. The result of this was that several expository traditions arose to try to explain the teaching of the new texts, the more cohesive of these forming distinct schools.[118]

The new sūtras appeared over several centuries, from the 1st century BCE through to at least the middle of the first millennium of the common era. All the earliest Mahāyāna sūtras were composed in a Middle Indo-Āryan (MIA) language, which was later Sanskritized, probably under the impact of the Gupta dynasty (c.320–540CE) which adopted Sanskrit as its official language. The older verse portions of these sūtras survive in a MIA/Sanskrit mix, usually called Buddhist

Hybrid Sanskrit, whilst the accompanying prose introductions are often in normal Sanskrit, suggesting that they are possibly explanatory in character. The youngest sūtras are written entirely in normal Sanskrit. No defined Mahāyāna canon was produced to compare with the Tripiṭaka of the non-Mahāyāna schools, not least because the general principle governing Mahāyāna teaching was inclusive rather than exclusive. For this reason the Mahāyāna accepts and reveres all the sūtras of the Tripiṭaka in addition to its own. Mention is made within some Mahāyāna sūtras of the twelve *aṅgas*, or factors, under which the Tripiṭaka itself may have been organized in its earliest form.

Many of the Mahāyāna sūtras describe themselves as *vaipulya*, meaning 'expanded', in the sense that they are often many times longer than the longest sūtras of the Tripiṭaka, and also that they each embody a comprehensive perspective on the Dharma as a whole, one which implies acceptance and knowledge of the teachings of the mainstream scriptures. It is not clear whether these texts were originally oral or literary compositions. It is likely that, on account of their great length, individual monks would only have been able to memorize one or two of these new scriptures, in place of the complete collections from the Tripiṭaka learnt by the *bhāṇakas* of the non-Mahāyāna schools. The Mahāyāna sūtras, like those of the Tripiṭaka, have been the subject of commentaries that have been produced both in India and in other countries.[119]

ORIGINS

It is an integral feature of the Mahāyāna tradition that, whilst there may be differences of emphasis between the Mahāyāna and Hīnayāna sūtras, they were all taught by the historical Buddha Śākyamuni. Whereas the sūtras of the Tripiṭaka were accepted as having been taught in the hearing of ordinary mortals, the Mahāyāna sūtras were said to have been taught on a refined, archetypal level of existence, to a more exalted audience consisting of divine beings, the Buddha's most advanced human disciples, and the various magnificent celestial Bodhisattvas such as Mañjuśrī, Avalokiteśvara and Mahāsthāmaprāpta. There is even a tradition of an alternative 'First' Council at which all the Mahāyāna sūtras were recited, presided over by the Bodhisattva Mañjuśrī, that took place upon the same archetypal level of reality at which the sūtras themselves had first been revealed by Śākyamuni.

However, linguistic, textual, social, and sometimes doctrinal evidence provided by the texts themselves suggest composition at a later date and, most decisive of all, they consciously criticize some of the teachings and practices of the Hīnayāna which they clearly see as pre-existent.

Several factors may be adduced in explanation of the appearance of these 'new' sutras. Firstly, there is the possibility that the Mahāyāna sūtras may well record genuine teachings of the historical Buddha which were not collected into the Tripiṭaka, and which only began to become prominent several centuries after the death of the Buddha. The story of Purāṇa at the First Council suggests one way in which this may have happened. The possibility remains that the advent of writing as an acceptable medium for the preservation of the Buddhavacana at around this time (e.g. the Pāli Tripiṭaka was recorded in writing in 17BCE) played an important part in the preservation and dissemination of discourses extraneous to the Tripiṭaka, whether or not they originated with the Buddha himself. Secondly, several Mahāyāna sūtras are connected with profound meditational experience, and one at least, the *Pratyutpanna Sūtra*, teaches a *samādhi* in which one will see one or many Buddhas, hear them teach, and after which one will be able to communicate that teaching to others.[120] Thirdly, the principle upon which something might be regarded as an expression of the Dharma is far broader in the Mahāyāna. Śāntideva quotes the *Adhyāśaya-saṁcodana Sūtra* on four qualities of a teaching by which it comes to be seen as the word of the Buddha: (a) It should be connected with the truth, (b) It should be concerned with the Dharma, (c) It should bring about renunciation of moral taints, (d) It should reflect the qualities of nirvāṇa, not saṁsāra.[121] Rather than regarding the canon as being closed to further additions, in the way that the Tripiṭaka was supposed to have been at the First Council, the Mahāyāna clearly adopted an inclusive attitude, expressive of an openness to any teachings which were effective – itself a reflection of the new doctrine of *upāya*, '[skilful] means' (see below).

Some 600 Mahāyāna sūtras have survived to the present day, either in Sanskrit or in Tibetan and Chinese translations. In the following survey various groupings are suggested based on the nature of the teachings of the sūtras, but it should be borne in mind that, with only a few exceptions, these groupings were not self-conscious, and that many sūtras cut across any categories that are narrower than the general category of 'Mahāyāna'.

PRAJÑĀPĀRAMITĀ SŪTRAS

The Prajñāpāramitā sūtras, or Perfection of Wisdom sūtras, are a body of self-consciously related works dealing with the subject of the new *prajñā*, or wisdom, taught by the Mahāyāna. Instrumental in the origins of the Mahāyāna itself, some texts from this category are among the earliest Mahāyāna sūtras, probably originating in the 1st century BCE. Four phases have been identified in the growth of this body of texts:[122]

(a) 100BCE–100CE: the *Ratnaguṇasaṁcayagāthā* and the *Aṣṭasāhasrikā* (8,000 lines).

(b) 100–300CE: a period of elaboration that produced versions in 18,000, 25,000, and 100,000 lines (and possibly the *Vajracchedikā*).

(c) 300–500CE: a period of condensation, producing, among others, the *Heart Sūtra* (although there is some evidence to suggest that this particular text was originally written in Chinese and then translated back into Sanskrit.[123])

(d) 500–1000CE: a period producing texts showing Tantric influences.

The sūtras themselves offer no elaborate philosophical argument – just the assertion of the true way of things, which is that nothing has ultimate existence, not even the purportedly real *dharmas* of the Abhidharma analysis. A characteristic device of these sūtras is the creation of paradoxes by switching between the conventional and the ultimate perspectives. The Perfection of Wisdom sūtras, and their *dharmaśūnyatā* position, were not accepted by all the adherents of the Bodhisattva Path.[124]

THE *SADDHARMA-PUṆḌARĪKA SŪTRA* OR *LOTUS SŪTRA*

The earliest date ascertainable for this sūtra is between 100BCE and 100CE. It is a composite text, showing an overall division into two sections, the first relating to *upāya* and *ekayāna*, and the latter to the life-span of the Buddha. *Upāya*, or skilful means, is the central teaching of the sūtra, and describes the way in which the Buddha adapts his teaching to the disposition (*adhimukti*) of his hearers, which means that the value of a teaching is relative to its result. This doctrine became the prime means used to account for the varied teachings of the sūtras, since those which were not thought to teach the ultimate truth, *paramārtha-satya*, were seen as *upāya* of the Buddha. The teaching of *ekayāna*, one way, maintains that the three *yānas*, the *śrāvaka-yāna* (the 'way' of the 'hearers' or disciples of the non-Mahāyāna schools), the *pratyekabuddha-yāna* (the 'way' of Buddhas who achieve Awakening on their own, and do not teach), and the *bodhisattva-yāna* are not separate approaches leading to distinct goals, but are only one *yāna*, identified as the *bodhisattva-yāna*, the path of Mahāyāna practice embodied in the Six Perfections, and leading to full and perfect Buddhahood. The previous *yānas* were just *upāya*, accommodations made by the Buddha to the various abilities and levels of spiritual development of different people. Among the reasons for the extensive popularity of this sūtra must be included its dramatic format and extensive use of parables to illustrate *upāya* and *ekayāna*. Great advantages are said to arise for those who praise and disseminate the sūtra, and in China and Japan it was thought to possess magical powers.

When the ancient Buddha Prabhūtaratna appears, in chapter 11, he reveals that this sūtra is not new, but has been preached frequently in past world ages. His appearance also shows that more than one Buddha can exist in the same place at the same time, contradicting the previously held view that not more than one Buddha can appear in the same world-system at once. It also affirms that a Buddha is not inaccessible after his parinirvāṇa, since Prabhūtaratna died aeons ago. This demonstrates that even Śākyamuni Buddha's death was an *upāya*. In reality his life-span is inconceivably long, as a result of his immense accumulation of merit over innumerable past lives.

In this respect the *Saddharma-puṇḍarīka* could be seen as developing the *lokottaravāda* teachings of the Mahāsaṅghikas. The new understanding of the life of the Buddha offered in this sūtra, combined with the possibility of visionary experience expounded in other Mahāyāna sūtras, accounts for the growth of numerous archetypal Buddhas in addition to the historical Buddha Śākyamuni. In their turn, these Buddhas became the focus for devotional cults. This practice was present from the earliest period of the Mahāyāna, and is witnessed and exemplified by those sūtras dedicated to the exposition of the Pure Land of Amitābha (see below). The nature of these 'visionary' Buddhas was later systematized in the Trikāya doctrine of the Yogācārin School. Most important among the archetypal Buddhas were Amitābha and Akṣobhya, who formed a triad with Śākyamuni, and to whom were attributed three attendant Bodhisattvas, Avalokiteśvara, Vajrapāṇi, and Mañjuśrī respectively.

SUKHĀVATĪ-VYŪHA SŪTRAS

The *Sukhāvatī-vyūha Sūtras* describe and explain the origin of the Pure Land of the red Buddha Amitābha, 'Infinite Radiance', who is also mentioned in the *Lotus* and *Pratyutpanna Sūtras*. In the *Larger Sukhāvatī Sūtra* the Bodhisattva Dharmākara takes forty-six vows, in which he undertakes to build a 'pure land' in which beings shall be able to practise the Dharma with the greatest of ease. This land, called Sukhāvatī or 'blissful', is described in great detail, in a way that suggests that the sūtras were to be used as guides to visualization meditation, and also gives an impression of a magical world of intense visual, and sonorous delight. Presided over by Dharmākara, who has by now become the Buddha Amitābha, beings may be born in this world purely through devotion to him. This is possible because he can now transfer to them the immense merit that he has accumulated in order to fulfil his vows. Those who wish to be reborn there must be pure in conduct, must think continuously of Amitābha, praising him, recounting his virtues, and repeating his name. They must firmly believe in the efficacy of his vow, and must visualize him in his Pure Land. Once there, Sukhāvatī provides the very best conditions for spiritual practice, such that Enlightenment is assured.

The *Sukhāvatī-vyūha Sūtras* were very popular in Kashmir and Central Asia, where indeed they may have originated. They were transmitted to China at an early period (the larger sūtra being translated into Chinese in 223CE), where they were highly influential, and formed the basis of the Ching-t'u School. Whilst there developed Pure Land schools devoted to the praise of Amitābha and entry to his Pure Land, it is clear that devotion to Amitābha was general and widespread. He is mentioned in the 2nd century CE by Nāgārjuna,[125] who in China is traditionally regarded as the first Patriarch of the Pure Land tradition.

THE *VIMALAKĪRTI-NIRDEŚA SŪTRA*

The *Vimalakīrti-nirdeśa Sūtra*, or 'Sūtra on the Discourse of Vimalakīrti', recounts, with wit and drama, the preaching to an audience of Bodhisattvas and bhikṣus by the layman Vimalakīrti. As such it represents the most extreme assertion of the validity of lay Buddhist practice beside that of the formal Saṅgha and the danger of superficial judgements based on external appearances. Doctrinally it propounds a

Wisdom teaching very similar to that of the Perfection of Wisdom sūtras. It also discusses the purification of the *buddha-kṣetra*, the Buddha-field, or field of influence of an individual Buddha, and so has some connection with Pure Land teachings. Possibly composed some time before 150CE, it became extremely popular in China and Japan, where it was thought more compatible with the ethics of social duty and filial piety.

SAMĀDHI SŪTRAS

A number of important Mahāyāna sūtras teach profound *samādhis*, or meditational attainments. These include the *Samādhirāja Sūtra*, the *Pratyutpanna Sūtra*, and the *Śūraṅgama-samādhi Sūtra*, of which the last two are among the earliest known Mahāyāna sūtras. This suggests that profound meditational experience had played a major role in the early Mahāyāna movement. The first of these, the *Samādhirāja Sūtra*, is very extensive, and is based on a dialogue between the Buddha and a young man, Candraprabha, and incorporates a number of stories of previous lives of the Buddha of some literary merit. The second of these sūtras describes a *samādhi* in which one can see Buddhas, hear them teach the Dharma, and then disseminate those teachings. The *Śūraṅgama-samādhi Sūtra* contains an exposition of the concentration of the *śūraṅgama*, the 'heroic advance', by which the Bodhisattva attains fullest Awakening, yet can also perform numerous deeds demonstrating the Dharma within saṁsāra.

CONFESSION SŪTRAS

Two sūtras reflect the significance given to confession in the Mahāyāna, perhaps by way of a critique of the formalism of monastic confession at the *upavasatha* ceremony. The *Triskandha Sūtra*, also found as a chapter of the early *Upālipariprcchā*, is a short text by which confession is made to the thirty-five 'Confession' Buddhas, and came to play an important ritual role in Mahāyāna Buddhism, being recommended for daily recitation by Śāntideva.[126] The original core of the *Suvarṇa-prabhāsa Sūtra* was the third chapter concerned with confession to the Buddhas, though over subsequent centuries numerous other miscellaneous chapters were added, many of them concerned with the protection of the sūtra by deities.

The *Avataṁsaka* (or *Buddhāvataṁsaka*) *Sūtra*

The *Avataṁsaka Sūtra* is a large composite work. The Chinese translations of this work appear to have incorporated a considerable amount of material originally circulating independently, some sections having been translated into Chinese by Lokakṣema in the latter half of the 2nd century CE. It is thought to have been collated into its present form by the middle of the 4th century.[127] This sūtra also contains two other sūtras which circulated independently, and have survived in their original Sanskrit. Those are the *Daśabhūmika Sūtra*, which teaches the ten *bhūmis*, or stages, of the Bodhisattva's career, and the *Gaṇḍavyūha Sūtra*, which describes the search made by the young man Sudhana for the true *kalyāṇa-mitra*, or spiritual friend. The Buddha Vairocana appears in the *Buddhāvataṁsaka Sūtra*, most notably in the 'Gaṇḍavyūha' chapter, which was the source for the cult of that Buddha later embodied in the *Mahāvairocanābhisaṁbodhi Tantra* of the *caryā* class of tantras. Both sūtras are thought to date from the 1st or 2nd century CE. The *Avataṁsaka* as a whole teaches the doctrine of interpenetration (and the Tathāgatagarbha), and was highly influential in Chinese Buddhism, forming the basis of the Hua-yen School, and hence also in Japan and Korea.

Idealist Sūtras

The idealist sūtras, to use a non-traditional term, are an extremely important group which teach the doctrine of *cittamātra*, or 'mind-only'. They were expounded as teaching the ultimate truth by the Yogācārin School, and are dealt with in the chapter on that school.

Tathāgatagarbha Sūtras

These consist of a number of sūtras which teach the presence of the Tathāgatagarbha, the 'embryo of the Tathāgata', in all beings. They are dealt with in the chapter on the Tathāgatagarbha doctrine.

Collected Sūtras

There are two very large sūtras which consist of collections of shorter texts. The *Mahāratnakūṭa Sūtra* contains forty-nine works, though the original core of the Sūtra was the forty-third, the *Kāśyapa-parivarta*. The bulk of these subsidiary sūtras take the form of *paripṛcchās*, or questions asked of the Buddha by an interlocutor, but there is no overall theme to their teachings. It includes sūtras on the Perfection of Wisdom, the Pure Lands, Vinaya, the Tathāgatagarbha, et al., including some which appear separately elsewhere. Whilst some sections are very early, it is thought that the collection as a whole was organized at some time after the 5th century, and possibly in Central Asia.[128] The *Mahāsaṁnipāta Sūtra* contains seventeen shorter sūtras, one of which was in circulation before 150CE, whereas the collection as whole was probably organized in or after the 5th century.

TRANSMIGRATION SŪTRAS

Included in this group are a number of sūtras which describe actions leading to the various spheres of existence, e.g. the *Saddharma-smṛtyu-pasthāna Sūtra*, and those, such as the *Śālistamba Sūtra*, which examine the twelve *nidānas*, or links of the *pratītya-samutpāda*, 'dependent origination'.

'DISCIPLINE' SŪTRAS

Several Mahāyāna sūtras set forth in a more systematic manner the principles which should guide the conduct of the Bodhisattva. These include the *Kāśyapa-parivarta Sūtra*, the *Bodhisattva-prātimokṣa Sūtra*, also known as the *Upālipariprcchā Sūtra*, and the *Brahmajāla Sūtra*.

SŪTRAS DEVOTED TO INDIVIDUAL FIGURES

Many sūtras appeared devoted to extolling the nature and virtues of individual Buddhas and Bodhisattvas. Mañjuśrī's Pure Land is described in the *Mañjuśrī-buddhakṣetra-guṇa-vyūha Sūtra*, Avalokiteśvara's compassion is lauded in the *Kāraṇḍa-vyūha Sūtra*, whilst the medicine Buddha, Bhaiṣajyaguru, appears in at least four sūtras which include his name in their title. The Bodhisattva Kṣitigarbha, who descends into the hell realms to save beings there, is the subject of several sūtras originating in Central Asia, as is the future Buddha, Maitreya, and the Buddha Akṣobhya's Pure Land is described in the *Akṣobhya-vyūha Sūtra*.

13

The New Spiritual Ideal: The Bodhisattva

If any single factor could be taken to distinguish the Mahāyāna from the non-Mahāyāna schools, then the ideal of the Bodhisattva would be the most appropriate. In the non-Mahāyāna schools the only Bodhisattvas that were recognized were the successive rebirths of the being who was to be reborn as Siddhartha Gautama and whose previous existences are recorded in the *Jātaka* books of the *Khuddaka-Nikāya*, and Maitreya, the present Buddha-to-be. The only religious goal recognized was that of the arhat, or membership of the Ārya-Saṅgha, though later sources began to speak of a figure known as the *pratyekabuddha*, a person who had realized Awakening independently, like a Buddha, but who did not teach. A Bodhisattva, literally a 'Bodhi-being', but perhaps, in origin, a term meaning 'committed to' or 'intent upon Bodhi', is someone who pursues the goal of full and perfect Buddhahood, rather than arhatship, and in the Mahāyāna this goal is presented as the ideal goal for which all Buddhists should strive. Moreover, the Bodhisattva is someone who aims for full Buddhahood for the benefit of all living beings, hence the common appellation Bodhisattva Mahāsattva – Bodhisattva referring to their personal aspiration to Enlightenment, and Mahāsattva, 'great being', to their aspiration to help other beings.

Without doubt the Bodhisattva ideal represents a resurgent emphasis upon compassion, and implicitly accuses the representatives of the non-Mahāyāna tradition, the śrāvakas, and their goal of arhatship, as lacking in this quality. Whether or not this was true of the non-Mahāyāna Saṅgha at this time, it should be pointed out that compassion had been a major element of the historical Buddha's life and teaching, as is illustrated by many episodes from his life. Therefore the Mahāyāna emphasis represents something of a reassertion of what had been inherent in the Buddha's teaching, if imperfectly understood by some, since the earliest times. The Bodhisattva ideal was, indeed still is, the commitment to Enlightenment which recognizes the equal importance of wisdom and compassion. The Bodhisattva seeks personal salvation through wisdom, but that salvation is achieved for the sake of aiding all sentient beings, out of compassion for them. The Bodhisattva seeks to become a Buddha because only a Buddha has the knowledge and means to save the maximum number of beings.

Three factors are said to characterize the Bodhisattva: a profound, non-dual wisdom, an extensive compassion, and the presence of the bodhicitta, the 'mind of, or will towards, Enlightenment'. The bodhicitta is not just an intellectual thought about Enlightenment, but a force or urge which completely transforms the life of the future Bodhisattva, such that its arising is likened to being reborn within a new family.[129] It is described by Nāgārjuna as something entirely outside the five skandhas, in other words, something outside mundane existence.[130] Various methods were developed to cultivate the bodhicitta. One of the most widely used is the *anuttarapūjā*, 'supreme worship'. The earliest account of this method is to be found in the final chapter of the *Gaṇḍavyūha Sūtra* (translated into Chinese by the 4th century, possibly as early as the 1st or 2nd century CE), which also circulated separately, under the title of the *Bhadracarīpraṇidhānagāthā*, the 'verses on the vows of conduct of Bhadra'. The *anuttarapūjā* consists in the cultivation of seven spiritual moods or experiences: worship of the Buddhas, salutation to the Three Jewels, Going for Refuge, confession of one's faults, rejoicing in the merits of others, requesting the teaching, and the transference of one's merit to others.[131] Another early practice, recommended by Vasubandhu (4th century), consists of four reflections: the recollection of the Buddhas (affirming the possibility of Enlightenment), seeing the faults of conditioned existence (reinforcing one's desire to gain release from it), observing the sufferings of sentient beings (thus cultivating compassion), and contemplating the virtues of the Tathāgatas – including *buddhānusmṛti* practices and visualization.[132] Śāntideva (8th century) is associated with a method, found in his *Bodhicaryāvatāra*, known as the 'exchange of self and others', and based on the final section of the *anuttarapūjā*. Here, the practitioner takes upon himself or herself the sufferings of all other beings, and in return dedicates body, speech, mind, and all merits to their benefit.[133]

THE BODHISATTVA PATH

The Path followed by the Bodhisattva is extremely long and arduous, and conceived as lasting for many lifetimes, through many aeons. The Bodhisattva pursues this path by practising what are called the six *pāramitās*, or perfections: *dāna* or giving, *śīla* or morality, *vīrya* or energy, *kṣānti* or patience, *samādhi* or meditation, and *prajñā* or wisdom. Through the cultivation of these perfections the Bodhisattva becomes a Buddha, and they form the basis for expositions of the Bodhisattva's career, as found in Śāntideva's *Bodhicaryāvatāra* and Āryaśūra's *Pāramitāsamāsa*. Some traditions add a further four, possibly in order to correlate the perfections with the *bhūmis*, or stages. These are *upāya* or skilful means, *praṇidhāna* or the vow to achieve Buddhahood, *bala* or power, and *jñāna* or knowledge. All the Bodhisattva's actions, i.e. their practice of the first five perfections, are sealed with the Perfection of Wisdom, i.e. the direct perception of the emptiness of all *dharmas*, *dharmaśūnyatā*. This means that the Bodhisattva realizes the ultimate unreality of the beings that he or she saves. This compassion for ultimately unreal beings is the *mahākaruṇā*, 'Great Compassion', of the Bodhisattvas and Buddhas – mentioned in many Mahāyāna sūtras and described in detail in a number of Mahāyāna treatises.[134] The six perfections make up the two *bodhi-saṁbhāra*, 'accumulations' or 'equipments' for Bodhi. The first of these, the *puṇya-saṁbhāra* or 'accumulation of merit', consists in the cultivation of the first five *pāramitās*. The *jñāna-saṁbhāra* is achieved through the sixth *pāramitā*, the perfection of wisdom.

Various accounts of the stages of the Bodhisattva's Path are given in the sūtras and śāstras of the Mahāyāna. The most ubiquitous of these is one which describes ten *bhūmis*, or stages, through which the Bodhisattva passes on the way to full and perfect Buddhahood. Several differing accounts of these exist, including one from the pre-Mahāyāna *Mahāvastu* of the Mahāsaṅghika School,[135] but that which gained the broadest acceptance was outlined in the *Daśabhūmika Sūtra*, a text which took its name, 'The Discourse on the Ten Stages', from this teaching. The stages named are: the Joyful, the Stainless, the Luminous, the Radiant, the Difficult to Conquer, the Face to Face, the Far Going, the Immovable, the Good Intelligence, and the Cloud of the Dharma. The first stage is entered only after the arising of the bodhicitta, and each stage thereafter is accompanied by rebirth in increasingly exalted realms, with increasingly resplendent form and virtues. In the sixth stage the Bodhisattva acquires the insights by which to become an arhat, though by the power of the Bodhisattva vow, *praṇidhāna*, he or she continues towards full Buddhahood through perfecting skilful means, *upāya*. By the eighth stage the Bodhisattva is irreversible, and can adopt various bodies for the purpose of teaching. In the ninth stage, the Good Intelligence, the Bodhisattva masters all aspects of the Dharma, and in the tenth, the Cloud of Dharma, acquires the ability to manifest multiple bodies to teach different beings, along with other magical powers. Beyond the tenth *bhūmi* lies the state of full Buddhahood.

Later Mahāyānists, such as Kamalaśīla, working in the monastic universities of northern India, developed a schema for the Bodhisattva Path which incorporated all these elements, and which still forms the basis for the understanding of the Path in some Tibetan schools. The basis of this schema was a system of five 'paths', with which were integrated the *pāramitās* and the *bhūmis*. The first path is that of Accumulation, consisting of the practice of the perfections, and is entered upon the arising of the bodhicitta. The second path, that of Preparation, is marked by a deepening insight into emptiness; the third, that of Seeing, by direct, full understanding of *prajñā*, whereupon the Bodhisattva enters upon the first *bhūmi* and the Ārya-Saṅgha; the fourth path, that of Development, involves the passage through all the remaining Bodhisattva *bhūmis*, whilst the fifth path, that of No More Learning, is the stage of Buddhahood.

It should be stressed that the Bodhisattva's determination to proceed through all these arduous stages arises from a desire to develop all mundane and psychic abilities in order to be able to help other beings more effectively. The resulting accomplishments mean that there is progressively less difference between the Bodhisattva in the higher stages of the Path and the fully awakened Buddha, with the result that Bodhisattvas of the higher *bhūmis* came to be worshipped to the same degree as Buddhas. Such Bodhisattvas, best described as archetypal Bodhisattvas, are no longer identifiable with ordinary human beings, since they have been practising the Path for many lifetimes, and have been reborn in more refined mundane realms incalculable times. Bodhisattvas of this type, e.g. Avalokiteśvara, Mañjuśrī, and Maitreya, become major actors in the Mahāyāna sūtras, and the subject of new forms of meditation concerned with their visualization. The *sādhana*, a formal set of instructions for invoking such a figure through visualization, became an increasingly important part of Mahāyāna practice.

Popular accounts of the Bodhisattva ideal have it that the Bodhisattva forgoes full Buddhahood in order to save living beings. It should be clear from the foregoing that this is a distortion of the true state of affairs. The Bodhisattva is motivated by compassion, and for this reason should not turn away from Enlightenment, because Buddhahood is the most effective state in which to help other beings. Moreover the implication that nirvāṇa is a place separate from the world, to which the Enlightened person 'goes', is denied by the Mahāyāna metaphysic which sees both saṁsāra and nirvāṇa as characterized by emptiness, and thereby not different from each other.

14

The Mahāyāna Schools I: The Madhyamaka

By tradition, the Mahāyāna sūtras were not the product of the literary activity of Buddhist schools. Rather, the various Mahāyāna schools developed out of the need to expound the meaning of particular sūtras, or groups of sūtras. The literary products of the schools are termed *śāstra* or 'treatises', as distinct from *sūtra*, because they are works of exposition. The Indian Mahāyāna schools grew out of an attempt to systematize the teachings of two groups of sūtras. The Madhyamaka School clarified and drew out the implications of the Perfection of Wisdom sūtras, whilst the Yogācārin School systematized the teachings of a group of what might be called 'idealist' sūtras, to use a non-traditional term. Together, the Madhyamaka and the Yogācāra represent a coherent strand of doctrinal development that reaches back to the Abhidharma via the Perfection of Wisdom sūtras. They form the two Mahāyāna representatives of the four 'philosophical' schools of Buddhism that are enumerated by later Buddhists and non-Buddhists alike. Both of these schools have had many exponents in Indo-Tibetan and Far Eastern Buddhism, and through a complex process of interaction have tended to dominate the later development of much Mahāyāna Buddhist doctrine. Later schools often align themselves more or less closely with the classical position of one of these two. In particular, Śāntarakṣita (c.680–740CE) synthesized the teachings of the Yogācāra and Madhyamaka Schools in his *Tattvasaṁgraha*, and his disciple, Kamalaśīla (c.700–750CE), argued that this synthesis, known as the Yogācāra-Svatāntrika Madhyamaka position, was superior to that of either school on its own.

Traditionally the founder of the Madhyamaka School was the illustrious Nāgārjuna who was born in the Vidarbha region of Maharashtra during the 2nd century CE, but after his monastic training at Nālandā lived in Andhra. He is associated with the Sātavahana dynasty of the Deccan, since there survives a letter by him to a king of that period. A considerable body of work attributed to him survives, the principal text being his *Mūlamadhyamaka-kārikā*, 'Fundamental Verses on the Middle Way'. The other name associated with the founding of this school is Āryadeva, who came from Sri Lanka, for whom a smaller body of work survives. His major work is the *Catuḥśatakakārikā*, the 'Four Hundred Verses'. One could say that his works complement those of Nāgārjuna, since he places greater emphasis upon the Bodhisattva Path than is apparent in the works of his predecessor. In later centuries, in the challenging and intellectually refined atmosphere of the major monastic universities at Nālandā, Valabhī, and so on, the Madhyamaka School itself divided up into sub-schools – the main division being that between the Prasaṅgika and Svātantrika Madhyamaka. The teachings of the former, still propounded by the present dGe-lugs Order of Tibet, were set out by Buddhapālita (c.470–540CE). The teachings of the Svātantrika Madhyamaka School were expounded by Bhāvaviveka (c.500–570CE), as part of a critique of Buddhapālita – a critique which was in turn rebuffed by Candrakīrti (c.600–650CE). Śāntideva, the author of the *Bodhicaryāvatāra*, was an 8th century adherent of the Prasaṅgika Madhyamaka.

The Perfection of Wisdom sūtras, the scriptural basis of the Madhyamaka School, are not systematic treatises. They simply assert their teachings – often with the use of paradoxical metaphor and imagery. The Madhyamaka School represents an attempt to systematize the teaching of these sūtras. The most important of these is that of *dharmaśūnyatā*, i.e. the emptiness of all *dharmas*. The central axiom of the Madhyamaka teaching is that all things are *śūnya*, 'empty', of inherent existence, *svabhāva*. Nāgārjuna argued that nothing at all, including the Abhidharma *dharmas*, had *svabhāva* – nothing existed independently of external conditions. It is important to understand that Nāgārjuna did not regard this teaching as being nihilistic. Instead he demonstrated that it represented a Middle Way between eternalism and nihilism, since it acknowledged the conventional existence of objects that arise within the continuous flux of *pratītya-samutpāda*, 'origination by dependence [upon conditions]'. He maintained that, whilst nothing has *svabhāva* and therefore nothing has ultimate existence, the world in which we live does exist as the product of passing conditions. He attacked the idea of inherent existence, not conventional existence. The conventional world is real, not illusory, but is radically impermanent (i.e. lacking *svabhāva*), and can only be described as conventionally true. The acknowledgement of the two truths, i.e. the *paramārtha-satya*, or ultimate truth of the universal absence of *svabhāva*, and the *saṁvṛti-satya*, or relative truth of the conventional world, constitutes a Middle Way between eternalism and nihilism. This position is reflected in the very title of his major work, *The Root Verses on the Middle Way*, and also in the name Madhyamaka, which literally means 'middling'.

The claims which the Madhyamaka School is attacking are those which assert that there exists something which has *svabhāva*. By definition *svabhāva* is something which should resist analysis, i.e. is irreducible and independently existent, but Nāgārjuna shows that, when searched for, all the objects of the conventional world simply dissolve away as they are reduced to their component parts (whether spatial or temporal), and as these component parts themselves can be shown to be dependent upon each other, they too have no ultimate existence. Viewed in this light, Nāgārjuna was simply reasserting the original doctrine of *pratītya-samutpāda*. 'We consider that emptiness is origination by dependence [upon conditions].'[136] This is confirmed by the fact that at no point in the *Mūlamadhyamaka-kārikā* does he draw upon a Mahāyāna sūtra as a scriptural authority, but instead refers repeatedly to identifiable sūtras from the *Āgamas* of the non-Mahāyāna schools.[137] His analysis demonstrating the absence of inherent existence is applied to *pratītya-samutpāda* itself, and even to the Buddha and nirvāṇa. Everything lacks *svabhāva* or inherent existence.

Nāgārjuna was accused of destroying the Dharma by such reasoning, but this he denied. On the level of *paramārtha-satya*, ultimate truth, the everyday world does not exist, i.e. it lacks *svabhāva*. Conventionally it does exist, and it is on the conventional level of existence that the teachings of Buddhism are relevant and effective. Indeed, if Enlightenment is to be possible, then the ordinary world must be lacking in *svabhāva*, or else it would be fixed and unchanging – for what has *svabhāva* must by definition remain unchanged. In other words Nāgārjuna replied that to assert that anything does have *svabhāva* is to destroy the Dharma, because then Enlightenment becomes impossible. As soon as anything is said to have a permanent unchanging essence, radical change becomes impossible. To avoid confusion, it is important to understand that, for Nāgārjuna and the Indian Mādhyamaka, *śūnyatā*, 'emptiness', is, in itself, only an abstraction. It is an epistemological ultimate, i.e. it is that which is ultimately true, and therefore that which is ultimately knowable about things. It is not a 'thing' in itself, still less a 'thing' which is supposed to have *svabhāva*, or ultimate existence. It has no ontological status. Hence emptiness itself is described as being empty – *śūnyatā* is *śūnyatā*.

The Madhyamaka School did not set out to formulate any kind of philosophical system. Nāgārjuna himself insisted that he had no thesis of his own. All he did was analyse critically the claims made by all others with regard to ultimate existence – even those claims made by other Buddhists. He did not offer any metaphysical propositions, only the total, universal absence of inherent existence – *śūnyatā*. The Prasaṅgika form of Madhyamaka uses reasoning to show that the claims made by an opponent are in some way incoherent or unacceptable to them – in particular by demonstrating that the opponent's position, when carried to its fullest extreme, entails undesired consequences, *prasaṅga*, and even absurd contradictions. The general thrust of the Prasaṅgika approach (and fully consistent with the claim that it propounds no thesis or metaphysic of its own) is to undermine critically the views of the opponent, by the use of a *reductio ad absurdum* argument. Here also lies the difference between the Prasaṅgika and the Svātantrika positions, because the latter felt it was essential to substantiate such arguments by setting them in the context of logical inference that would be recognized by other Buddhist and non-Buddhist traditions. It held that one had to use arguments that are based on independent and valid logical inference, *svatāntra-anumāṇa* – hence its name.

The Madhyamaka School distinguished between innate and acquired conceptions or ideas of *svabhāva*. The acquired ideas of inherent existence are those which have been learnt, such as the existence of a god or a soul. All that is needed, in the longer term, is to show that whatever thing or being is endowed with *svabhāva* is, in fact, merely conditioned by external factors. Because these are acquired, learnt intellectually or by social conditioning, they can also be refuted by discussion or argument. Innate conceptions of *svabhāva*, on the other hand, are those which determine behaviour at a fundamental level – everyday behaviour in which, whatever we claim to think, we still treat the objects of the conventional world as ultimately existent entities. This innate conception of *svabhāva* is a reflection of the unenlightened state of our own mind. The only cure for this is not rational argument, but sustained meditation on the emptiness of all conditioned things. Be that as it may, the overall orientation of the Madhyamaka approach, especially as represented in the dGe-lugs Order of Tibet, is towards rational debate and the use of the discursive mind to establish the truth of *śūnyatā*.

15

The Mahāyāna Schools II: The Yogācāra

WITH THE YOGĀCĀRIN SCHOOL we come to the fourth of the major schools of Buddhist philosophy, the others being the Sarvāstivādin, the Sautrāntika, and the Madhyamaka. The Yogācārin School is associated with the teachings of a number of idealist sūtras, the earliest of which is the *Saṁdhinirmocana Sūtra* (c.2nd century CE). The later *Laṅkāvatāra Sūtra* (4th century CE) also propounds the Yogācārin doctrine. A number of sūtras, such as the *Pratyutpanna* (c.1st century CE) and *Daśabhūmika* (pre-3rd centuries CE) *Sūtras*, contain idealist elements. The founder of the Yogācārin School was the great scholar Asaṅga (c.310–390CE), who, according to legend, received a number of the seminal treatises of the school directly from Maitreya, the future Buddha, in the Tuṣita *devaloka* (wherein Maitreya is said to reside). These texts include the *Madhyāntavibhāga*, the *Mahāyānasūtralaṁkāra*, and the *Abhisamayālaṁkāra*. He is also ascribed with personal authorship of several other works, including the *Mahāyānasaṁgraha*, the *Abhidharmasamuccaya*, and the *Yogācārabhūmi*. The *Yogācārabhūmi* is probably the earliest Yogācārin treatise, in part contemporary with the *Saṁdhinirmocana Sūtra*, and very likely the work of several authors.

The other great commentator associated with the origins of the Yogācārin School was Vasubandhu (c.320–400CE), the author of a larger number of works including the *Trisvabhāva-nirdeśa*, the *Viṁśatikā*, and the *Triṁśikā*. Traditionally he was also the author of the *Abhidharmakośa*, although, if this was the case, it dates from a period prior to his conversion to a Mahāyāna viewpoint. (It is possible that there were two Vasubandhus.[138])

Both of these teachers lived during the first years of the brilliant Gupta period (c.320–c.540CE) in which medieval Indian culture reached its peak of sophistication and creativity within a peaceful and prosperous society which itself showed considerable influence from Buddhism. It was a period that also saw the founding of the Buddhist monastic University at Nālandā. This became the training centre for generations of Buddhist thinkers, where ambitious educational schemes were realized amongst thousands of students, and the Dharma received its most intellectually sophisticated formulations. The Yogācārin and later Madhyamaka schools reflect this brilliance and sophistication.

The Yogācārin School had a specifically historical perspective on the significance of its doctrines, since it saw them as a final resolution of the Buddha's teaching. In particular it saw them as an antidote to the grasping at extreme views into which it considered earlier Buddhist schools to have fallen. Śākyamuni Buddha's first teaching, to the five ascetics at the Deer Park at Vārāṇasī, was traditionally described as the 'first turning of the Wheel of the Dharma'. This, say both the Yogācārin and the Madhyamaka Schools, was misunderstood in such a way as to allow the development of the erroneous grasping at 'existents', or *dharmas*, of the Abhidharma schools. This grasping at *dharmas* was counteracted by the teachings of *śūnyatā* and *prajñā* in the Perfection of Wisdom sūtras,[139] and was formulated by Nāgārjuna and his successors in the Madhyamaka tradition. However, in the eyes of the Yogācārins, this too promoted an extreme view, because it over-emphasized the non-existence of *dharmas* and, by virtue of this, passed over into a nihilistic position in which it denied the real existence of anything. The Yogācārin School therefore saw its own sūtras as being the 'third turning of the Wheel of the Dharma', presenting the true, final, and ultimate, or *paramārtha*, teaching of the Buddha.[140]

To substantiate this claim it adopted the already established hermeneutic of distinguishing between texts which were *neyārtha* and texts which were *nītārtha*. It described the teachings of the Tripiṭaka and the Prajñāpāramitā sūtras as *upāyas*, or skilful means, and as such they were *neyārtha*, which means they needed 'drawing out', that is they needed interpretation in order to be understood properly. They were not speaking the literal truth, which is why those who took them literally were prone to fall into the extremes of eternalism or nihilism. Its own idealist sūtras, however, were classified as *nītārtha*, 'whose meaning is drawn out', that is, they taught the literal truth, and therefore needed no interpretation in order to be understood properly. The purpose of this new turning of the Dharma Wheel was to reaffirm the Middle Way – the Middle Way between existence and non-existence, eternalism and nihilism.

'Mind-only', or *cittamātra,* is the principal doctrine of the Yogācārin School. As is suggested by the name Yogācāra, meaning 'the practice of yoga', its origin may well have been in connection with experience in yoga, or meditation. This is further suggested by the provenance of the works received by Asaṅga from Maitreya. The *devalokas* are regarded as the objective counterparts of the higher mental states experienced in *dhyāna,* or meditative absorption, and since Maitreya is supposed to reside in the Tuṣita *devaloka,* it implies that Asaṅga 'encountered' Maitreya in meditation. In this connection we should remember that Asaṅga's homeland, Gandhāra, and also Kashmir in particular, were the home of a number of meditation schools, which took the Bodhisattva Maitreya as their patron and chief object of devotion. Furthermore, Asaṅga, dissatisfied with his training within the non-Mahāyāna Mahīśāsika School, had practised meditation for a period of twelve years prior to his visions of Maitreya. In the *Saṁdhinirmocana Sūtra,* the Buddha states that both the images perceived in meditation and externally perceived objects are *vijñaptimātra,* merely ideation.[141] 'Ideation' means the 'product of ideas' or 'activity of the mind', so the Buddha is saying that ideas or mental objects perceived during meditation, and the objects of the ordinary world, are the product of the activity of the mind.

If the 'mind-only' doctrine was the product of reflection upon meditational experience, this, in turn, may help us to understand that what is being said by this school of thought is not that everything is made of mind (as though the mind were some kind of universal matter), but that the totality of our experience is dependent upon our mind. The proposition is that we can only know or experience things with our mind. Even sense experience is cognized by the mind, therefore the things that we know, every element of our cognition, is essentially part of a mental process. Nothing cognized can be radically or fundamentally different from that mind. If they were fundamentally different from each other, they would be cognitively inaccessible to each other.

So the Yogācārin School disagreed with the Madhyamaka position. More specifically, it thought the Madhyamaka to be nihilistic and, in so far as the latter claims that nothing has ultimate existence, to have strayed from a Middle Way between eternalism and nihilism. By contrast the Yogācāra gave expression to a more positive or concrete description of reality, and, though doubtless inspired by meditational experience, partly reacting against the apparent nihilism of the Madhyamaka *śūnyatā* teachings. (The Madhyamaka replied that the Yogācārin School merely misunderstood the Madhyamaka doctrine of *śūnyatā*!) The Yogācārin School held that there is indeed something which really exists, which really does have *svabhāva*, and that is the mind. It is empty, *śūnya*, in that it is free from duality, empty of any conception of subject and object. *Śūnyatā*, according to the Yogācāra, is freedom from duality. We can see that the Yogācārin School has revised the meaning of *śūnyatā*. Although meaning 'absence of inherent existence' in the Madhyamaka, to the Yogācārins it means 'absence of duality between perceiving subject and perceived object'. This difference of interpretation arose directly from the sūtra material upon which these two schools based their understanding and exposition of the Dharma. (Nor was this the only transformation of meaning for the term *śūnyatā* in the Mahāyāna. In the Tathāgatagarbha doctrine, the 'One Mind' was described as *śūnyatā* because it is empty of phenomenal impurities.)

The Three Natures

In the light of their teachings concerning the real existence of mind, the Yogācārin School also elaborated the concept of *svabhāva*, formulating the doctrine of the *trisvabhāva*, the 'three own beings' or 'natures'. Everything knowable about the way things really are, everything that can be the object of cognition, can be classified under these three natures. According to this teaching the primary aspect of the 'way things really are' is the *paratantra-svabhāva*. This is the 'dependent' (*paratantra*) nature, and it is that which really exists. It therefore possesses *svabhāva* in the sense criticized by the Madhyamaka. We could also say that it is an ontological absolute, except in so far as it is, essentially, a mental process, i.e. it is the continual flow of mutually conditioned and conditioning mental events which make up consciousness. In other words, it is the process that is *pratītya-samutpāda* viewed from a mind-only perspective. It is called the 'dependent' nature by virtue of this process of mutual conditioning, because the elements of which it is constituted are dependent on each other for their existence. It is beyond the grasp of the unenlightened mind, which creates the duality of the false, 'imagined' nature.

The *parikalpita-svabhāva*, or 'imagined' nature, is the kind of existence which the unenlightened person ascribes to the everyday world. It is unreal, and only has a conventional existence, which is projected by the activity of the unenlightened mind. It is the perception of subject and object, characterized by our experience of ourselves as separate, discrete beings in opposition to an objective external world. It is the product of the falsifying activity of language which imputes duality to the mutually dependent flow of mental *dharmas*. These dualistic phenomena are really only 'imagined', *parikalpita*.

The third nature is called the *pariniṣpanna-svabhāva*, 'perfected' or 'absolute' nature. Unlike the last it is the highest truth, the Yogācārin School's epistemological ultimate, because it is 'the way things really are' as understood by the Enlightened mind. It is the truth that ultimately all things are completely lacking in duality, even though they appear to the unenlightened mind under the guise of dualism. In his *Trisvabhāva-nirdeśa*, Vasubandhu offers an analogy in an attempt to make the difference between the three natures clear.[142] It is, he suggests, like a magician who takes a piece of wood, and through his magical spells makes it appear to his audience to be an elephant. The 'dependent' nature is like the piece of wood – it is what is really there. The 'imagined' nature is like the elephant – a misperception of reality. The perfected nature is the fact, or the true perception, that there is no 'elephant' in the piece of wood.

In East Asia the *trisvabhāva* doctrine received a radically different interpretation.[143] There the relationship between the three natures came to be seen as a progressive sequence, through which practitioners move as they gain a deeper understanding of the 'way things really are'. The 'imagined' nature is the world of everyday experience, in which we, as 'real' beings, grasp on to 'real' objects. It is the world of duality between non-existent subject and object, as perceived by the spiritually undeveloped. The character of the phenomena upon which we mistakenly project these delusions of duality is 'dependent' because it arises on the basis of causes and conditions – the flow of mutually conditioning *dharmas* of the *pratītya-samutpāda*. Perception of this *svabhāva* is therefore closer to an understanding of the way things are, in that it understands the impermanent and dependent nature of the 'imagined' reality of ordinary perception. However, even this is a limited realization, which is in turn subordinated to the realization of the 'perfected' nature, which is understood to be the pure, unchanging, ultimate Reality that underlies the impermanent 'dependent' nature. East Asian Yogācārins therefore understood the *parinişpanna-svabhāva* as an ontological absolute. Doubtless, in so doing, they reflected some influence from the *tathāgatagarbha* doctrine.

Unlike the Madhyamaka, the Yogācāra developed a metaphysical and psychological system, in part to give a coherent framework to the meditational experiences which were embodied in the 'mind-only' sūtras. In particular, the positive ontological status given by the Yogācārin School to the dependent nature is necessitated on the one hand by the need to counteract the spiritually disastrous extreme of nihilism, and on the other by the logical necessity for there to be a really existent substratum upon which the erroneous perception of the imagined nature is based. It was fiercely criticized by the Madhyamaka for holding this position. (See, for example, chapter 9 of Śāntideva's *Bodhicaryāvatāra*.)

Yogācārin Practice

The seminal treatise of the school, Asaṅga's *Yogācārabhūmi*, reflects its author's training within the non-Mahāyāna schools prior to his transition to the Yogācārin viewpoint. It is modelled on preceding meditation and practice manuals of the same name, produced within Kashmiri Sarvāstivādin circles.[144] Typically, Yogācārin practice manuals introduce the practitioner to mindfulness meditation upon body, feelings, thoughts, and *dharmas*, both in oneself and in others. Through this, insight into the non-difference between self and others arises. Further meditations help undermine, at successively more subtle levels, the mental activity which gives rise to the perception of duality, and the practitioner thereby passes on, with the aid of *śamatha* meditations, through the remaining Paths and Bodhisattva *bhūmis*.

The critical process involved is described in psycho-spiritual terms as one of *āśraya-parāvṛtti*, a 'turning about in the basis'. The 'basis' referred to here is the deepest level of consciousness, the *ālaya-vijñāna*, the '[store]house' or 'receptacle' consciousness. This is, in its pure state, the undifferentiated flow of mind that is the *paratantra-svabhāva*. In its defiled state it is the subconscious collectivity of *bīja*, or 'seeds', which are 'sown' by previous moments of consciousness, and which 'perfume' future moments of consciousness with perceptions of duality, and thereby constitute the means by which *karman* operates. (We can see here the influence of the Sautrāntika School upon Mahāyāna thought.) This function of the impure *ālaya-vijñāna* is also alluded to in its name, which also means 'clinging consciousness'. The purification of the *ālaya-vijñāna* of seeds purifies the other levels of consciousness (they enumerate seven) of *vijñapti*, or 'ideation'.

The Yogācārin School also describes the process by which the dependent nature comes to be seen as the imagined nature, i.e. how the *ālaya-vijñāna*, as the fundamental level of consciousness, comes to be transformed into the six sense consciousnesses, by a process known as the 'threefold transformation of consciousness'. In doing this it freely incorporated the Abhidharma analysis of the perceived world, adapted from the non-Mahāyāna schools.

THE TRIKĀYA DOCTRINE

The Yogācārin School was also responsible for developing a teaching which elaborated the nature of the Buddha Jewel, and proposed that there are 'three bodies', *trikāya*, of the Buddha. The *dharmakāya*, 'dharma-body' or the *svabhāvikakāya*, 'body of own being', is the pure, non-dual flow of consciousness experienced by the Enlightened person. As such it is or has 'dependent' nature, *paratantra-svabhāva*, which means that it is ultimately real. It is mind, completely and utterly pure of any conception of duality. From the mundane viewpoint it is the collection of good mental qualities which make up or characterize the mind of a Buddha. The *saṁbhogakāya*, 'body of complete or mutual enjoyment' is the Buddha that appears in Pure Lands to help beings attain liberation, and therefore it is also the Buddha that teaches the Mahāyāna sūtras. In this sense it is the most important body of the Buddha in religious terms, and also because it is the Buddha of devotion – the archetypal Buddha of visionary experience. The *saṁbhogakāya* is also the form in which Bodhisattvas treading the path of the Six Perfections finally attain full Buddhahood, and the archetypal Bodhisattvas are understood to be *saṁbhogakāya* forms. This body, or *kāya*, is only relatively true or real, because it has *parikalpita-svabhāva*, or 'imagined nature' only, i.e. it participates in the world of duality. Even so, it is an excellent and perfect subtle body, having the 112 marks of the traditional *mahāpuruṣa*, or 'superman'. The *nirmāṇakāya*, 'transformed or created body', is the body of the historical Buddha, who was nothing more than the magical creation of an archetypal, *saṁbhogakāya* Buddha. This being the case, it too is of the nature of *parikalpita-svabhāva*. The function of this illusory form is that it teaches those who do not follow the Mahāyāna.

Various systems of Buddha bodies were developed by later teachers and schools, all directly based upon the Yogācārin Trikāya, but often increasing the number of bodies. The dGe-lugs Order, a Madhyamaka school of Tibet, propounds a system of four bodies, and there are others describing five.[145] Mention should be made here of the epigraphical evidence that survives from this period, and which suggests that medieval ideas on the nature of the Buddha were not expressed exclusively by such sophisticated doctrines as the Trikāya. It has become apparent that parallel to the development of the Trikāya doctrine there also arose the widespread view of the Buddha as a living personal presence and permanent resident within many monasteries, mirrored by the provision of specific and elaborate accommodation for him in the form of his *gandhakuṭī*, or perfumed chamber, and, in the rock-cut *leṇa* or caves, the addition of a shrine in the back wall containing a Buddha image. Whilst these developments are best evidenced at the very monastic sites which are also associated with the development of the theory of the three bodies of the Buddha, i.e. Nālandā and Valabhī, the exact nature of the relationship between the two phenomena is not known.[146]

The Mahāyāna Schools: Epilogue

Nālandā, and later the universities established by the Pāla kings, became outstanding national and international educational institutions offering an extensive syllabus alike to Buddhist monks and laymen and to non-Buddhists. At its peak Nālandā catered for 10,000 students, who could choose from as many as one hundred lectures in a day (although we are also told that the bulk of teaching took the form of tutorials and debates). Not only was Buddhist philosophy taught there, but also the ideas of other Indian religions, with the result that there was considerable interaction, and hence refinement, of ideas.[147] As an aspect of this process, and parallel to the development of the Yogācārin School, the monastic universities also witnessed the growth of a tradition of Buddhist Logicians. This was initiated by Dignāga (5th–6th centuries), a pupil of Vasubandhu, his main work being the *Pramāṇasamuccaya*. Much of his thought was reworked by Dharmakīrti (7th century) in a commentary on the *Pramāṇasamuccaya* called the *Pramāṇavārttikā*. Since Buddhism is founded on a quest for knowledge of things as they really are, it was considered essential to be able to establish what were valid sources of knowledge. The main concern of the Buddhist Logicians was to establish these valid means of knowledge, or *pramāṇas*, for which purpose they engaged in detailed philosophical debate with non-Buddhist opponents. Though often associated with the Yogācārin or Sautrāntika Schools because of passing references to doctrines of those schools in their works, the doctrinal affiliation of these teachers is not easy to discern, since the focus of their thought is so narrow. However, the impact of their work was such that, in the later university syllabuses (as are still maintained in modern Tibetan Buddhism), the investigation of valid sources of knowledge became the basis of training, essential to study and practice, which preceded even that of the Abhidharma analysis.

In origin at least, the Mahāyāna schools were not diversions from the major task of treading the Path to Enlightenment. In each case their concern was to rationalize and systematize the teachings of a group of sūtras, which were regarded as being the words of the Buddha. In each case they were trying to establish the exact nature of the 'Right View' which forms the first stage of the Eightfold Path of the Noble Ones. Enlightenment is frequently described as achieving a state in which one 'sees things as they really are', and much of the doctrinal debate that developed in the Mahāyāna was an attempt to establish what the 'way things really are' really was. Later generations, however, seemed to become embroiled in scholastic debate and sophisticated but abstruse attempts to synthesize the teachings of all the different sūtras and schools.

16

The Tathāgatagarbha Doctrine

From the perspective of Madhyamaka teaching, the Tathāgatagarbha doctrine seems paradoxical. Whereas Nāgārjuna had identified nirvāṇa and saṁsāra on the basis of their common lack of *svabhāva*, or inherent existence, the Tathāgatagarbha affirmed this identity on the opposite basis. Whereas to the Madhyamaka all things are *śūnya*, empty, of *svabhāva*, the Tathāgatagarbha doctrine emphasized an indestructible, permanent core to all beings, which really exists, and is the basis of mundane and transcendental reality. This basis was termed the Tathāgatagarbha, the 'womb' or 'embryo' of the Tathāgata, the seed of Buddhahood that lies in all beings and which is uncovered through spiritual practice to shine forth at Enlightenment. Whilst earlier Tathāgatagarbha texts understand this in terms of merely a potential within sentient beings, the later tradition interpreted it rather more substantially, as that 'thing' the existence of which enables the unenlightened person to become Enlightened. It was the presence of this Tathāgatagarbha in all beings that encouraged the Buddha to try to teach beings the Path, for he could see that each and every being has thereby the capacity to become a Buddha. According to the Tathāgatagarbha perspective, this was the true significance of the episode in which Brahmā Sahaṁpati asked the Buddha to teach.[148] The substantialist interpretation was not without its practical religious (as distinct from doctrinal) problems, since the idea that each of us 'contains' Buddhahood was sometimes understood in such a way as to undermine the value of spiritual practice as a means of self-transformation. If practitioners thought they were already Enlightened, there would be little point in making any strenuous effort.

The Tathāgatagarbha was not a school in the same sense as the Madhyamaka and Yogācāra, neither having the same intellectual impact either inside or outside the Buddhist fold (perhaps because of its similarity to some Hindu teachings), nor, as far as we can tell, attracting any separate and exclusive allegiance from proponents.[149] In fact, there seems to have been considerable debate as to whether it was really distinct from the Yogācāra, both doctrines originating in the same period and sharing some root texts by Asaṅga. Moreover, there was an increasing tendency for Tathāgatagarbha literature to equate the Tathāgatagarbha with the *ālaya-vijñāna* of the Yogācāra. In fact the degree to which this equation is made is one of the bases upon which historians have tried to date Tathāgatagarbha texts, and we shall be tentatively following this schema here.[150] The doctrines of the Tathāgatagarbha appear to have had little influence on Indian Buddhist thought prior to the 11th century.

The earliest Tathāgatagarbha sūtras are the *Tathāgatagarbha Sūtra* and the *Śrīmālādevī-siṁhanāda Sūtra*, both of which might date from as early as the 3rd century CE. The *Tathāgatagarbha Sūtra* is very short, consisting of little more than nine similes by which the manner in which the Tathāgatagarbha is hidden within mundane reality is explained. The Buddha says there, 'Thus, in spite of their being covered with defilements, transmigrating from one existence to another, they [living beings] are possessed of the Tathāgatagarbha, endowed with virtues, always pure, and hence are not different from me.'[151] The *Śrīmālā-siṁhanāda*, or 'Discourse on the Lion's Roar of Queen Śrīmālā', which some have argued is derived from a Mahāsaṅghika source,[152] is longer, and has as its hero the Buddhist queen, Śrīmālā. Receiving her prediction to Buddhahood from the Buddha, Śrīmālā makes ten great vows, and preaches a doctrine of *ekayāna*, one way, as well as the Tathāgatagarbha. Whereas for the Madhyamaka *śūnyatā* referred to the emptiness of inherent existence, and for the Yogācāra it referred to the emptiness of duality, i.e. the absence of subject and object, the *Śrīmālādevī-siṁhanāda Sūtra* explains that emptiness refers to the absence in the Tathāgatagarbha of any defilement. When freed from this defilement, this emptiness of defilement becomes apparent, and that which is freed of defilement is known as the *dharmakāya*, for it is this pure undefiled element which is the essence of the Buddhas.[153]

A third sūtra important for the exposition of Tathāgatagarbha ideas is the Sanskrit version of the *Mahāparinirvāṇa Sūtra*. Though sharing the same name this is not another version of the *Mahāparinibbāna Sutta* that occurs in the Pāli Canon, though it does claim to relate the final events of the Buddha's life. It is very long and, though undoubtedly composite, dates from some time between 200 and 400CE. The *Mahāparinirvāṇa Sūtra* is particularly noteworthy for its teaching that there is in reality a self! In a fashion entirely in keeping with the exegetical practices of the other schools of the Mahāyāna, the *Mahāparinirvāṇa Sūtra* says that the doctrine of *anātman* was an expedient, a skilful means, or *upāya*, adopted by the Buddha to help eradicate selfhood in its narrow, grasping, unenlightened sense. Therefore the sūtras that expound this doctrine are *neyārtha*, i.e. they need to be interpreted in order to be properly understood. For its own part the *Mahāparinirvāṇa Sūtra* claims to expound a secret teaching of the Buddha that had not been preached before. This teaching is the truth that there is a 'Great Self', which is the permanent element underlying mundane reality. (This may seem highly reminiscent of the Pudgalavāda, though there is no evidence of any direct link between the two teachings.) Whereas the Madhyamaka, in line with the Perfection of Wisdom sūtras, had emphasized the negative qualities of Buddhahood, the *Mahāparinirvāṇa Sūtra* maintains that this had led to a one-sided understanding of Enlightenment and reality, and so duly tried to correct this imbalance by placing greater emphasis on positive qualities of Enlightenment. Thus, whereas earlier schools (both Mahāyāna and non-Mahāyāna) had stressed that delusion lay in seeing permanence where there is impermanence, happiness where there is suffering, self where there is no self, and purity where there is impurity, the *Mahāparinirvāṇa Sūtra* maintains that the opposite is also true – it is delusion to see impermanence where there is permanence, suffering where there is happiness, no self where there is a self, and impurity where there is purity.[154] In reality there is something which is permanent, blissful, pure, and of the nature of a self, and that is the Tathāgatagarbha – a really existent, pure element totally beyond narrow egotistic greed, hatred, and delusion.

Another important text for the Tathāgatagarbha doctrine was the *Ratnagotravibhāga* of Maitreyanātha, with its commentary attributed by Chinese tradition to Sāramati – both dating from the 3rd or 4th century CE. Sāramati, regarded as the first systematizer of Tathāgatagarbha thought, explains that reality, here termed *tathatā*, or suchness, has two modes or states. Buddhahood is the pure, undefiled *tathatā*, whereas the everyday world is the manifestation of *tathatā* in a defiled state. For the unenlightened, this pure *tathatā* that underlies mundane reality is the Tathāgatagarbha.

None of these texts mentions the *ālaya-vijñāna*. The second stage in the development of Tathāgatagarbha thought and literature is marked by several texts which mention the *ālaya-vijñāna*, but give no account of its connection with the Tathāgatagarbha. Among these one can include the *Mahāyānasūtralaṁkāra*. The final phase, in which the Tathāgatagarbha and the *ālaya-vijñāna* are fully identified, is represented by the *Laṅkāvatāra Sūtra* and the *Ta-sheng ch'i-hsin lun*, usually translated as '*The Awakening of Faith in the Mahāyāna*', which though ascribed to Aśvaghoṣa, an Indian author of the 2nd century CE, was probably composed in Central Asia or China. This latter treatise came to be particularly influential in eastern Asian Buddhism and the Hua-yen School of China, where the Tathāgatagarbha doctrine was regarded as a fourth turning of the Dharma Wheel.

Whilst superficially the Tathāgatagarbha doctrine may seem to negate several central tenets of basic Buddhism (and was certainly criticized for doing so by non-Tathāgatagarbha Buddhists), it can be seen, in contrast to the Madhyamaka, as an aspect of the persistent trend in Buddhism that attempts to describe Buddhahood in positive terms, and was to play a significant role in the syntheses of the doctrine by the Tibetan Buddhist orders.

However, this simple juxtaposition of Madhyamaka and Tathāgatagarbha does little justice to the complexity and richness of the latter's contribution to the broader development of Mahāyāna Buddhism. Having discussed the identification made between the Tathāgatagarbha and the *ālaya-vijñāna*, suggesting a close link between Tathāgatagarbha thought and the Yogācāra (in implicit contrast to the Madhyamaka), we cannot forget that there was considerable continuity between the Madhyamaka and the Yogācāra, with their shared concern with emptiness, and perhaps the Tathāgatagarbha doctrine, with its substantialist character, should instead be contrasted with these two together. Then again, all three doctrinal traditions might be seen in a complementary light. Whilst the Madhyamaka established the cognitive content of Enlightenment, the Yogācāra emphasized spiritual practice as the means by which we move to that state from our present one of unenlightenment, whilst the Tathāgatagarbha doctrine seeks to explain how this movement, or transformation, is even possible.

17

The Tantra and Vajrayāna Buddhism

The Tantra and, later, the Vajrayāna, were esoteric traditions, and, unlike the preceding traditions, their teachings were only available to those Buddhists who had received the appropriate initiations. Furthermore, the texts produced by this movement are themselves so rich in symbolism as to make them virtually unintelligible without commentary from a teacher, which should only be acquired by someone who has received *abhiṣeka*, or initiation, within the Tantric lineages. The following discussion will be of a more general nature.

The Tantra was a pan-Indian phenomenon. It consisted of a movement towards the employment of ritual magic and yoga, or meditative techniques, in an antinomian spirit, to gain secular and religious goals. The Buddhist Tantra seems to have developed mainly within the context of the Mahāyāna, and even though it was to give rise to the third great phase of Indian Buddhist history, the Vajrayāna, it consciously retained this affiliation at all times. (There is evidence of a non-Mahāyānist Tantra in South-east Asia, although it is not known how widespread this was.) The Vajrayānist Buddhist therefore works within the framework of the Mahāyāna Bodhisattva ideal, striving for Buddhahood for the sake of all sentient beings. The greatest emphasis in the Vajrayāna is upon magical ritual, and it is the development of this that chiefly distinguishes it from previous forms of Buddhism. The more philosophical understanding of the nature of reality was taken over from mainstream Mahāyāna with little change. Reflecting the Tathāgatagarbha doctrine and the Mahāyāna identification of saṁsāra and nirvāṇa, the initiate sees himself as already Enlightened. The Yogācāra doctrine of mind-only was also crucial, given the central role assigned to meditation in tantric ritual, such that all things, including mundane objects, are seen as symbols of the reality perceived by the Enlightened mind. The practitioner cultivates an attitude in which every aspect of the illusory everyday world is understood as a manifestation of Enlightened awareness.

Great emphasis is placed on immediate results, the intention being that the initiate attempts to gain Enlightenment not as the result of many lifetimes spent practising the Perfections, but now, in this very lifetime. With this distinction in mind, some Vajrayāna texts refer to the non-Vajrayāna Mahāyāna as the *Pāramitāyāna*, the 'Way of the Perfections'. The principle of Going for Refuge is retained, but reinterpreted in terms of the direct experience of the Tantric practitioner. Thus the Buddha Jewel is seen as embodied in one's guru, from whom one receives initiation and instruction, the Dharma Jewel is one's *iṣṭadevatā*, one's 'chosen deity', i.e. the Buddha or Bodhisattva into whose maṇḍala one has been initiated and whose figure one visualizes, and which is the most direct experience one has of the Dharma; and the Saṅgha Jewel is the *ḍākiṇī*, the 'ogress' who is the inspiriting spiritual influence which is Saṅgha, or spiritual community, at its highest and best. The Vajrayāna begins with the root emotions of hatred and greed, treating them not as hindrances to spiritual growth but as powerful vehicles of the Bodhisattva ideal. The deeply seated urge towards biological procreation is harnessed to the generation of the bodhicitta; the ingrained response of destruction towards those things that threaten the mundane ego is redirected towards all defilements that obscure one's innate Buddhahood.

As a system of religious practice, and as the means whereby one might bypass the lengthy preparation of cultivating the Perfections, the Vajrayāna uses ritual magic to attain the spiritual goals of Mahāyāna Buddhism. The basis of this magic is the symbolic identification of the body and actions of the initiate with aspects of the cosmos, both mundane and spiritual. On the basis of this identification, through the manipulation of the physical and subtle body, the initiate can manipulate the outer world. More importantly from the soteriological perspective, but on the same principle, through the manipulation of the outer world the practitioner can also transform the inner world of their subtle body, for there is no difference to the Tantric initiate between the inner and outer worlds. Thereby they can gain *siddhi*, or success, be it in a mundane matter or in a matter of the highest spirituality.

The highest levels of Tantric practice (the so-called *anuttarayoga*; see below) involve the galvanizing and manipulation of the energies of the entire psycho-physical organism, for which reason a complex system of energy channels within the body was identified. This process is linked with a form of sexual yoga, involving ritual copulation with a female *śakti* (lit. 'power'), or consort, designed to stimulate the arising of the bodhicitta, symbolized by the practitioner's semen. Needless to say, such practices, performed literally, involved breaking the monastic *prātimokṣa* rule enjoining total celibacy, and so some later Tibetan tantric tradition (following Atīśa) emphatically maintains that this language is entirely symbolic – the female partner symbolizing transcendental wisdom, the male partner *upāya*, or skilful means. However, this symbolic interpretation was not universal, and there is an earlier Vajrayāna tradition which described the ideal Vajrayānist as performing an external (i.e. public) Hīnayāna practice, a private Mahāyāna practice, and a secret Vajrayāna practice. Archaeological evidence supports the proposition that the highest levels of Tantric practice were not public until very late, c.10th–11th centuries, and that even then they were still able to cause misunderstanding and offence. The Tibetan pilgrim Dharmasvāmin, who visited Bodh Gaya in the 13th century, describes 'Ceylonese Śrāvakas' who publicly denounced the Vajrayāna, burned Tantric texts, and destroyed an image of a *heruka*, or wrathful male Buddha, from a Tantric shrine there.[155] There is also evidence of a reciprocal segregation on the part of Tantric practitioners, some of whom forbore to spend more than seven days at a time in the company of śrāvakas.[156]

The history of the Vajrayāna is highly obscure, as is so much else in the story of Indian Buddhism, but historians have been able to identify several stages in its development. The first evidence of the emergence of features which can be considered Tantric dates from as early as the 2nd century CE, and consists of chapters from various Mahāyāna sūtras devoted to *dhāraṇī*, long sequences of unintelligible syllables, to which are attributed various powers. These are clearly related both to the mantras of the Mahāyāna and to the *parittā* – texts, such as the *Mettā Sutta*, recited for protection by non-Mahāyāna Buddhists. The earliest tantras, from the *kriyā* tantra class, were being translated into Chinese from the 3rd century. However, this early phase, sometimes referred to as the Mantrayāna, was probably a private minority interest, which for a long time had no great impact on the Buddhist community as a whole.

By the 8th century this situation had been transformed, and the Vajrayāna was sufficiently well known to have begun to stimulate commentarial activity within the great universities. This transformation is undoubtedly connected with the arising of the Pāla dynasty of Bihar and Bengal (760–1142CE), which established the new universities at Vikramaśīla and Odantapurī. These became centres for the new movement, and it was largely from here that Buddhism was taken to Tibet. It may also be seen in terms of a revival, as a response to the decline in Buddhism noted by Yuan-tsang in his tour of India in the 7th century. It should be stressed that at all stages there were Tantric practitioners living in monasteries as fully ordained monks, observing the same Vinaya as did the other monks (adherents of both the Mahāyāna and non-Mahāyāna schools) into whose *nikāya* they had been ordained. This second stage could be said to mark the origin of the Vajrayāna proper, in which the symbolism, the terminology, and much ritual was established. Most prominent, and most multifaceted, among these symbols, and moreover responsible for its name, is the *vajra*, the diamond or thunderbolt – symbolizing the powerful, indestructible, cutting nature of wisdom, and also the pure, undefiled state of Buddhahood innate within all beings (showing the influence of Tathāgatagarbha ideas). The state of Buddhahood is also symbolized by the figure Vajrasattva, associated with innate purity and representing the non-dual state of realization that integrates the vision of emptiness and pure consciousness, of the Madhyamaka and Yogācāra schools respectively.

Within the Vajrayāna two further stages have been identified. The first of these, called by some scholars the Sahajayāna, is associated with the activities of a group of *mahā-siddhas*, 'great adepts', traditionally numbered at eighty-four, who appeared in the 9th to 12th centuries. These were accomplished yogins who travelled around the countryside in the manner of holy wizards (there was probably a strong shamanistic dimension to *siddha* activity), who apparently were not necessarily based in a monastic context at all, sometimes accompanied by a low-caste consort with whom they performed their Tantric rituals and yoga. Their ideology was that of the Vajrayāna, and they extolled, in mystic songs, the *mahāsukha* or 'great bliss' (*nirvāṇa*) that is *sahaja*, 'co-emergent' or 'simultaneously arisen', with the bliss arising from the union of yogin and consort which leads, through yogic techniques, to the union of *upāya*, skilful means, and *prajñā*, wisdom.[157] The term *mudrā* or 'seal' is also commonly used by the *siddhas* in this context. On its own, or as the compound *karmamudrā*, 'action seal', it is used to denote the female consort; in the expression *mahāmudrā*, it is synonymous with *mahāsukha* or nirvāṇa.

Through their life-style some *siddhas* challenged and ridiculed the complacency and external ritual of the religious establishment in the monastic universities. Their antinomian approach to the religious quest, as well as the sexual symbolism and practice of the later Vajrayāna, also suggests some desire to shock. Indeed, the breaking of taboo was a major component of Vajrayāna practice – among which one could include the emphasis on copulation with low-caste women, the use and particularly the eating of flesh (especially that of dogs and corpses) and other impure substances, and the frequenting of cremation grounds, all of which were highly polluting and repugnant to brahmaṇical orthodoxy. Whether this should be taken to suggest that established Buddhism was itself absorbing these values at this time is not clear. Certainly there must have been many Brahmin converts within the monasteries, and it is known that there were non-Buddhists who were students at the main Buddhist universities. It is quite possible that they may have brought their socially conditioned preoccupations with them. The relationship between these *siddhas* and representatives of the monastic establishment is well illustrated by the story of Nāropa. As the abbot of a monastery he is firstly confronted, and then challenged, by Tilopa, the *mahā-siddha*. Accepting the limited nature of his spiritual realization revealed to him by Tilopa, he pursues the *siddha*, who eludes him for some time before bringing Nāropa to full realization outside of a monastic context.

The final and late stage of development is associated with a text called the *Kālacakra Tantra*, which appears to have been compiled by the mid-11th century, and is the last tantra known to emerge within India itself. It is written in classical Sanskrit, unlike the earlier phases of tantras which are written in a mixture of Prakrit and *saṁdhyābhāṣā*, or 'allusive speech', both of which are difficult to decipher and understand. This, in conjunction with its attempt to provide a comprehensive synthesis of all deities within three highly complex maṇḍalas, including Hindu deities, suggests that it was the product of a learned monastic context rather than compiled by a *siddha*. It introduces political and astrological elements not found in earlier texts, for example, the synthesis of worship of Buddhist and Hindu deities conceived as a means of halting the contemporary Muslim invasions. Teachings concerning the *ādibuddha* or 'primordial Buddha' appear for the first time in the *Kālacakra Tantra*.

The literature of the Vajrayāna is massive. Individual texts are called tantras, a term like sūtra, meaning 'thread', and the earliest examples are attributed to Śākyamuni Buddha – supposedly from another, esoteric turning of the Dharma wheel only perceptible to highly advanced beings. For this reason they are regarded as the word of the Buddha, and are included with the sūtras in the Tibetan and Chinese collections of Buddhavacana. The Tibetan canon contains translations of almost 500 tantras and over 2,000 commentaries to such works. Generally they are concerned with instructions for elaborate rituals and meditations. By a later Tibetan systematization, there are four classes of tantras: *kriyā* tantras or 'tantras of action', *caryā* tantras or 'tantras of observance', *yoga* tantras or 'tantras of union', and *anuttara* tantras or 'ultimate tantras' (usually, but incorrectly, referred to as *anuttarayoga* tantras).[158]

The *kriyā* tantras form a very large category of texts which appeared between the 2nd and 6th centuries CE. They include some of the earliest tantras, and were the first to be translated into Chinese (from the 3rd century onwards) e.g. the *Mahāmegha Sūtra* (prior to 439CE). *Kriyā* tantras – such as the *Mahāmegha Sūtra*, which is concerned solely with rain-making – unlike the remaining classes of tantras, are essentially instrumental in character, utilized for exclusively secular purposes. Because of their non-soteriological nature, the *kriyā* tantras were not superseded by the later classes of tantras. They are distributed between four kulas or 'families': the *tathāgatakula*, the *padmakula*, the *vajrakula*, and the *sāmānyakula*, and each centres on the worship of one of a large number of Buddhas, Bodhisattvas, and deities. Many are based around *dhāraṇīs*. Included in this class are the *Āryamañjuśrīmūlakalpa*, the *Subāhuparipṛcchā Sūtra*, and the *Aparimitāyurjñānahṛdayadhāraṇī*, along with many others.

The *caryā* tantras form a small class of texts that probably emerged from the 6th century onwards, comprising the *Mahāvairocanābhisaṁbodhi Tantra* (c.600) and a few ancillary texts. As a class, it is therefore almost entirely centred upon the worship of the Buddha Vairocana, although it is still concerned with gaining *siddhis*, or mundane powers. Unlike the *kriyā* tantras, however, the *siddhis* are obtained through a process of visualization of oneself as Vairocana.

The *yoga* tantras likewise centre on Vairocana, and include the *Sarvatathāgatatattvasaṁgraha Tantra* (c.700CE), the *Sarvadurgatipariśodhana*

Tantra, and, reflecting a cult of the Bodhisattva Mañjuśrī, the *Mañjuśrī-nāmasaṁgīti*. Together with the *caryā* tantras they form the basis of Shingon, the Japanese Tantric school.

The fourfold Tibetan classification, in which there is a final class of *anuttara* tantras, seems to have been imposed on a more complex reality that existed in India.[159] It incorporates at least two classes of tantra, which in origin clearly saw themselves as consecutively superseding or replacing previous tantras. The first of these are the *yogottara* tantras, or 'higher tantras of union', also described as 'father tantras' or '*upāya* tantras', which are concerned primarily with the worship of the Buddha Akṣobhya and his consort Māmakī, utilizing the imagery and ritual of sexual intercourse. The practices of the *yogottara* tantras, and those which followed them, are described as non-dualistic, in that they enjoin a deliberate transcendence of social and religious conventions regarding dualities of what is permissible and impermissible. They include the *Guhyasamāja Tantra*, dating probably from the 8th century.

The *yogottara* tantras were superseded by a class of tantras, dating from the late 8th century, which describe themselves in contrast as 'mother tantras' or *prajñā* tantras. These are still centred around the Buddha Akṣobhya, but he is worshipped in his wrathful forms (known as *herukas*) with female consorts, and is accompanied by retinues of *ḍākiṇīs*. He is usually visualized in a cremation ground. Generally speaking, female figures are as important as male figures, if not more so, in these tantras, and this is reflected in the name used for this class: *yoginī* tantra. These tantras are also called *yogānuttara-* or *yoganiruttara* tantras, i.e. 'ultimate tantras of union'. The first tantra of this class of which we know is the *Saṁvara Tantra*, translated into Tibetan in the 8th century. Other members of this class, such as the *Hevajra Tantra*, the *Saṁvarodaya Tantra*, and the *Caṇḍamahāroṣaṇa Tantra*, seem to have appeared only in the 10th century. The *Kālacakra Tantra* (11th century) is sometimes classed as an *advaya* tantra or 'non-dual' tantra which supersedes all previous classes of tantras.

Similarities between *yoginī* tantra figures and Śaivite tantra figures have been noted for a long time, but it has been established only recently that some *yoginī* tantras were undoubtedly transcribed from Śaivite tantras and adapted to Buddhist purposes by a Buddhist redactor.[160] This textual evidence is reinforced by the well known similarities of rituals and iconography. This is not to say that these higher tantras are non-Buddhist, since it was always a part of the Buddhist tradition to incorporate deities from other religious traditions, and transform them so as to complement or serve the soteriological purposes of Buddhism.

By later systematization, these four classes are regarded as forming a hierarchy through which the practitioner has to rise in due order. Access to, and practice of, a tantra always requires prior initiation by a qualified master. Individual *sādhanas*, or instructions for the visualization of a figure, usually incorporate elements from both early Buddhist and Mahāyāna practice, amongst which one can include the *brahmavihāras*, Going for Refuge, confession of faults, the Bodhisattva vow, cultivation of the bodhicitta, and the transference of merits.[161]

Other characteristic literary products of the Vajrayāna include various compendia of *sādhanas*, such as the *Sādhanamālā*, and also collections of the songs of the *mahā-siddhas*, such as the *Caryāgīti* (12th century), which contains *dohas* by many *siddhas*, and the *Dohakośa*, which is a collection of songs by the *siddha* Saraha (9th century). Several Tantric manuals are devoted to the exposition, for the purposes of visualization, of groups of complex maṇḍalas, or circular diagrams, which are two-dimensional diagrams of ritual temples for specific Buddhas, accompanied by their entourages. Characteristically such maṇḍalas might depict a central figure flanked by four others at the cardinal points. In this context the triad of three Buddhas, Śākyamuni, Amitābha, and Akṣobhya, known from the earlier Mahāyāna, is supplemented by two others, Ratnasaṁbhava and Amoghasiddhi, whilst Śākyamuni is replaced by Vairocana. In the higher tantras the central position of Vairocana is taken over by Akṣobhya.

The Vajrayāna was taken to Tibet, particularly after the collapse of northern Indian Buddhism under Muslim invasion, where it was embraced by the Tibetans. Though it was taken to China in the early 8th century it did not prosper there, since the Chinese found the sexual content of the *yogottara* tantras unacceptable. By contrast Tantric practice (excluding the *yogottara*) gained a firm foothold in Japan, where it flourished in the guise of the Shingon School.

18

The End of Buddhism in India

The end of Buddhism in India was undoubtedly precipitated by the Muslim invasions of the 12th and 13th centuries, but there were several respects in which it was already suffering a decline, and was thereby vulnerable to the impact of Islam.

Firstly, there had already begun an intermingling of Hindu and Buddhist ideas, which for the ordinary person made a clear differentiation between them difficult. On the one hand, there had been for several centuries a mutual critical dialogue between the two religions which had served to refine their respective philosophies – but refine them in a way that made them more abstract and less easy for the layperson to differentiate. On the other hand the developments of the Tantra, giving rise to a host of Buddha, Bodhisattva, and *dharmapāla* figures, must have made Buddhism seem little different to the outsider or the non-specialist from orthodox (or Tantric) Hinduism, with its multiplicity of deities. There was even to some degree an absorption of Buddhism by Hinduism, as reflected in the Vaiṣṇavite doctrine of the Buddha as an avatar of Viṣṇu, which appeared for the first time shortly before the Muslim invasions took place. Even the Pālas, who regarded themselves as Buddhists, also prided themselves on their full observance of caste dharma – the Hindu regulations governing all aspects of social interaction.

Allied with this was the degree to which Buddhism seems to have become a religion for specialists, particularly monastic specialists occupying the increasingly grand universities which had been built under the sponsorship of the Gupta and Pāla patron kings. At its height, Nālandā was supported by tithes from one hundred villages, and offered free training to as many as 10,000 students, both Buddhist and non-Buddhist. Whilst Buddhism had become increasingly associated with centralized, monastic learning, Hinduism remained based in the village, the brahmin purohita ministering to the religious needs of his fellow householders. The Buddhists, by contrast, were free from any immediate economic dependence on the communities around them through the cumulative effect of generous endowments from past lay followers and royal patrons. Perhaps they lost touch to some degree with popular culture, ceasing to proselytize, and turning inward towards subtle philosophical debate and Tantric ritual. Even the Hindu ascetics were mere wanderers, as had been the first Buddhists, and thus were free from this dependence upon monastic organization and the necessary royal patronage which had become the lot of the Buddhists. It seems that Hinduism underwent a further resurgence during the centuries preceding the Muslim invasions, with the spread of Vaiṣṇavism in the south, Śaivism in Kashmir, and philosopher-teachers hostile to Buddhism, such as Śaṅkara and Kumārila, teaching across the country and gathering influential followings. Although there are possible indications that the caste distinctions at the core of Hindu society had infiltrated the Buddhist Saṅgha (as happened in Sri Lanka), one should not forget that Buddhism had implicitly denied their validity by offering ordination to all regardless of caste. This opposition was expressed directly in Aśvaghoṣa's *Vajrasuci*, in which the author undermines the basis of caste by drawing upon anomalous episodes in the Hindu scriptures.

Finally, the support of royalty was itself ambiguous in its benefits. Nālandā, so heavily sponsored by Harṣa (606–647CE), was later neglected by the Pāla dynasty, who instead favoured the monastic universities that they themselves had founded – Vikramaśīla and Odantapurī. Nor were kings necessarily reliable in their undertakings, for they not only changed their religious allegiances, but could also be usurped and replaced by others hostile to the Dharma.

The beginning of the end of Indian Buddhism started in the 8th century, with the first Muslim forays into India, such as that which destroyed the town and the Buddhist university at Valabhī. These were checked by local Indian rulers, so that the Turkish invaders made only gradual advances into the mainland over the next four centuries, as successive kingdoms fell to their troops. As local Indian rulers did not achieve any successful alliance against the Muslim threat, and in some cases tragically underestimated the danger represented by the foe at their borders, a decisive breakthrough was made in the 12th century, when the Muslims extended their destructive presence across the whole of the north of the subcontinent. In 1197 Nālandā was sacked. Vikramaśīla followed suit in 1203. Muslim historians record that the universities, standing out upon the northern Indian plains, were initially mistaken for fortresses, and were cruelly ravaged, the libraries burnt, and the occupants murdered before they could even explain who and what they were.[162] Before long the Ganges basin, the traditional heartland of Buddhism, was under the control of Islamic rulers.

The universities themselves were destroyed almost at a stroke, for the central principles of non-violence presumably hindered any military defence on the part of the Buddhist communities. But Buddhist groups survived in small pockets in northern India for several more centuries. A Tibetan pilgrim, Dharmasvāmin, seeking scriptures among the ruins of Nālandā, found a monk called Rāhulaśrībhadra teaching Sanskrit grammar to a handful of pupils in 1295.[163] Most refugees escaped to South-east Asia via Burma, or to Tibet, or to southern India. Largely unaffected by the Muslim encroachments upon northern India, Buddhist institutions in southern India survived for several more centuries, until slowly succumbing to a resurgent Śaivism from the 8th or 9th centuries onwards. There is evidence to show that Theravāda Buddhism survived in Karnataka until at least the 16th century[164] and Tamil Nadu until as late as the 17th century.[165]

Part 2

Buddhism Beyond India

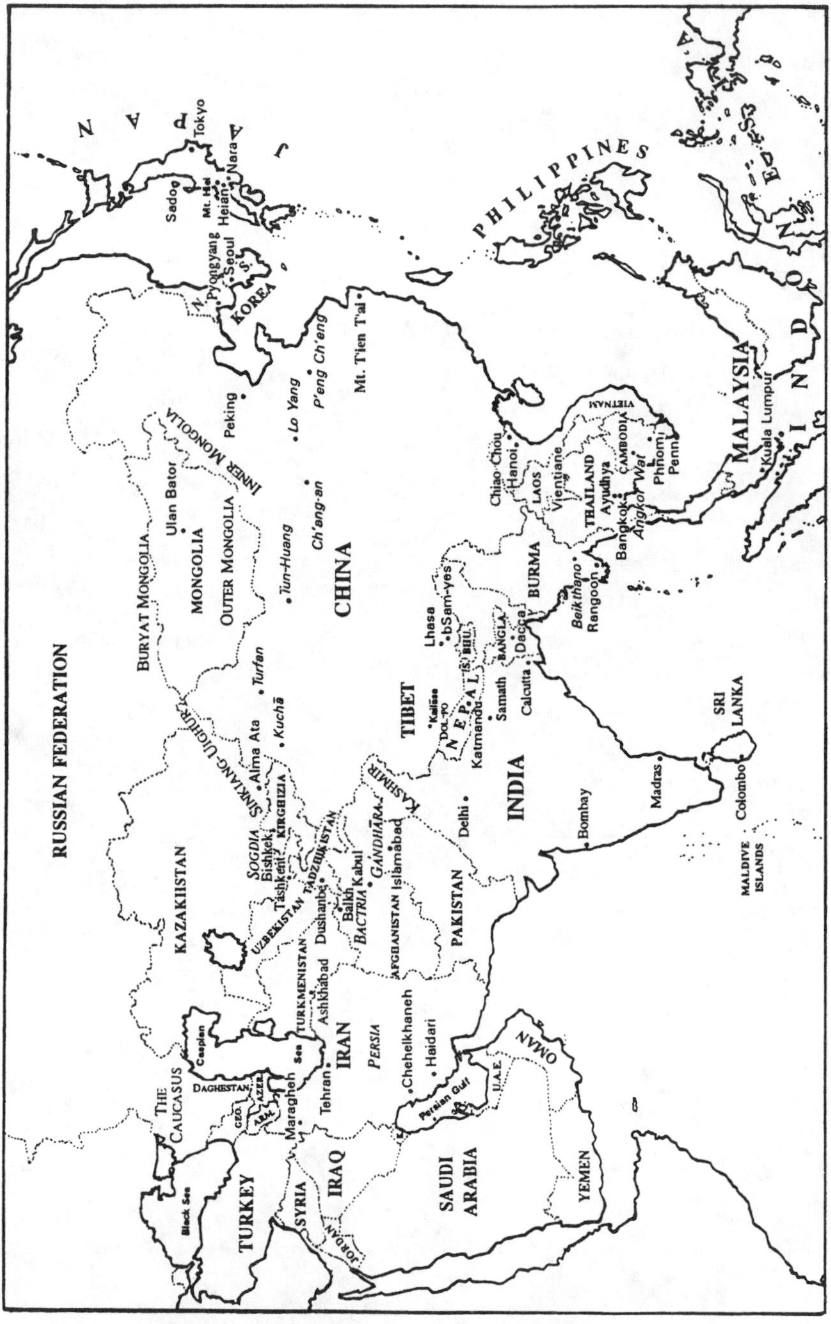

These maps are provided to offer general geographical orientation only. Countries are described by their modern political boundaries; ancient states and sites are given in italics.

19

Buddhism in Sri Lanka

The story of Buddhism in South-east Asia begins with the introduction of the Dharma to Sri Lanka. Whilst there is a legend that the Buddha himself visited the island, historical contact dates from the mission sent by Aśoka, c.247BCE, in response to overtures of friendship from the Sri Lankan king, Devānaṁpiyatissa, 250–210BCE. He became a fervent patron of the new religion, and is associated by tradition with the founding of the Mahāvihāra monastery, the planting of a seedling of the Bodhi Tree there, and the building of the great stūpa at Anurādhapura, the Thūpārāma Dāgaba, for the Buddha's collar-bone relic. It appears that a close identification was soon formed between the state and Sinhala culture, with Buddhism as the established, or state-sponsored, religion. This meant that Buddhism in Sri Lanka quickly acquired a nationalist significance which was cultivated both by monks, who thereby enjoyed royal favour, and by the kings, who enjoyed a reciprocal legitimation of their political power from the monks. From the start, Buddhism in Sri Lanka was a monastic phenomenon, and its early history on the island was dominated by the interplay of rivalry between different *vihāras*, or monasteries, which at various times each enjoyed the patronage of the monarch, and thereby sought dominance over the Saṅgha as a whole. The form of Buddhism that Mahinda brought was apparently that of the Sthaviravāda, and this came to be dominated by a later sub-sect, called in Pāli the Theravāda. Since *thera* is the Pāli equivalent of the Sanskrit *sthavira*, 'elder', the Theravāda subsequently identified itself with the earliest Sthaviravāda, and claimed to preserve the Buddha's original Dharma-Vinaya.

The first competitor to the Mahāvihāra was the Abhayagiri Vihāra, built by the king Vaṭṭagāmaṇī (29–17BCE) after the repulsion of Tamil invaders from the island. It was also in the final year of this king's reign that the Tipiṭaka was written down for the first time, since the recent warfare had threatened the total extinction of the Saṅgha, which up to then had been the sole vehicle for its preservation. Conflict of interest soon developed between the Mahāvihāra and the Abhayagiri Vihāra, since the king had given the new *vihāra* to an individual monk with the result that the monk was expelled by the Mahāvihāra for breaching the Vinaya rule that forbids such possession. Consequently the monk broke off relations with the Mahāvihāra, taking a body of disciples to the Abhayagiri Vihāra. The two institutions went their own ways, conducting an ongoing rivalry for the favour of successive monarchs. A second split occurred in the 4th century, when the king, Mahāsena, came under the influence of a southern Indian Mahāyānist monk, and as a result apparently wished the Mahāvihāra to become Mahāyānist too. The occupants of the *vihāra* refused and left, and the king destroyed the *vihāra*, building the Jetavana Vihāra for the Mahāyānists. The next king gave his patronage once more to the Mahāvihāra, who had their monastery rebuilt and were reinstated there, and under him was instituted the Mahinda festival, a celebration of the 'purification' of the *sāsana*. Thereafter, for several centuries, these three establishments vied for patronage and supremacy, the Abhayagiri Vihāra more open to the influence of Mahāyāna ideas, the Mahāvihāra stressing its own ultra-orthodoxy. With each *vihāra* there was an associated *nikāya*, or ordination lineage. This situation continued until the 12th century when the Saṅgha was 'purified' and united under the dominance of the Mahāvihāra by the king Parakkama Bāhu I (who simply abolished the other two lineages).

In addition to the recension of the Tipiṭaka written down there, among the most notable examples of the literature produced in Sri Lanka are the chronicles, the *Dīpavaṁsa* and *Mahāvaṁsa* (of the 4th and 5th centuries respectively), which clearly demonstrate the combination of religion and nationalism that so characterizes Sri Lankan Buddhism. There are also the works of Buddhaghosa, an Indian monk who travelled to Sri Lanka in the early 5th century. Once there, he first compiled a large compendium of doctrine, the *Visuddhi-magga*, or 'Path to Purity', arranged according to the *sīla*, *samādhi*, and *paññā* structure of the path. He then summarized the commentarial material on the Vinaya and most of the Sutta Piṭaka, which had been arriving in Sri Lanka until the 1st century CE from the Indian mainland. (There appears to have been a strong Theravādin presence in Tamil Nadu until as late as the 17th century.[166]) Through this work, Buddhaghosa exerted a major formative influence upon the doctrine of the Theravāda orthodoxy on the island, and mainstream Theravāda teaching as we know it today, i.e. the teaching of the Mahāvihāra, is largely the result of his synthesis. There also survives in Chinese translation a compendium called the *Vimutti-magga*, 'Path to Liberation', which parallels the *Visuddhi-magga*, and may have been compiled at the Abhayagiri Vihāra. Of equal interest must be the *Buddhāpadāna* from the *Khuddhaka-Nikāya*. Composed in the 1st or 2nd century CE, before the suppression of the Mahāyāna in the 3rd century, it shows some influence of teachings similar to those of the *Sukhāvatī-vyūha Sūtras* of the Mahāyāna. There is also reliable evidence of the introduction of Mahāyāna Tantric texts to Sri Lanka by the 9th century, and there are reports from European visitors in the 18th century which appear to describe monks engaged in the recitation of mantras and using rosary beads, or *mālās*.[167] It is clear that non-Mahāvihāra Theravāda Buddhism in Sri Lanka and throughout South-east Asia may well have exhibited tantric elements, although – in the aftermath of the successful Mahāvihārin proselytizing of the region – the main textual evidence for this survives largely in Cambodia. This Tantric element did not reflect Mahāyāna influence, but rather the pan-Indian development of Tantric techniques in Buddhism. In the predominantly non-Mahāyāna milieu of South-east Asia these Tantric techniques were applied to the doctrines and practices of the Thera-vāda, and scriptural authority sought in the Pāli Canon, producing what has been called a 'Tantric' Theravāda. However, it is clear from sculptural evidence alone that the Mahāyāna was fairly widespread throughout the country, although the modern account of the history of Buddhism on the island presents an unbroken and pure lineage of Theravāda. (One can only assume that similar trends were transmitted to other parts of South-east Asia with Sri Lankan ordination lineages.) Relics of an extensive cult of Avalokiteśvara can be seen in the present-day figure of Nātha.[168]

Other interesting developments of this period include the *paṁsu-kūlikas*, or 'rag-robe wearers', monks drawn from all Sri Lankan *nikāyas*, who chose to adopt the permitted ascetic practice of wearing robes made from rags, and live in separate monasteries. Noted from the beginning of the 8th century, they appear to have succumbed to the pull of royal patronage by the 11th century and pass out of the records by the 12th. Of more lasting significance is the distinction, first appearing in the 6th century, but formalized by the 12th century 'purification' and reorganization, and still applicable today, between village-dwelling monks and forest-dwelling monks. The latter, termed *araññavāsins*, preferred to live in quieter forest monasteries or hermitages, where they could pursue a more rigorous life-style of meditation and study. Considerable economic resources were directed towards the Saṅgha through royal patronage, which often took the form of land grants made to individual monasteries, with the result that these became, collectively, the major land-holder on the island during this period. The extraordinary wealth of the Saṅgha is reflected in the numbers of monks reported by Chinese pilgrims who visited Sri Lanka – Fa-hsien reports that there were 60,000 in the 5th century. Further signs of heavy royal patronage were to be seen in the extensive architectural developments of sites such as Polonnaruva, financed by the enormous landholdings of the monastic community.

The reforms under Parakkama Bāhu I involved the expulsion from the Saṅgha of monks who refused to observe the Vinaya and the organization of the Saṅgha under a *saṅgharāja*, or 'king of the order', and beneath him two *mahāsthaviras*, i.e. two elders of more than twenty years ordination, to direct the village and forest dwelling monks on the island. This reorganization had a revitalizing effect, in part reflected by the generation of a new stratum of sub-canonical literature in the form of sub-commentaries on the commentaries of Buddhaghosa and Dhammapāla, and chronicles, or *vaṁsa*, of the Buddha's relics and stūpas. A continuation of the *Mahāvaṁsa*, called the *Cūlavaṁsa* or 'lesser chronicle', was begun in the 13th century.

During the 10th and 11th centuries the Sri Lankan Saṅgha was disrupted by invasions of the island by Cola kings of Tamil Nadu in southern India. It was during this period that the bhikkhunī Saṅgha, the community of nuns, died out. Since the concept of ordination in Buddhism rested upon the unbroken transmission reaching back (in theory) to the Buddha, the demise of the nuns' community meant that this transmission had stopped, and by definition it could not be revived. Similar situations eventually obtaining in all Theravādin countries, women could no longer join the Theravādin monastic Saṅgha. There is little doubt that this situation really reflects the reluctance of the bhikkhu Saṅgha to allow women to share their privileges, since it is known that a branch of the Sri Lankan bhikkhunī Saṅgha, transplanted to China in the 5th century from where it could have been reintroduced into any part of South-east Asia, has survived even to the present day.[169] After a further Tamil incursion King Parakkama Bahu II (13th century) invited Theravādin monks from Tamil Nadu to Sri Lanka to help restore the Saṅgha on the island.

The later history of Buddhism in Sri Lanka continues this story of decline and revival. After the persecution of a 16th-century Śaiva king, the Dharma had to be reintroduced on two occasions in the 17th century, both times from Theravādin communities in Burma. By the 18th century there were no celibate monks, since, through revisions made to the Vinaya (under the auspices of the monarchy) allowing the personal possession of property by members of the Saṅgha, the monasteries had become the hereditary property of nominally ordained family lineages. Also by this time ordination was determined by caste, and largely restricted to members of the land-owning class. The 19th century saw the extensive contact of Buddhism with British colonial officials and later Protestant missionaries – a contact that was to exert some influence towards the reform and revival of the Saṅgha.

20

Buddhism in South-east Asia

Though later to be universally dominated by the Theravāda form of Buddhism, the early history of the Dharma in South-east Asia is more piecemeal and eclectic. The later history of Buddhism in the region is characterized by a strong correlation of religious and national identity, and the promulgation of an ultra-orthodoxy derived from the works of Buddhaghosa, on the model of developments in Sri Lanka at the Mahāvihāra.

Burma

The region occupied by the modern state of Burma was to play a crucial role in the spread of Buddhism in the region, and indeed seems to have been the first mainland country outside India to come under its influence, a mission being sent by Aśoka (3rd century BCE) to the Mon peoples of Lower Burma and Thailand. It is to be assumed that the two monks Soṇa and Uttara took some form of the Sthaviravāda. Subsequent missions from Sri Lanka and southern India arrived in the 1st century CE, and firmly established a Theravādin presence amongst the Mons.

The ancestors of the modern Burmese people occupied the region by moving southwards from their homeland in the eastern Himalayas, and had established the first Burmese kingdom, the Pyu, in central Burma by the 3rd century CE. Upper Burma received its first contacts with Buddhism through land missions from northern India, which arrived during the 3rd to 5th centuries, bringing with them the teachings and practices of the Sarvāstivāda and Mahāyāna and, by the 7th century, Tantric influences too. Through geographical proximity to southern India and Sri Lanka, the Theravāda was also established in central Burma. The earliest monumental remains of Buddhism in the Pyu city of Beikthano date from the 4th century and indicate strong links with the Buddhist communities of Nāgārjunakoṇḍa, probably based upon trade.[170]

This situation persisted until the unification of upper and lower Burma under the Burmese king Anawratā (11th century) who brought Theravāda monks to Upper Burma from the conquered Mon kingdom (partly corresponding to Lower Burma), and gave them control of the Saṅgha throughout the country. Their influence, which represented the older Theravāda preserved by the Mon, was augmented by that of a Burmese monk, Chapaṭa, who had received ordination in Sri Lanka in the reformed Mahāvihāra Saṅgha of Parakkama Bāhu I. Thereafter royal support for the Theravāda was strong, and in the 15th century the role of *dhammarāja*, 'king of the Teaching', initiated by King Dhammaceti, with its attendant authority over all the country's monasteries, was given to whichever monk was acting as personal preceptor to the king in power. This coincided with the reformation of the ordination lineages. Hitherto there had been four separate traditions identified with Sri Lankan and Burmese sources. These were now unified under a single lineage introduced by eighteen monks who had been sent to the Mahāvihāra of Sri Lanka. Contacts with Sri Lanka were strong, monks going there on pilgrimage. However, it should not be assumed that Burmese Buddhism is exclusively Theravādin. The popular cult of a Sarvāstivādin arhat, Upagupta, still survives in Burma, as also in parts of Thailand and Laos.[171] A major, though not the earliest, source for this legend is the *Lokapaññatti*, a primarily cosmological text composed in Lower Burma in the 11th or 12th century. Another important Burmese work is the *Saddanīti*, the definitive grammar of Pāli, written by the monk Aggavaṁsa in the 12th century.

Application to the study of the Buddhist scriptures has been a feature of Burmese Buddhism. This has resulted in a particularly reliable transmission of the whole Pāli Canon there, although the Burmese have shown greatest interest in the Abhidhamma. Notable expression of the same trend was shown in the Fifth and Sixth Buddhist Councils, convened in Mandalay in 1871 and Rangoon in 1954–56 respectively, at both of which the canon was thoroughly revised.

CAMBODIA

Cambodia, like the other regions of South-east Asia, received considerable cultural influence from India, and as a result witnessed an intermingling of Śaivism and Buddhism in the early years. Mahāyāna Buddhist communities had been established since the 2nd century CE, and by the 5th century were being heavily patronized by Śaivite kings. After a period of repression in the 7th century, a succession of Vaiṣṇavite and Śaivite kings identified themselves as Bodhisattvas, giving strong support to the Buddhist communities. Considerable wealth was lavished upon temples, including the famous Angkor Wat, although it appears that the drain that patronage on this scale made upon the country's resources led to two revolts in the 12th century. Despite a Mahāyāna revival in court circles in the same century, a gradual conversion of the populace to the Theravāda began at the same time, possibly under Thai influence. The first dated evidence is an inscription of c.1230. By the 14th century the first king with a Theravāda affiliation, Jayavarman Parameśvara, came to the throne, and the older court Mahāyāna practices finally died out with the invasion of the capital by a Thai army in 1431. The Dhammayutika *nikāya* was introduced into Cambodia in 1864.

Cambodia also preserves the main evidence for a form of esoteric Theravāda Buddhism, sometimes called 'Tantric' Theravāda.[172] The origin of this phenomenon is not understood in detail, although it seems unlikely that it came from an external Mahāyānist or Śaivite source as it relies entirely upon the Pāli Canon for scriptural reference. It is more likely the natural expression of the Tantric developments occurring throughout India, when confined to a non-Mahāyāna environment. This form of Theravāda, which like all tantra was accessible only through initiation, appears to have been structured around a complex system of correspondences between the human body, the cosmos, and esoteric knowledge. Mantras were widely used, as we might expect. The most widely known literary product of this tradition, although not recognized as such for some time, is *Yogāvacara's Manual*, one of a number of more or less closely related meditation manuals.

THAILAND

Part of the region occupied by the modern states of Thailand and Laos was Mon, and shared the Theravādin influence on the Mon of Burma. During a period of Cambodian dominance, in the 11th and 12th centuries, Thailand received Mahāyāna and Hindu influences, and also assimilated the influx of the Thai peoples into the region from southern China. Both Thailand and Laos became independent kingdoms in the 13th century, and both were the recipients of Theravāda missions in the 14th century – Thailand from Burma, and Laos from Cambodia – although it is very likely that there was considerable influence prior to this from the Theravāda of the Mon people whose homeland they were settling. Royal interest in Buddhism in Thailand is exemplified by King Lu Thai who took full ordination in 1384, and is known to have undertaken to attain Buddhahood in order to help his subjects achieve freedom from saṁsāra – thus suggesting some Mahāyāna influence. The composition of a text known as the *Tribhūmigāthā*, or 'Verses on the Three Realms', which describes the character of the three realms of Buddhist cosmology and the ethical disposition of those reborn in them, is also dated to the reign of this king.

With the establishment of a new royal dynasty at Ayudhya in 1350, Brahmanism to some extent matched Buddhism as an influence at court, and although the latter remained the state religion, it was conflated with Brahmanical practices. The apparently benevolent and more exclusive interest that had characterized relations between the state and the Saṅgha of the previous century was lost. Increasingly, the Saṅgha came to be seen as a source of legitimation for the state. During the reign of King Paramatrailokanāth (1441–81), Thais were sent to Sri Lanka to receive ordination and returned with Sri Lankan monks to establish a new ordination lineage in Thailand, and in the early 18th century monks from Thailand went to Sri Lanka to ordain bhikkhus, and so established the Siyam *nikāya* there, by way of reviving the Sri Lankan Saṅgha.

The destruction of the capital and almost all the Buddhist institutions at Ayudhya by a Burmese army of occupation in 1761 necessitated a widespread revival when the country was reunited under Thai leadership in 1767. The new king, Tak Sin, himself educated by a Buddhist monk, purified the Saṅgha (dismissing even the *saṅgharāja*), limited the influence of Brahmanism at court, and ensured that a complete copy of the Tipiṭaka was restored to the capital city. A reform sect known as the Thammayutika *nikāya*, the 'ordination lineage in accordance with the Teaching', was founded with the patronage of the monk-prince Mongkut (1824–51), partly under Sri Lankan influence. Under Mongkut's kingship, beginning in 1851, the better-educated monks of the minority reform movement gained preferential position in society, causing considerable tension between them and the representatives of the older unreformed Mahānikāya. Under Thai influence the Mahānikāya and Thammayutika *nikāya* spread to both Laos and Cambodia.

The countries considered so far reveal a pattern in which, between the 12th and 15th centuries, a normative Saṅgha structure, and Theravāda doctrine based upon that of the Mahāvihāra in Sri Lanka, is adopted by emergent states as a means of legitimation. The perceived connection between state and religion is clearly derived from the Sri Lankan model, which itself derives some inspiration from the example of Aśoka and his intervention in the Saṅgha connected with the Third Council. In part this influence was undoubtedly beneficial, many kings trying to emulate the example of the Buddhist *dhammarāja*, who rules in righteousness. Nor should it be forgotten that, as in Tibet and Japan, Buddhism was to play a crucial role in the introduction of higher culture into these countries.

VIETNAM

Vietnam stands somewhat outside the pattern of the other South-east Asian countries, in that it was dominated by the Chinese cultural sphere of influence, especially in the north of the country, even after its political independence was won in the 10th century. The first Buddhists to arrive came as fugitives from the turbulence of the Three Kingdoms period in China (c.189CE), but there were further missions from both Mahāyāna and non-Mahāyāna schools in the 3rd century. Because of its geographical position, Vietnam benefited from the traffic of merchants and missionaries along the sea route between China and India. Buddhist missionaries, travelling by sea from India and other southern Asian countries, will doubtless have stopped over in Vietnam *en route* for China. Indian, Tibetan, and Chinese monks likewise came to Vietnam by sea from China. Buddhism was also transmitted to Vietnam from more proximate sources, including the kingdom of Campā (on the east coast of Vietnam), which had been founded in part by Indian colonists in the 2nd century CE (until absorbed by Vietnam in the 15th century), and from Cambodia. Both countries supported both a syncretic Śaiva-Mahāyāna Buddhism and Theravāda Buddhism, although Campā probably had a Theravāda presence from as early as the 3rd century, whilst Cambodia received the Theravāda as late as the 12th century.

Three characteristic forms of Buddhism developed under largely Chinese influence: the A-Ham (*āgama*) tradition, dating probably from the 2nd century; the Thien (Ch'an) tradition, introduced in the 6th century; and a Pure Land school, involving the worship of Amitābha, which was popular amongst ordinary people, the former two being restricted to the monasteries. After some initial success, Hīnayāna forms of Buddhism gave way to the influence of the Mahāyāna. After the 12th century an amalgamation of Thien and Pure Land arose which thereafter characterized Vietnamese Buddhism to the 20th century. Reflecting the different points of entry of the religion to Vietnam, northern Vietnamese Buddhism was generally based on the Chinese canon, whereas that of South Vietnam was based on the Pāli Canon in the Cambodian script.

INDONESIA

Indonesia likewise falls outside the South-east Asian pattern. According to Fa-hsien, who visited Sumatra in 414CE, no evidence of Buddhism was to be found, but by the 6th century the Śailendra dynasty had become Mahāyānist, and I-Tsing found Mahāyāna Buddhists there when he visited in 690, and monks observing the Mūla-sarvāstivādin Vinaya in the main, with some from the Sammitīya *nikāya*. Among a number of stone monuments built under the Śailendras, the most magnificent evidence of the vigour and wealth of Buddhist patronage during this period is that at Borobudur. It forms a vast symbolic maṇḍala-city, containing seventy stūpas enclosing statues of Vairocana Buddha and a wealth of relief carvings illustrating scenes from the *Gaṇḍavyūha Sūtra*, the *Lalitavistara*, and the *Divyāvadāna*. A hybrid tantra, containing Buddhist and Śaivite elements and enjoying royal patronage, developed during the 12th and 13th centuries, but this was ousted along with the rulers by an Islamic rebellion in the 15th century.

21

BUDDHISM IN CENTRAL ASIA AND KASHMIR

THE HIMALAYAS FORM AN ALMOST INSUPERABLE BARRIER between the heartlands of Buddhism in India and the lands to the north and east. The initial diffusion of the Dharma to these regions followed the silk route, beginning by the same passes of north-western India which had played so crucial a role in so many phases of the subcontinent's history. The result was that the enormous region known as Central Asia, stretching from the republics of Turkmenistan, Uzbekistan, and Tadzhikistan in the west to the Chinese Autonomous Region of Sinkiang-Uighur in the east, and the state of Kashmir to the south-west, played a vital role in the development of Buddhism in China and Tibet. Central Asia was the main route for the transmission of Buddhism to China, from about the 1st century CE, and to Tibet from the 7th century. Yet despite its importance, little is known of the history of this diffusion, especially since, between the 8th and 14th centuries, the entire region succumbed to the rule of Muslim invaders, although the process of 'Islamification' was in a number of areas very slow, and Buddhism may have survived in some form in Chinese Central Asia until the 17th or 18th centuries,[173] and in Afghanistan until the 19th.[174]

The key to the importance of this area was the presence of trade routes, largely concerned with the export of silk to India and Europe, which, via the passes of north-western India, linked China with the Mediterranean. Merchants, many of them from Sogdia, who established settlements along this route, acquired languages for the purpose of trade, especially with the Chinese, and were substantially instrumental in the translation of Buddhist texts into their language in the early centuries of the common era. The region was divided at this time into a number of kingdoms, often centred around important oasis settlements such as Khotan, Kuchā, and Turfan, each of which also became an important centre of Buddhist learning. Ethnically the region was very mixed, with Greeks, Indians, and Iranians to the south and west, and Turks and Chinese to the north and east. Inevitably there were many languages in use in the area, including eastern Iranian and Turkic dialects, Tibetan, Chinese, Prakrit, and Sanskrit.

The earliest phase of Buddhist missionary activity may well have been undertaken by Dharmaguptaka monks. The evidence that we have for this includes a version of the *Dharmapada* in the language that they used, now called Gandhārī Prakrit, surviving in a single manuscript dating from the 1st or 2nd century CE, found at Khotan. We also know that it was their version of the *Dīrghāgama* which was translated into Chinese between 410 and 413CE, and it was also the Dharmaguptaka Vinaya that was observed by Chinese monks. A later phase of Sarvāstivādin influence began under the patronage of the Kuśāna kings, particularly Kaniṣka, which disseminated characteristic Sarvāstivādin works, including many Abhidharma texts, in Buddhist Sanskrit. By the 4th century there also appears to have been a centre of Mahāyāna learning at Khotan.

Great innovations undoubtedly arose from the intermingling of early Buddhism and the Mahāyāna in Kashmir. Under the guidance of Sarvāstivādin teachers in the region, a number of influential meditation schools evolved which took as their inspiration the Bodhisattva Maitreya. This doubtless reflects the fact that Maitreya, the future Buddha, is recognized as a Bodhisattva by both the Mahāyāna and the non-Mahāyāna schools, and was therefore able to exert a universal appeal in a milieu where the two traditions mixed. The Kashmiri meditation schools were undoubtedly highly influential in the arising of the *buddhānusmṛti* practices, concerned with the 'recollection of the Buddha(s)', which were later to become characteristic of Mahāyāna Buddhism and the Tantra. Maitreya's popularity was clearly linked with meditational experience, and it seems likely that he may have been the object of visionary experiences cultivated through meditation. His popularity is attested throughout the Central Asian region, a sūtra devoted to him being found at Turfan and enormous statues erected at the border of each kingdom along the trade routes. The Buddha Amitābha also gained a widespread devotional following in this region, eventually ousting Maitreya, and it is possible that the *Sukhāvatī-vyūha*

Sūtras were composed here. Kashmir was also the home of Saṅgharakṣa, a Sarvāstivādin meditation teacher who was a contemporary of Kaniṣka and who wrote a meditation manual entitled the *Yogācārabhūmi*, which was to be the model for the later text of the same name by the Mahāyānist, Asaṅga.

At the eastern end of the silk route, in what is now western China, is Tun-huang, the site of an extensive complex of rock-cut caves, containing many Buddhist wall-paintings and statues. It was the birthplace of Dharmarakṣa, the most important translator of Buddhist texts into Chinese before Kumārajīva. Whilst many Central Asians were involved in translation work, the most illustrious was Kumārajīva (344–413CE), the son of a Kuchean mother and Indian father, who translated many early Buddhist and Mahāyāna works into Chinese. His translation of the *Lotus Sūtra* was regarded as particularly good (it seems probable that he was the first translator who was fully competent in both Sanskrit and Chinese) and became the definitive Chinese version. Central Asia is also associated with several discoveries of Buddhist manuscripts, most notably at Tun-huang, Turfan, and Gilgit (northern Pakistan). These have provided us with the earliest manuscripts we possess for a number of important sūtras. Since these manuscripts contain what are sometimes shorter versions of much later manuscripts recovered from Nepal, they demonstrate how many sūtra texts are in fact composite creations, that grew through a process of accretion over the centuries.

22

Buddhism in China

Buddhism was first brought to China during the 1st century CE. It came from the west, from Central Asia, with merchants and Central Asian Buddhists. It did not, as in South-east Asia and Tibet, function as the vehicle for higher culture, since China had already acquired a high degree of literate civilization. China also had its own indigenous religions, well established in society and, each in its own way, having some influence on the character that Buddhism was to take in their homeland. The older of these religions was Taoism, associated with a founder Lao-Tzu (b.604BCE), which was primarily concerned with the extension of life through alchemy and the worship of a number of deities. The second of the indigenous systems was that of Confucianism, itself based on the 'sayings' of Confucius (551–497BCE), which stressed the ideals of social utility, the veneration of elders, and learning. Confucianism particularly encouraged a view of cultural superiority on the part of the Chinese, seeing no virtue whatsoever in the import of a 'barbarian' religion from the west, i.e. India.

The first phase of Buddhist contact, up to the 4th century, made little impact upon Chinese religious life. The activities of the Buddhists, the majority being non-Chinese Central Asians, revolved largely around the translation and study of a miscellaneous stream of Buddhist texts that were imported via the western trade routes. Up to 220CE this activity was centred on a monastery in Lo Yang, where meditation manuals, compiled by the meditation masters of Kashmir and north-western India and largely concerned with the meditation practices typical of the non-Mahāyāna schools, were thought to resonate with the indigenous Taoist interest in mental and physical alchemical techniques. The first sūtra to be translated at this period was the *Sūtra in Forty-Two Sections*. Foremost among those involved in this work was An Shih-kao, a Parthian, who arrived in Lo Yang c.148, and worked with a team of non-Mahāyāna monks. However, he did have contemporaries who were engaged in translating Mahāyāna sūtras, notably An-hsuan, another Parthian, and Lokakṣema, an Indo-Scythian (post-168), eleven of whose translations have survived.[175] Translations from this early period all suggest a minority interest, perhaps from amongst some fringe cult groups, in which there was probably no clear differentiation between lay and ordained.[176] After the fall of the Han dynasty in 220, the situation changed and many more translations were made, including those of numerous Mahāyāna sūtras. However, little is known of Buddhism in this period other than that it was not the interest of the educated Chinese upper classes.[177] Less still is known of the early Buddhist centres at P'eng Ch'eng (on the lower Yangtze River) in east China, and at Chiao Chou in southern China (now in North Vietnam). There is little doubt that the latter must have been initiated through sea trade contact with southern Asia, and it is possible that the same source accounts for the eastern centre too.

A second phase of development was initiated by the collapse of the northern part of the Chinese empire under the hands of Hun invaders, c.320. The Chinese court fled to the south, and until the end of the 6th century China was divided between numerous unstable regimes. In the contrasting atmospheres of these two regions Buddhism made great advances. In the northern region, ruled by various foreign dynasties, Buddhism, itself a foreign religion, could oppose the pro-Chinese Confucianism, and so had considerable appeal. As a result it received royal encouragement (albeit with the usual attendant problems of close association with the state). For this reason, in the northern region, the foreignness of Buddhism was less problematic, and the translation and study of Indian source materials continued, even though this emphasized the non-Chinese origins of Buddhism. This was facilitated by the proximity of Central Asia, which still functioned as the main route for the introduction of Buddhism to China. By the 5th century '30,000' monasteries were recorded, housing '2,000,000' monks. Particularly notable was the arrival in Ch'ang-an of the Kuchean monk Kumārajīva, the first translator competent in all the necessary languages, who organized a large and prolific translation bureau and introduced Indian Madhyamaka Buddhism to China.

In the south, however, a brilliant indigenous cultural life, a downturn in the fortunes of Confucianism, and the growth of interest in Taoism, combined with the physical suffering caused by the political situation, stimulated a vibrant and open-minded intellectual life in which Buddhism became attractive to the educated Chinese upper class for the first time. This was helped by the physical isolation from contacts with the west via Central Asia, which discouraged any emphasis upon the Indian origins of Buddhism (something less acceptable in the Chinese-ruled south), and resulted in forms of Buddhism in which Buddhist doctrines had been more thoroughly integrated with Chinese ideas. For the first time indigenous forms of Chinese Buddhism had begun to appear. An interesting consequence of the lack of direct contact with Indian Buddhism was that Chinese Buddhists, reading the chapter on meat-eating from the *Laṅkāvatāra Sūtra*, understood strict vegetarianism to be a part of the Vinaya rule. By c.400 there were almost 2,000 monasteries in the south, and for the first time Buddhism began to become the target of bitter Confucian attempts to have the 'barbarian' religion expelled from the country. The high point of Buddhist popularity in the south was marked by the emperor Wu (502–549CE) who became a Buddhist layman, banned Taoism, and forbade animal sacrifice. It was also during this period that the Indian monk Bodhidharma, the founder of the Ch'an school, came to China.

The third phase in the development of Chinese Buddhism coincides with the reunification of northern and southern regions under the Sui and T'ang dynasties, from the 6th to the 10th centuries. At this point the two tendencies identified in the second phase of development began to intermingle. Unification also meant that Central Asia could once more act as a corridor for the transmission of Buddhist ideas from the west to the heart of China, which it continued to do until this route was cut by Muslim incursions in the mid-7th century. Overland access encouraged a resurgence of Chinese pilgrims journeying to India, including Hsüan-tsang (629–645CE). Once the overland route was cut, such journeys were made by sea, via South-east Asia, as did I-Tsing (635–713CE). Whilst the end of the period was marked by a severe repression of Buddhism by resurgent Confucian and Taoist forces, it is generally regarded as the high water mark of Buddhism in China, during which it exercised its deepest degree of influence upon Chinese culture, and received the greatest amount of patronage within society. It was during this period that a number of Chinese Buddhist schools appeared. Generally speaking, these fell into two main groupings. There were those based around the teachings (which usually meant the texts) of Indian Buddhist schools and teachers, and there were those that were the product of native Chinese genius.

INDIAN SCHOOLS IN CHINA

Various Indian Buddhist schools, familiar from our discussion of Indian Buddhism, were transplanted to China in more or less the same form as they had acquired in India. These included the San-lun tsung, literally, 'Three Treatise School', founded by Kumārajīva and based on three Madhyamaka treatises by Nāgārjuna and Āryadeva, and the Fa-hsiang tsung or Yogācārin School, founded by Hsüan-tsang in 645 on his return from India with the *Triṁśikā* or 'Treatise in Thirty Verses' of Vasubandhu. Less significant were the Chu-she tsung or '(Abhidharma-)Kośa School', founded after, and concerned with, the exposition of the translation by Paramārtha, c.565, of the *Abhidharmakośa*, and the Lu tsung or 'Disciplinary School', founded by Tao-hsuan in the 7th century and concerned with the exposition of the monastic Vinaya. The Tantra was also introduced into China by three Indian monks in the 8th century, though it was not influential, and thought to be indecent by the Chinese on account of the sexual imagery of the higher tantras.

INDIGENOUS CHINESE BUDDHIST SCHOOLS

One of the unique problems facing Chinese Buddhists was the enormous influx of textual material from all periods of Buddhist development, all claiming to represent the true, ultimate teaching of Śākyamuni Buddha. Clearly there was an urgent need to assimilate this diverse material, to reconcile the varying and sometimes apparently contradictory teachings it contained, and identify the one basic truth taught by the Buddha. Unlike Tibet, China did not directly benefit from the systematizing activities of the great monastic universities of the Pāla period (c.760 onward), since overland access to northern India was cut in the 7th century, significantly reducing the contact it was possible for China to have with the Indian mainstream. Moreover, unlike their Pāla counterparts, the Chinese monks worked under the disadvantage of using translations, rather than texts composed in their native tongue. The characteristic Chinese response to this challenge tended to take one of two forms. On the one hand, some teachers founded schools based on the teaching of a single sūtra, which was regarded as proclaiming the ultimate truth, with all the other teachings of the Buddha, regarded as *upāya*, graded into a hierarchy beneath this in a schema known as a *p'an chiao*. This response paralleled that of the mainstream Indian schools, in that, like them, these Chinese schools grew out of the exposition of particular sūtras. On the other hand, and in contrast to the first approach, there was the teaching of a direct path to Enlightenment which transcended doctrinal debates and represented a radical rejection of the value of scholasticism. The former tendency gave rise to the main scholastic schools of Chinese Buddhism, such as the Hua-yen and T'ien-t'ai, whilst the latter is exemplified by Ch'an, and perhaps to a lesser extent by Ching-t'u.

T'IEN-T'AI

This school was named after the abode, Mount T'ien-t'ai, of its founder Chih-i (538–597CE). As the result of his pioneering *p'an chiao* work, Chih-i came to the conclusion that the *Lotus Sūtra* was the final, ultimate teaching of the Buddha. All sūtras, he said, were propounded by the Buddha in one of five chronological stages. The first stage was that of the preaching of the *Avataṁsaka Sūtra*, which lasted three weeks, the second was that of the *Āgamas*, which lasted twelve years, the third was that of the Vaipulya sūtras, which lasted eight years, the fourth, that of the Perfection of Wisdom sūtras, lasted twenty-two years, and the fifth stage was that of the *Lotus* and *Mahāparinirvāṇa Sūtras*, which were the final utterances of the Buddha before his parinirvāṇa. The inclusion of the *Mahāparinirvāṇa Sūtra* with the *Lotus Sūtra* was necessary because it was by definition and by tradition the discourse delivered immediately before the Buddha's parinirvāṇa.

Chih-i reasoned that, since the *Lotus Sūtra* was too sublime for the understanding of some disciples, the Buddha had also provided the *Mahāparinirvāṇa Sūtra*. The association of these two sūtras meant that something of the latter's Tathāgatagarbha doctrine was assimilated to the principal teachings of the *Lotus Sūtra*, along with classic Yogācāra teachings, including a version of the *trisvabhāva* doctrine known as the 'threefold truth'. Particularly characteristic of the T'ien-t'ai synthesis was the teaching of the interpenetration of all existent things in all the different realms. This is so because all things partake of a single organic unity, which is the One Mind – in its defiled state producing the phenomena of the everyday world, in its pure state Buddhahood. The ultimate conclusion to which this trend leads was reached by the Ninth Patriarch of the T'ien-t'ai School, Chan-jan (711–782CE), who taught that since everything was a manifestation of the one absolute mind, all things, even dust grains and blades of grass, contain the Buddha-nature.

Hua-yen

The Hua-yen School has as founder Fa-tsang (643–712CE), who like Chih-i propounded a *p'an chiao* schema, but in which the final, ultimate teaching of the Buddha was the *Avataṁsaka Sūtra*. The basic teachings of the Hua-yen School are set out in a treatise composed by Fa-tsang, entitled *Essay on the Golden Lion*. This title refers to an incident in which, summoned by the empress Tse-t'ien to explain the teachings of the *Avataṁsaka Sūtra*, Fa-tsang used a statuette of a golden lion to demonstrate the fundamental principles of the sūtra. The gold, he explained, is like the *li*, or noumenon (also identified with Buddha-nature), which is the inherently pure, complete, luminous essence which is mind, while the form of the lion is like the *shih*, or phenomenon (*dharma*). Fa-tsang was himself influenced by a text called the *Awakening of Faith in the Mahāyāna*, and seems to have understood the ultimate teaching to be something very similar to the Tathāgatagarbha doctrine expounded there. The *li* has no particular form of its own. It is empty of own-nature (*svabhāva*), though it always takes some form, in accordance with conditions, and it is these forms that are *shih* or 'phenomena' (*dharmas*). This means that all phenomena (*dharmas*), whilst remaining distinct, are the full and perfect expression of the noumenon (Buddha-nature). Moreover, all phenomena (*dharmas*) are therefore mutually identified and interpenetrated by all other phenomena because, as all phenomena are noumenon (which is single and indivisible), it means that *each* phenomenon is *all* phenomena, because each phenomenon is a part of something which is indivisible. Since this is so hard to grasp, Fa-tsang illustrated this principle with the example of a Buddha image placed between ten inward facing mirrors. The image is reflected in the mirrors, as are those reflections, and the reflections of the reflections, and so on, revealing an infinite, mutually interconnected web of identity.

Because Hua-yen teaches that Buddha-nature is already present in all beings, and furthermore that, through the interpenetration and identity of all things, Buddhahood is present right from the start of one's spiritual career, it also taught sudden Enlightenment. Enlightenment already exists, and is not caused by cumulative spiritual practice. This does not mean that spiritual practice was abandoned by followers of Hua-yen, but more that it was seen as a provisional expedient which helped to uncover what was really there. Because of this advocacy of sudden Awakening, Hua-yen is sometimes seen as the philosophical underpinning for Ch'an.

CH'AN

Ch'an is the Chinese pronunciation of the Indian word *dhyāna/jhāna*, 'meditative absorption', and the Ch'an School was centred upon the practice of meditation. Whilst its inception is attributed to an Indian monk called Bodhidharma (c.470–520CE), it traces back from him a lineage of masters, each Enlightened by a direct, mind-to-mind transmission derived from Mahākāśyapa, who, according to legend, reached Awakening when he saw Śākyamuni silently holding up a flower. Bodhidharma is counted as the First Chinese Patriarch. The Sixth Patriarch was the famous Hui Neng (638–713CE), whose story and teachings are contained in the *Platform Sūtra*, compiled c.820. His status as Patriarch was disputed, and it appears that Ch'an divided into several lineages or transmissions during the T'ang dynasty. The most important of these transmissions were the *Lin-ch'i*, which emphasizes sudden Awakening and the use of *kung-an* (Japanese, *kōan*), and the *Ts'ao-tung*, which advocated 'just sitting' meditation and a gradual path to Enlightenment. The *kung-an*, or 'public record', is an account of a historical dialogue between an Awakened master and a disciple which led to that disciple's Awakening. Often these are highly paradoxical. In practice they are assigned to individual students by their master for contemplation. If skilfully chosen such contemplation can lead the student to an experience of Awakening. The Ch'an schools developed a distinctive monastic rule over and above the Vinaya, which particularly emphasized work as an integral part of the monks' daily life. The emphasis in Ch'an is on personal Awakening, less stress being placed on the Bodhisattva ideal. Despite the emphasis on meditative experience unmediated by intellect and learning, the Perfection of

Wisdom sūtras are particularly important for the Ch'an schools, though the *Laṅkāvatāra*, *Śūraṅgama*, and *Vimalakīrti-nirdeśa Sūtras* are also widely used and respected, and a connection is often made between Ch'an and Hua-yen.

Ching-t'u

Whilst the Ch'an traditions stressed the personal effort or 'self-power' required to gain Enlightenment, Ching-t'u stressed its opposite, 'other-power'. The 'other-power' referred to here is the effort made by the Buddha Amitābha. Ching-t'u means 'the field which purifies' and is the Chinese translation of Pure Land. Ching-t'u is the school of Pure Land Buddhism, based upon the *Sukhāvatī-vyūha Sūtras*. Its roots go back to the earliest transmission of Buddhism to China in the 2nd century, and the practice of the worship of Amitābha is by no means restricted to Ching-t'u, but its foundation as a school is attributed to its First Patriarch, T'an-luan (476–542CE), who was converted from Taoism by the Buddhist monk Bodhiruci in 530. His treatises on the worship of Amitābha form the core of Ching-t'u doctrine. The goal of this school is to gain rebirth in Sukhāvatī, the Pure Land of the Buddha Amitābha, so all practices are oriented towards this end. These include prostration, *nien fo*, reflection upon Sukhāvatī and Amitābha, making the resolution to be reborn in Sukhāvatī, and the transference to others of merit gained. *Nien fo*, the 'invocation of the Buddha' involves the repetition of the phrase *nan-mo a-mi-t'o fo*, 'Homage to Amitābha Buddha'. Attention was also concentrated on Avalokiteśvara, as the Bodhisattva emanation of Amitābha, whose name was translated as Kuan Yin, 'The Hearer of Sounds'. By a popular confusion with his Tantric consort, Pāndaravāsinī, who is depicted clad in white, Kuan Yin came to be depicted as a white-clad female figure.

The Final Phase of Chinese Buddhism

The final phase of development of Chinese Buddhism was initiated by the vigorous persecution under the Taoist emperor Wu-tsung in 845. Neither the T'ien-t'ai nor the Hua-yen schools survived, probably because of their dependence on monastic specialists who bore the brunt of the persecution. Ch'an and Ching-t'u, with their more popular followings, survived and slowly recuperated, finding their place in an increasingly Confucianized society, in the company of Confucianism and Taoism, and at the popular level in a fusion of all three. During a short period of Mongol rule (1215–1368) Tantric Tibetan Buddhism was introduced to the former Chin (northern) and Sung (southern) courts, where it continued to be patronized (during the Ch'ing dynasty) after the Mongol influence had ceased, largely for the sake of political claims towards Tibet and Mongolia. The Ming dynasty (1368–1662), initiated by Chu Yuan-chang, who linked the new imperial dynasty with the arrival of the next Buddha, Maitreya, gave some support to Ch'an and Chung-t'u, and their popularization. The early Ch'ing dynasty (1662–1911) patronized the Tibetan Buddhism of the dGe-lugs Order, originally introduced during the Mongol period although it remained the cult of the Imperial court. The T'ai-p'ing or 'Great Peace' rebellion of 1851–64 in southern China, which espoused a form of Protestant Christian theism, was virulently anti-Manchu (the ruling Ch'ing dynasty), and as a result disastrously persecuted all Buddhist institutions within the territory that it seized, with the consequence that Buddhism had to be reintroduced from Japan. The early 20th century saw a revival of Chinese Buddhism, led by T'ai-hsu (1899–1947), in reaction to contacts with modern industrial powers and Christian missions to China.

From an early period, beginning with Tao-an in 347, the Chinese had catalogued the Buddhist texts that had been translated into Chinese. Eighteen such catalogues survive to the present day. The Chinese Tripiṭaka is enormous, since, where there were several translations of a single sūtra, all would be included – as distinct from Tibet, where variant translations were standardized and duplications survive by accident rather than design. The Chinese invented printing in the 8th century, and this was used for the reproduction of sūtras. The oldest known printed book in the world is a copy of the *Diamond Sūtra* or *Vajracchedikā*. The first complete printed edition of the Tripiṭaka was produced towards the end of the 9th century. Texts of different classes are arranged together in the Chinese Tripiṭaka, the sūtras (early and Mahāyāna) coming first, but no definitive organizational principle was devised for the Chinese canon.

23

Buddhism in Korea

Buddhism was first introduced into Korea by Chinese monks in the late 4th century. Its diffusion was slow as there was strong popular allegiance to the indigenous shamanistic religion, and it was only in the 6th century that Buddhism reached the south-east of the country, and official acknowledgement of its introduction dated only from 528. The 6th and 7th centuries saw the introduction of many Chinese schools of Buddhism, particularly when the practice of sending Korean monks to China became widespread. From the late 7th to the mid-10th centuries Korea was unified as a single political entity under the Silla kingdom, in the course of which Buddhism became an established social institution. This period also saw the first introduction of Ch'an Buddhism from China.

The Koryo period (935–1392) was that of the greatest expansion and influence of Buddhism within Korea. Monasteries were patronized by the state, and the entire Chinese Buddhist canon was collected and reproduced. However, the end of the 14th century saw the introduction of a new dynasty of kings, the Yi, who were generally Confucian in allegiance and who initiated five centuries of increasing repression. The number of monasteries and monks was reduced by royal decree, the various schools were reduced to two by a process of enforced amalgamation, and monks were denied access to the capital. By the 19th century Korean Buddhism was severely reduced from its popularity and influence during the Koryo period. The effect of several centuries of denial of access to the capital city, and the impossibility of social advancement for members of the Saṅgha, had encouraged a movement away from cities into isolated mountain monasteries. These provided amenable conditions for the Sonjon, or Meditation School, which preserved an ancient form of Ch'an and was the dominant form of Buddhism to survive there. The fortunes of Buddhism were only to revive from the late 19th century onwards, under Japanese influence.

24

Buddhism in Japan

The official date for the introduction of Buddhism to Japan is 552CE. It came as part of an overture of peace from a Korean king who wanted to cultivate some political stability in the neighbouring Japanese archipelago. It seems that the gift was a welcome one, for the Japanese leadership, recently emerged from a period of internecine strife between warring clans, was seeking some moderating influence that would help ameliorate the tensions and feuds amongst the aristocracy. Moreover, as contacts with Chinese Buddhism grew, and China itself recovered from several centuries of its own internal division, the Japanese aristocracy clearly saw Buddhism (in the context of Chinese culture) as a civilizing influence. For this reason Buddhism was encouraged by Japan's new rulers, as it brought to their own relatively uncultured islands Chinese literacy, arts, and sciences, and its own principles of non-violence and co-operation, all of which contributed to a positive transformation of Japanese society.

The result of this policy was that for several centuries Buddhism was largely the preserve of the Japanese aristocracy, having little contact with the populace but many of the attendant disadvantages of political patronage. This policy was exemplified by Prince Shōtoku (574–622CE) who wished to centralize the state under imperial power on the model of the Chinese empire, and to encourage Buddhism as a cultural stimulus. The most concrete product of this ambition was the interaction which he initiated with the Chinese court. He also introduced to Japan the Seventeen Article Constitution, combining Confucian and Buddhist principles, which effectively formed a state religion. It appears that his interest in Buddhism was not purely expedient, and that he had some understanding of its doctrines. To him is attributed a commentary upon three major Mahāyāna sūtras: the *Vimalakīrti-nirdeśa, Śrīmālādevī-siṁhanāda,* and *Saddharma-puṇḍarīka (Lotus) Sūtras.*

While the trends established by Shōtoku continued, the capital of Japan was moved to Nara in 710, where royal patronage of Buddhism increased. The effect of this was to stimulate the desire for wealth and power on the part of the Buddhist monks, and the period saw an increase in corruption, intrigue, and the general politicization of Buddhist circles. The Buddhism of this period was dominated by six schools, all imported from the Chinese capital at Ch'ang-an, all based upon Indian schools and textual traditions, and with little interest in proselytizing. An exception to this was the monk Gyōgi (c.670–749CE), who lived as a recluse in the countryside, performing magical deeds for the benefit of the populace. The Buddhist institutions of this period were almost entirely subservient to the desires of the government (the Saṅgha being listed as a government department!). A network of state-funded temples was built in each province, and in 749 the massive bronze statue of Vairocana Buddha was erected in Nara.

In 794 the capital was moved to Heian (modern Kyoto), where it was to stay until the end of the 12th century. The imperial bureaucracy of the previous period was to some extent replaced by a diffusion of power amongst several powerful clans, and the Buddhists of the period tended to identify themselves with the interests of these families. Whilst the earlier part of the period saw the introduction of two new schools from China, by the end of the 9th century political contact with China had stopped. The first of these new schools was that of Tendai (Chinese, T'ien-t'ai) a syncretic form of Buddhism which took the *Lotus Sūtra* as the final, ultimate teaching of the Buddha, and was brought to Japan by the monk Saichō (767–822CE), also known as Dengyō Daishi. After considerable difficulty he was able to establish an ordination lineage at Mount Hiei, separate from that of the Nara schools. The second was Shingon, a form of Tantric Buddhism, the name of which is derived from the Chinese term for mantra. This was brought from China by another monk dissatisfied with Nara Buddhism, Kūkai (774–835CE), also known as Kōbō Daishi. Two further factors of significance that emerged during this period were an increasing syncretism between Buddhism and the native Shinto religion (which lasted through to the 19th century), and an increasing mood of pessimism, doubtless fed by political instabilities, which saw society in a state of irreversible and terminal decline. This view was formalized as the *mappō* theory, in which, as described in some late Buddhist texts (e.g. the *Mahāparinirvāṇa Sūtra*), Buddhism itself was to decline through three stages, the last of which had already begun. Doubtless confirming this view, the Nara Buddhist schools became even more corrupt in this period, and before long both Tendai and Shingon had been assimilated to state interests and influence.

JAPANESE FORMS OF BUDDHISM

The Kamakura period (1185–1333) was remarkable for the emergence of characteristically Japanese forms of Buddhism. This was in part stimulated by the break from Chinese influence that had begun in the Nara period, and which had encouraged the assimilation of Chinese Buddhism to the Japanese character and culture. All the new schools shared certain features: a strong emphasis upon faith on the part of the practitioner; strong, charismatic founders dissatisfied with the established forms of Buddhism; an emphasis upon a single, practical teaching which would ensure Awakening; and a popular appeal, which shifted the centre of gravity of Japanese Buddhism from the sphere of aristocratic patronage towards the populace. The simplicity which marks all these new schools was a reflection both of a reaction against the confusing and corrupt diversity of the non-indigenous forms of Buddhism, and of a growing belief in the *mappō* theory, which seemed to require the development of simple and fail-safe religious practices which could be performed even by the people of the present corrupt age. It should not be forgotten that Japan at this time was riven by civil war and famine. The suffering and calamity caused were seen as further evidence of the decline of the age. Some of the new teachings also derived inspiration from Chinese models, once contact was eased with the continent.

The first of the new schools to appear were associated with Pure Land Buddhism and the worship of the Buddha Amitābha; in Japanese, Amida. They did not represent the first appearance of such practice in Japan, since worship of Amida had been current for some centuries, and to some extent was accepted as a part of several different traditions, including Tendai. In particular, during the Heian period (794–1185) there had been an upsurge of wandering holy men, known as *hiriji*, living an unconventional life outside of monasteries and teaching simple practices, particularly the worship of Amida. However, the Pure Land School as such, known as Jōdo, was started by Hōnen (1133–1212).

Dissatisfied with the Tendai teachings of Mount Hiei, Hōnen eventually discovered the work of a previous Japanese Pure Land Buddhist, Genshin, and that of the Chinese teacher Shan-tao. Under the combined impact of these two he began to teach that salvation was only possible through the recitation, with faith, of Amida's name, i.e. the *nembutsu* – Namu Amida Butsu. All other practices were secondary to this, for in the present corrupt age no one is capable of attaining Enlightenment through their own efforts, *jiriki*, but is in reality totally dependent upon the compassionate 'other-power', *tariki*, of Amida.

Hōnen was superseded by a pupil, Shinran (1173–1263), who took the principles of his master's teaching a step further. He taught that the *nembutsu* was to be considered not as spiritual practice but as an act of gratitude, for Amida had already created Sukhāvatī and all beings were already there. Rebirth in the Pure Land was therefore not the result of any action that we perform, but of the compassion of Amida. All that one could do was have faith in that compassion. To engage in spiritual practice, i.e. to exert 'own-power', represented a denial of the reality of Amida's realm and doubt of his ability to fulfil his vow. In making this absolute emphasis on 'other-power', *tariki*, Shinran maintained that he was only transmitting the ideas of his teacher, but whereas Hōnen had remained a monk, Shinran felt that such distinctions of life-style were irrelevant in the face of Amida's compassion, and so he rejected celibacy, and married. His disciples chose to observe fewer and fewer of the Vinaya rules and, in contrast to those following the Chinese practice of vegetarianism, meat-eating was common. This precedent had very broad repercussions on Japanese Buddhism as a whole, which increasingly tended to minimize the difference between monastic and lay life. A major result of this trend was that a married priesthood became the norm in many schools, with temples passed from father to son. Shinran called his school the Jōdo-shin-shū, 'True Pure Land School'.

The 12th and 13th centuries saw the introduction of Zen, or Ch'an, Buddhism from China. The first form to arrive was Rinzai (Chinese, Lin-ch'i), emphasizing the use of the *kōan* (*kung-an*), brought by the monk Eisai (1141–1215). Sōtō (Chinese, Ts'ao-tung), advocating zazen or 'just sitting' meditation, came later, introduced by Dōgen (1200–53). Both became popular, but in different spheres of society. Rinzai Zen was patronized by the samurai rulers and, being centred on the capital city, came to play an important role in the diffusion of Chinese culture into Japan. Sōtō Zen, on the other hand, found its support among the peasantry and, as a result, absorbed or developed a number of popular rituals for rites of passage, such as funeral ceremonies.

The last of the new schools to be discussed here had no foreign precedent, and therefore could be seen as the most Japanese development. This grew from the teaching of Nichiren (1222–82). Though trained as a Tendai monk, Nichiren was profoundly distressed by the appalling disasters, both natural and political, that characterized the Japan of his day, and felt that a different approach to spiritual practice was necessary. He came to the conclusion that these disasters were due to the disappearance of the true teaching of Buddhism from the land, and that, for Japan to survive, this true teaching had to be reintroduced. He identified the true teaching with the eternal Śākyamuni Buddha of the *Lotus Sūtra*, and asserted the identity of Śākyamuni Buddha both with the *Lotus Sūtra* itself and with all sentient beings. Furthermore, he went so far as to claim that all other forms of Buddhist practice were positively harmful, and agitated for their suppression by the rulers for the sake of the well-being of Japan. He identified himself with the Bodhisattva Viśiṣṭacārita, praised in the *Lotus Sūtra* by the Buddha as the Bodhisattva who will restore the true teaching after its future disappearance. Since he was repeatedly persecuted for his views and eventually exiled to the island of Sado, he also identified himself with the persecuted Bodhisattva, Sadāparibhūta, from the same sūtra. The main spiritual practice advocated by Nichiren was the recitation of the *daimoku*, *Nam myō hō renge kyō*, 'Homage to the Lotus Sūtra'. Nichirenism was to become popular among members of the merchant class.

The 14th to 16th centuries saw considerable unrest in Japan, in which the monasteries themselves were heavily involved – many having their own private armies! As a result of their interference in political affairs several monastic centres were destroyed by the secular authorities during the 16th century, including those of the Jōdo-shin-shū, the Shingon, and the Tendai. From the beginning of the 17th century Japan was ruled by a military dictatorship which imposed a total cultural isolation from the rest of the world. In the resulting stagnation, Buddhism was to suffer a sharp move towards formalism and nominal membership, not least since every citizen was required to register as a member of a local Buddhist temple in order to prove that they were not Christian. Notable individuals, such as Hakuin (1685–1768), stand out against this sad backdrop. Whilst there was a numerical expansion during this time, there was considerable corruption amongst the Buddhist 'priests', and sometimes groups interested in serious practice were forced to meet in secret. The situation only began to change under the impact both of the new Meiji dynasty (1867), under which Shintō became the official religion, and of modernist influences from outside Japan.

25

Buddhism in Tibet

Tibetan Buddhism is remarkable for having preserved until the 20th century the unbroken tradition of the monastic universities of northern India, a tradition which, since the Chinese invasion of 1959, has been transplanted to India and many Western countries. To understand the nature of this tradition one must look at its origins in the monastic milieu of the Pāla dynasty of India, which provided the definitive model for the Tibetan monastic system. The Indian universities and their Tibetan counterparts stressed a synthesizing approach to Buddhism, in which an attempt was made to categorize and incorporate all previous doctrines and practices, reconciling all differences in a universal system that covered all aspects of the Dharma-Vinaya. Grasping this synthesis in its entirety required an encyclopaedic knowledge of the sūtras and śāstras, or treatises, for which a training lasting many years was needed. Since the sūtras themselves were so apparently contradictory and thereby resistant to synthesis, they had of necessity to be approached by way of the commentaries and treatises of the great *ācāryas*, or teachers. It is for this reason that, in contrast to Chinese Buddhism, where individual sūtras were made the centre of doctrinal systems, Tibetan Buddhism places its characteristic emphasis upon the śāstras, giving them primacy over the sūtras in the monastic education programmes. (See Chapter 15 for further information on the Indian monastic universities.)

Linked with this heritage from the monastic universities of India was the concept of an elaborate path structure incorporating the cultivation of the bodhicitta, practice of the Perfections, completion of the Five Paths, and the passage through the Bodhisattva *bhūmis* towards full and perfect Buddhahood for the sake of all sentient beings. Spiritual progress was measured on a long and gradual path towards Enlightenment. However, contrasting with and complementing this sophisticated and complex systematization was the Tantric tradition, which, particularly amongst the *mahāsiddhas*, challenged the complacency of the monastic establishment and incorporated non-rational, magical rituals into Buddhist practice in the service of the quest for Enlightenment. Whilst the present account concentrates on the history of the Tibetan Buddhist orders, these were largely centralized organizations, and it should be remembered that there was a parallel, though by its nature ill-recorded, history of Tibetan Buddhism formed by the localized activities of Buddhist monk-priests, shamanic in character and only partly overlapping with the concerns of the history of the orders.[178]

The First Diffusion

Whilst there is some suggestion that Buddhism had begun a slow and piecemeal infiltration into Tibetan culture prior to the 7th century, the first significant contact occurred through the king Srong-btsan-sgam-po (pronounced *song sen gam po*; died c.650), who had two Buddhist wives, one from Nepal and the other from China. Moreover, this king was responsible for the considerable expansion of the Tibetan empire, incorporating parts of China that were already Buddhist. In the 8th century, the king Khri-Srong-lde-brtsan (pronounced *tree song detsun*) founded the first monastery, bSam-yes (pronounced *sam yay*), by inviting Buddhist teachers from India to his court. The monk who responded to the invitation, called Śāntarakṣita, a Yogācāra-Svātāntrika-Mādhyamika from the northern Indian university tradition, had considerable difficulty establishing the monastery, and retired to India, from where the king next called on the services of a Tantric yogin called Padmasambhava, who was rather more successful than Śāntarakṣita, since, it is said, he was able to subdue the local deities who had resisted the efforts of the scholar-monk. The significance of this episode is open to interpretation. It is known that there were factions opposed to the king, who identified themselves with the pre-Buddhist religious tradition, which was centred on ideas of sacred kingship, and which resisted the introduction of Buddhism. Perhaps it also reveals the relative weakness of the sophisticated intellect when faced with the need to transform relatively gross cultural phenomena. Be that as it may,

Padmasambhava later left Tibet, and Śāntarakṣita was able to return and continue his work in training the first generation of Tibetan monks, enlisting his Indian disciple Kamalaśīla in the task.

Even so, progress was not assured for the Indian missionaries, since Buddhist influences were making themselves felt from very different sources – namely Central Asia and China. The diversity of influences is well symbolized by the two wives of Srong-btsan-sgam-po, each a Buddhist, and each with accompanying missionaries from China and Nepal. By the time of King Khri-Srong-lde-brtsan (8th century), relations between representatives of the two traditions were acrimonious, and the arguments were to be resolved by a debate, or series of debates, held in the monastery at bSam-yes. The Indian party, representing the gradualist approach to Enlightenment, was championed by Kamalaśīla. The Chinese tradition was represented by a monk called Ho Shang Mahāyāna, who appears to have put forward a form of Ch'an teaching that led to sudden Enlightenment by cutting all mental discrimination. Eventually the king declared Kamalaśīla the victor, and that henceforth all Tibetan Buddhists should be practitioners of the Indian tradition. Ho Shang was banished.

It is probable that the king's decision was in part pragmatic, since the Indian party argued that the view of sudden Enlightenment undermined morality. If Enlightenment occurred suddenly, without the preparation of the gradual path that the gradualists advocated, then the practice of morality and the Perfections was pointless. This seems to have been a misrepresentation of Ho Shang's true position, for other sources indicate that he advocated practice of the Perfections and full monastic ordination. However, it is possible that the king was concerned that the religion should be a civilizing influence upon his people, and therefore chose that tradition which gave the greatest emphasis to morality. This was not the end of teachings of the type espoused by Ho Shang, however, for very similar ideas occur in those of the rNying-ma rDzogs-chen (pronounced *zog chen*; see below). This episode also illustrates the role that Buddhism was to play in bringing a higher culture to the Tibetan people. Tibetan culture was hitherto preliterate, and even the Tibetan alphabet was devised so as to permit the writing down of Buddhist scriptures. Kamalaśīla was to write three treatises, each entitled the *Bhāvanākrama*, 'steps of meditation', in which he summarized the Path as understood in the Indian universities, and also criticized Ho Shang's position. These, along with Atīśa's

Bodhipathapradīpa, were to become the main source for the Tibetan understanding of the gradual path.

For the first centuries of its development in Tibet the monastic tradition was characterized by considerable unity. Both then and thereafter, by royal decree, all monasteries observed a single Vinaya, that of the Mūla-Sarvāstivāda. However, the monarchical system which supported this growth was not itself stable, and by the mid-9th century the last of the pro-Buddhist sacred kings, Ral-pa-can (pronounced *relpa chen*) had been assassinated (c.838) and replaced by his brother, Glang-dar-ma (pronounced *lang darma*). He vigorously persecuted the Buddhists in his realm, until he too was assassinated (in 842) by a Buddhist monk who wished to preserve the Dharma from further attack. This period of persecution is regarded by Tibetan tradition as marking the end of the first diffusion of the Dharma in Tibet.

The Second Diffusion

Thereafter Tibet entered a phase of political fragmentation and internal division, during which Buddhism itself apparently suffered some kind of decline into lawlessness, accompanied by an upsurge of self-proclaimed *siddhas* roaming the countryside. By the 10th century the political situation had begun to stabilize, Buddhism began a slow recovery, and new monasteries and literary centres began to flourish. The old royal lineage surviving in the western region continued to support monastic scholarship and translation, a notable product of this being Rin-chen-bzangs-po (pronounced *rin chen zang po*; 958–1055), a prolific translator and builder of temples. However, more famous still was an Indian teacher, Atīśa, who was invited to Tibet in 1042. His impact upon the recuperating Buddhist community was enormous, and he is therefore associated with the initiation of the second diffusion of Buddhism to Tibet. Unlike the first diffusion, this second phase was characterized by an almost total reliance upon Indian sources of inspiration. Among his many works he composed a highly influential treatise on the Path called the *Bodhipathapradīpa* ('Lamp on the Path to Bodhi'), and his disciples formed the first Tibetan 'order', known as the bKa'-gdams (pronounced *ka dam*) Order, for which this was the root text. This second diffusion brought with it from the Indian universities the new *yogottara* and *yoginī* tantras. Introducing this new and shocking material to the Tibetans, Atīśa adopted a conservative policy, insisting that the sexual imagery and ritual were purely symbolic. Should a monk perform them literally, he would be in breach of the *parājika* rule of the Vinaya that enjoins total celibacy.

THE TIBETAN ORDERS

In the same period Tibetan Buddhists were also founding orders. The wealthy land-owning layman, Mar-pa, had travelled in India, where he had been instructed by the *mahāsiddha* Nāropa. Returning to Tibet with many texts he had collected on his journeys, he took pupils, among whom the most famous is the poet Mi-la-ras-pa (pronounced *mila ray pa*; 1040–1123). Mi-la-ras-pa was the composer of a large collection of songs in the style of the *dohās* of the Indian *siddhas*, and his biography has been a much loved source of inspiration to subsequent generations of Buddhists. Mi-la-ras-pa's disciple, sGam-po-pa (pronounced *gam po pa*; 1079–1153) founded the bKa'-rgyud (pronounced *kaa gyu*) Order, also known as the 'red hats', and was the composer of a *lam rim* ('stages on the Path') text known as the *Jewel Ornament of Liberation*. The bKa'-rgyud Order quickly spawned a series of sub-orders, such that the bKa'-rgyud Order as a whole needs to be seen as an affiliated group of lineages, rather than a single unified order. Generally, the bKa'-rgyud Order is associated with yogic practice *par excellence*, teaching the Six Yogas of Nāropa, which lead to the mystic *mahāmudrā*, or 'great seal'. Of particular note among its sub-orders is the Karma(-pa) Order (also known as 'the black hats'), which is credited with the innovation (in 1283) of finding the reincarnations of deceased lineage holders, and training them from childhood to reoccupy the position they had held in their last life. This practice, possibly introduced from India, was adopted by other orders, most notably the later dGe-lugs (pronounced *ge look*) Order, with its lineage holder, entitled the Dalai Lama. Another contemporary of Atīśa, 'Brag-mi (pronounced *drak me*; 992–1072), who studied Sanskrit in Nepal, and then the Tantra at Vikramaśīla under the *siddha* Śāntipa, founded the Sa-skya (pronounced *sakya*) Order.

It must be emphasized that these orders were not divided by any schism, i.e. differences over Vinaya, nor primarily by doctrinal difference, but more by virtue of the enormous emphasis placed, in Tibetan Buddhism, upon the guru or teacher (Tibetan, bla-ma; pronounced *lama*), and his relationship with individual disciples. This emphasis might be traced to Atīśa and the Indian Tantric tradition that he represented, who affirmed that the direct instruction of one's teacher should take precedence over instruction from the treatises. In this light the different Tibetan orders can be seen not as schools, in the sense familiar from either the early phase of Buddhism or the Mahāyāna, but instead as more or less loosely related lineages of transmission from guru to disciple. The transmission consisted of ordination, initiation, and instruction. The main characteristics that serve to differentiate the orders are the texts which they hold to be authoritative, the *yidam*, or 'deity', used for meditation, and, in some cases, specific spiritual practices or teachings developed by *bla-mas*, or teachers, within that tradition.

All the orders used the same terminology of emptiness and the Middle Path, and doctrinally they showed little difference except in their understanding of the nature of ultimate reality, where they tended to emphasize either a positive or a negative description. This debate was discussed in terms of the *gZhan tong* (pronounced *zhen tong*) and *rang tong* perspectives. The *gZhan tong* (literally 'other empty') position holds that there is an ultimately existent reality, which is a pure radiant consciousness, but that in the unenlightened state it is defiled by adventitious defilements. In truth, this reality is not empty of its own-being or inherent nature (*svabhāva*), but is empty of the defilements, which are wholly other to it. In other words the *gZhan tong* perspective takes the Tathāgatagarbha doctrine as *paramārtha-satya*, the ultimate truth, even though it insists that it is true Madhyamaka, and takes pains to derive its doctrinal stance from the works of Nāgārjuna.[179] This position contrasts directly with the *rang tong* perspective which is essentially that of the Madhyamaka as interpreted by the Indian representatives of the school, viz. that reality is not a really existing thing, but is the emptiness (*śūnyatā*) or absence of inherent existence, or own-being (*svabhāva*), in all things, including the *dharmakāya*.

In the course of the 12th century, and in response to the influence of the new orders of the second diffusion, there appeared the first signs of an order identifying itself with the first diffusion of Buddhism, calling itself the rNying-ma (pronounced *nying ma*) Order, the 'old order', and retrospectively claiming the *siddha* Padmasambhava as its founder. It seems likely that this was a response to the critical impact of the new orders, and was an attempt to define and preserve the older teachings and practices. Generally, these teachings reflect the character of the first diffusion, which incorporated elements from Chinese and Central Asian Buddhism absent in the second diffusion. Conspicuous among these, and the focus of much rNying-ma practice, is that of the 'Great Fulfilment' or rDzogs-chen, which incorporates Ch'an-like teachings derived from Central Asian and Chinese sources of a type which were rejected after the bSam-yes debates of the 8th century in favour of the Indian gradualists. Otherwise, in the rNying-ma schema, the rDzogs-chen corresponds to the third and ultimate division of the *anuttara* tantra, also known as *atiyoga*. The rNying-ma Order also preserves many tantras which were derived from India in the early period but were thought to be apocryphal by the second diffusion orders, and therefore not accepted as canonical. Whilst also acknowledged by the other orders, Padmasambhava is especially venerated by the rNying-ma Order, which elevated him to the status of a second Buddha. He is also regarded as being responsible for the composition of numerous texts and teachings, which were left hidden, ready to be found by later generations of practitioners. These texts were known as *gTer-ma* (pronounced *terma*), and there were a number of famous discoverers of *gTer-ma*, who were known as *gTer-stons* (pronounced *ter tön*). It should be pointed out that such discoveries included not just the recovery of physical texts from hiding places, but the 'discovery' of teachings in the depths of the mind. The most famous of these *gTer-ma* is the *Bar-do-thos-grol* (pronounced *bar do tö dol*), the *Tibetan Book of the Dead*. They also include the *Padma-bKa'i-thang-yig* (pronounced *padma kaitang yik*; 'the precepts of Padma') known as the *Life and Liberation of Padmasambhava*. Klong-chen-rab-'byams-pa (pronounced *long chen rap jyam pa*) was a prolific and original rNying-ma author who lived in the 14th century. Doctrinally, the rNying-ma Order often emphasizes a *gZhan tong* position as the ultimate reality.

The rNying-ma Order remained free from the political involvements that after a while began to preoccupy the new orders – probably because of its lack of centralization (five out of its six main monasteries were only founded in the 17th century) and an underlying lack of interest in secular power. In the vacuum left after the demise of the old sacred kingship of the Tibetan empire, the new schools of the second diffusion assumed political power, and within several generations had become hereditary power brokers, in which powerful abbots passed their demesne to a son or nephew – clearly, strict celibacy was no longer observed at this period. Pre-eminent among these was the Sa-skya

Order, which, Tibet having succumbed to Mongol domination in the 13th century, was given overlordship of the whole of Tibet. Since, within a generation, the Mongols became emperors over China too, the field of Sa-skya influence was immense. However, with the waning of Mongol power, the Sa-skya Order also lost influence, in particular to the bKa'-rgyud Order.

Closely associated in origin with the Sa-skya Order was an order that appeared in eastern Tibet in the 13th century, called the Jo-nang Order.[180] Its founder, one Yu-mo, received teachings in Kailāsa, and its systematizer, Dol-pu-pa, apparently lived in the Dol-po region on the border with Nepal. The Jo-nang Order adopted the Tathāgatagarbha doctrine as the ultimate truth, treating texts like the *Tathāgatagarbha*, *Śrīmālādevī-siṁhanāda*, and *Mahāparinirvāṇa Sūtras* as *nītārtha*, i.e. of definitive meaning, not needing interpretation. In doing so, it upheld a *gZhan tong*, or 'other empty', position, in opposition to the other second diffusion orders, which maintained the absolute truth of the Madhyamaka perspective, in which the Perfection of Wisdom sūtras are regarded as *nītārtha*. While the Jo-nang Order occupied what was apparently an isolated position, and was regularly caricatured as Buddhist brahmanism by its opponents, it enjoyed a high reputation and considerable support for a period of several centuries. Indeed, two of its number were teachers of the great Tsong-kha-pa. Perhaps most famous of its members is the Tibetan historian Tārānātha (born 1575).

The 14th century saw the finalization of the compilation of the Tibetan Buddhist canon by the great scholar Bu-ston (pronounced *poo tön*; 1290–1364), who completed work already begun at the monastery of sNar thang (pronounced *nar tang*). As there was no formally structured Indian Mahāyāna canon for the Tibetans to model their own collections upon, and as there was great need to establish some order upon the enormous collection of texts brought to Tibet over the preceding six centuries, they devised an arrangement which bore little if any connection with the arrangement of the Tripiṭaka of the Indian schools. They divided the materials they had into what they considered to be the genuine word of the Buddha on the one hand, called the *bKa' 'gyur* (pronounced *kan jyur*) or 'translated word', and on the other the works of commentators, which they called the *bsTan 'gyur* (pronounced *ten jyur*) or 'translated treatises'. The former was divided between sections on Vinaya, Perfection of Wisdom sūtras, other Mahāyāna sūtras, and tantras; to the latter were confined the śāstras, treatises, and the Abhidharma works of the Mahāyāna and non-Mahāyāna schools.

The youngest of the second diffusion orders was founded in the 15th century by a reformer called Tsong-kha-pa (1357–1419), who sought to return to the purity of Atīśa's original foundation. Thus identifying himself with the bKa'-gdams Order founded by Atīśa, he re-enforced the rule of celibacy, forbade the practice of father–son inheritance within monasteries, and generally excluded practices which had no Indian Buddhist precedent. In ten years (1409–19) he established three new monasteries, the first of the new dGe-lugs Order, near to Lhasa (pronounced *hlasa*), the capital of central Tibet. He also stressed learning, being greatly erudite himself, and composed among many other things an exhaustive *lam rim*, or text describing the stages of the path, based on Atīśa's *Bodhipathapradīpa*.

The dGe-lugs Order maintains that the Prasaṅgika Madhyamaka represents the best account of *paramartha-satya*, ultimate truth, although it also emphasizes an extensive grounding in logic and debate as preparation for meditation upon emptiness. It later took up the practice of discovering reincarnations of the heads of the order, and the third of these, bSod-nams-rgya-mtsho (pronounced *sirnam gyatso*), was named 'ocean' or *dalai* (a Mongolian term) by the Mongol Khan, and thereafter known as the Dalai Lama (his two predecessors being posthumously given the same title). The fourth Dalai Lama was himself a Mongol, ensuring the future devotion of Mongolian Buddhists to the dGe-lugs camp, whilst the fifth Dalai Lama gained political control of Tibet in the 17th century, after crushing the power-base of the rival Karma(-pa) Order. Subsequently, the Dalai Lamas have been in theory the leaders of the Tibetan people, though a number have ruled through regents, prior to gaining their majority. A further victim of the dGe-lugs Order in the 17th century was the Jo-nang Order, whose monasteries it took over and whose treatises were systematically burned. This substantially accounts for the low representation of the *gZhan tong* view among modern Tibetan orders.

The remaining noteworthy development was the Ris-med (pronounced *ree may*) movement of the 19th century, originating in eastern Tibet, which sought to draw attention back to the Indian sources of the Tibetan Buddhist tradition and reorientate the monastic education programme accordingly. Among its proponents were numbered 'Jam-dbyangs-mKhyen-brtse (pronounced *jamyang kyentsay*; 1820–92), and

Mi-pham (pronounced *me pam*; 1841–1912). In an attempt to reconcile doctrinal differences the Ris-med tended towards upholding a *gZhan tong* position which takes reality to be a really existent entity beyond the realm of rational thought and thereby undermines the ultimate validity of rational discourse and disagreement.

26

Buddhism in Mongolia

There is little doubt that Buddhism was initially introduced to Mongolia from Central Asia and China as early as the 4th century, although its later development there was almost entirely dominated by representatives of the Tibetan Buddhist orders. Indigenous Mongol religion was shamanistic, although it also reflected Persian religious ideas through its contact with the Manichaean Uighurs of Central Asia. Very little is known of the nature of Buddhism in Mongolia at this time.

The first phase of the transmission of Buddhism to Mongolia occurred as a result of the Mongol expansion of the 13th century, in which Mongol emperors secured vast territories throughout Asia. This expansion was accompanied by a policy of encouraging foreign statesmen and religious to attend the Mongol court (as hostages). As a result a large number of Tibetan Buddhists, mainly of the Sa-skya Order, gained influential footholds at court, where they stimulated general interest in their forms of Buddhism. Most notable among these was 'Phags-pa (pronounced *pak pa*; 1235–80), who managed to engage the interest of Kublai Khan (1260–94) who became a Buddhist himself, receiving initiation for the *Hevajra Tantra*. At this time the entire Mongolian court was converted to late Vajrayāna Buddhism, and one can speculate that the shamanic character of Tantric Buddhism had considerable appeal for the Mongols. By the time of the last Mongol emperor, several monasteries had been founded and a part of the Tibetan canon translated. However, Buddhism was still largely the interest of the Mongolian ruling class, and suffered a decline until the second phase of transmission.

The second and farther reaching phase of the transmission of Buddhism to Mongolia began with new contacts with Tibet resulting from military expeditions led into the eastern part of the country by Altan Khan (1507–83). The dGe-lugs Order, seeking political support in its struggle against the Sa-skya Order within Tibet, made overtures of friendship to the Altan Khan, and as a result of this the title of Dalai Lama, 'Great Ocean (of Wisdom) Lama', was conferred on the dGe-lugs lama, or teacher, bSod-nams-rgya-mtsho. Posthumous conferral of the same title upon two predecessors meant that bSod-nams was therefore the third Dalai Lama. Thereafter the success of the dGe-lugs in Mongolia was unchecked. The fourth Dalai Lama was himself a Mongolian, thus cementing the new religio-political link between the dGe-lugs Order and Mongolia. After their conquest of Tibet in 1641, the Mongols installed the dGe-lugs Dalai Lama as the secular authority in Lhasa.

The Ch'ing emperors of China (1662–1911), who were Buddhists themselves, also found Buddhism to be a suitable mechanism of control of their territories in Inner Mongolia. For this reason they heavily patronized Buddhist monasteries and temples in the region. By 1629 the Tibetan *bKa' 'gyur* had been translated into Mongolian. A translation of the *bsTan 'gyur* was completed in 1749. By the end of the 18th century the fortunes of Buddhism in Inner Mongolia took a downturn with the restriction of patronage from the Ch'ing emperors of China, although in the same period Buddhism began to spread for the first time from Outer Mongolia into the northern region of Buryat Mongolia, which had remained fully shamanistic until the 19th century.

27

Buddhism in Nepal

The modern state of Nepal incorporates a substantially larger geographical area than corresponds to the historical entity of Nepal. The latter is more appropriately identified with the Kathmandu valley itself, before the expansion of the country under the Gurkhas in the 18th century. It was only as a result of this expansion that the Buddha's birthplace, Lumbinī, falls within the borders of modern Nepal rather than the modern Indian state of Uttar Pradesh. The Buddhism of Nepal is the heritage of the Newars, a Mongoloid race, who speak Newari. The Gurkhas are Hindus, speaking an Indian language, now the official language of Nepal, called Nepali.

Nepal is first mentioned in a 4th century Gupta inscription, where it is described as a tributary kingdom. Its ruling dynasty were the Licchavi kings (300–870CE), who presumably claimed some link with the Licchavi kingdom of the Buddha's time. Although we know little of this early Nepal, it was undoubtedly within the cultural influence of India. A harmonious co-existence of Hinduism and Buddhism flourished there, as it did in the contemporary Gupta empire. During the 5th century the stūpas of Bodhnāth and Svayambhunath were built, and in the 7th century the Chinese pilgrim Hsüan-Tsang mentions that some 2,000 Hīnayāna and Mahāyāna monks lived in monasteries in the Kathmandu valley. There can be little doubt that developments in Buddhism taking place in India were transmitted quickly to Nepal, given its proximity to Bihar and Bengal, especially when those regions were the home of the Pāla dynasty, the last Buddhist dynasty of pre-Muslim India (c.760–1142).

The Tantric Buddhism that flourished in the Pāla kingdom, especially at the new monastic universities founded there under royal patronage at this time, was transmitted to Nepal. There it took firm root, eventually ousting any representation of non-Mahāyāna Buddhism. Scholars now look to modern Nepal as preserving some semblance of late Indian Buddhism and thereby offering a unique glimpse of the Buddhist practice and culture of India proper, which has not survived anywhere else. It must be said that quite to what degree Nepalese Buddhism preserves late Indian Buddhism, or merely exhibits its own unique developments, remains uncertain. The main features of Nepalese Buddhist culture include a harmonious co-existence of Hinduism and Buddhism, a caste structured Saṅgha (as also occurred in Sri Lanka, and was formalized in Nepal by royal decree in the 14th century), and the development of a married 'priest' caste of Tantric practitioners, who pass down the responsibility for the care of Buddhist temples within their own family. There are two castes of Buddhist priest. The higher caste is that of the *vajrācāryas*, 'teachers of the Vajra(-yāna)', the lower, that of the *śākyabhikṣus*, or 'monks of the Śākyan' (i.e. the Buddha). Although originally titles, they are nowadays used as the family names for members of both sexes, since a Nepali's right to use them is purely hereditary.

The three forms of Buddhism, Hīnayāna, Mahāyāna, and Vajrayāna, are regarded as consecutive levels of practice (a common enough interpretation). Hīnayāna practice is symbolized by a more or less nominal and brief ordination, usually for four days, as a bhikṣu. Through this ordination a boy gains membership of a particular monastery or temple, and inherits various life-long rights and duties associated with that establishment. From this Hīnayāna stage the practitioner is released so as to undertake Mahāyāna practice, i.e. to get married! Effectively he is now a lay practitioner, although this interpretation of Mahāyāna practice is undoubtedly out of keeping with Mahāyāna origins. The married householder continues his duties within his monastery or temple. On this basis, the practitioner is then free to take initiation into the Vajrayāna, a privilege to which he is entitled by birthright, i.e. as the duty of his Buddhist caste. The decline of celibate monasticism was slow, and it is known that there were celibate communities of monks in Patan as late as the 17th century.[181]

Because of its geographical location, Nepal was a natural conduit through which Buddhism was transmitted to Tibet. The flow of

Buddhists into and through Nepal dramatically increased under the impact of the Muslim invasions, since the country offered a natural and proximate refuge from the terror enacted upon the northern Indian plains. The Muslim invasion did not reach Nepal itself, so that its Buddhist heritage was able to survive and flourish in the Kathmandu valley. Many Tibetans used Nepal as a staging post *en route* to India, and the Tibetan monk Dharmasvāmin (13th century) studied there for several years before attempting to travel to the old homelands of Buddhism in India, which by that time had been overrun by Muslim invaders. Only after the Gurkha conquest of 1768 did Buddhism begin to feel any repressive political influence in Nepal. The Gurkhas, militaristic Hindus ousted from Rajasthan in India by the Muslim conquests there, and hitherto a minor political force in the west of modern Nepal, nurtured some ambitions to Hinduize their new territories, and at times engendered repressive policies towards the Buddhist Newars.

Apart from potential insights into the character of late Indian Buddhism, Nepalese Buddhists have also preserved the main, and often sole, source for the Sanskrit originals of many Buddhist texts, including most Mahāyāna sūtras. The larger proportion of this material is Tantric in character, but also prominent are manuscripts of the so-called *nava-dharma*, the nine Dharma texts used to symbolize the teaching in a ritual maṇḍala. These are the *Lalitavistara*, the *Gaṇḍavyūha*, *Laṅkāvatāra*, *Samādhirāja*, *Daśabhūmika*, *Suvarṇa-prabhāsa*, *Saddharma-puṇḍarīka*, and *Aṣṭasāhasrikā-prajñāpāramitā Sūtras*, and the *Guhyasamāja Tantra*. Buddhist temples have kept in relatively safe storage many thousands of manuscripts, some even of ancient Indian origin, copied in Nālandā and Vikramaśīla in the 10th or 11th centuries and carried to Nepal. One could say that the preservation of the bulk of the Sanskrit heritage of Buddhism is due to the Buddhists of Nepal. Without their efforts to copy and protect the manuscripts in their temples, the majority of Sanskrit Buddhists texts would be known to modern Buddhists from Tibetan and Chinese translations only.[182]

28

Buddhism in Persia

Our knowledge of the spread of Buddhism into Persia is still at a primarily speculative stage. This said, a summary of current views is relevant to any account of the history of Buddhism. There has been little archaeological investigation of potential Buddhist sites in modern Iran, and none at all, to my knowledge, further west into the Caucasus. The documentation of literary evidence for the influence of Buddhist literature on Persian and Arabic culture began in the 19th century. The assessment of the evidence for the influence of Buddhist monuments, and for a knowledge of Buddhism in practice, has begun only in the last few decades.

In the last century it was pointed out that the Buddhist *Jātaka* stories, via a Hindu recension under the title of the *Pañcatantra*, were translated into Persian in the 6th century at the command of the Zoroastrian king Khusru, and in the 8th century into Syriac and Arabic, under the title *Kalilag and Damnag*. The Persian translation was later translated into Greek, Latin, and Hebrew and was to form the basis of the collections of stories known as *Aesop's Fables* (compiled in the 14th century by a Byzantine monk), the stories of Sinbad, and the *Arabian Nights*. In the 8th century a life of the Buddha was translated into Greek by St John of Damascus and circulated widely in Christian circles as the story of Balaam and Josaphat. So popular was this story in medieval Europe that we arrive at the irony of the figure of Josaphat, this name a corruption of 'bodhisattva', being canonized, by the 14th century, and worshipped as a saint in the Catholic church.[183] Rashīd al-Dīn, a 13th century historian, records some eleven Buddhist texts circulating in Persia in Arabic translations, amongst which the *Sukhāvatī-vyūha* and

Kāraṇḍa-vyūha Sūtras are recognizable.[184] More recently portions of the *Saṁyutta* and *Aṅguttara-Nikāyas*, along with (parts of) the *Maitreya-vyākaraṇa*, have been identified in this collection.[185]

Whilst the Persian and Arab cultures of the area clearly appreciated the edifying stories of the *Jātaka* book, no Arabic, Persian, or other Middle Eastern translation of more scholastic literature is known to have survived. Accounts of Buddhism that we do have in Persian literature occur in the works of historians and geographers, and bear a distinctly anthropological cast. Relying upon anecdote, as such an approach was bound to do, these writers knew of *al Budd* (the Buddha) as an Indian idol, *al Būdāsf* (the Bodhisattva), and of the *sumaniyyas* (*śramaṇas*), one of two Indian sects (the other being the Hindus), but did not draw them together into a coherent account of Buddhism proper.[186] Persian literature, especially that from eastern Persia, draws both imagery and locale from Buddhist sites such as Merv and Balkh, although the interest in these derived considerably from their mysterious and even romantic desolation.[187] Knowledge of Buddhist ritual connected with the stūpa at Balkh is shown by the 10th century Persian historian, Ibn al-Faqīh, and Yāqūt, a Syrian historian of the 13th century.[188] That Persian knowledge of Buddhism should be so slight and even then restricted to that from Central Asia and Afghanistan is partly explicable in the light of the demise of Buddhism in India, a demise for which militant Islamic conquest was itself largely responsible. Buddhist influence upon Islam itself has been mooted through the mystical Sufi movements, at least one early leader of which, Ibrāhim ibn Ādham (8th century), came from Balkh.[189]

So much then for the Persian awareness of Buddhism. As for Buddhists themselves, any movement into Persia appears to have taken place during two periods, the former possibly beginning in the 3rd century BCE and lasting at least until countered by the eastward movement of Islam from the 7th century onwards; the latter, the result of the Mongol conquest of Iran in the early 13th century.

The first of these movements undoubtedly involved two mechanisms. Missionary activity in the area probably began in the reign of Aśoka. Legend records missions sent to Bactria and Gandhara, both in modern Afghanistan, and there is no doubt that the flourishing Buddhism of the area spilt over into Khurasan (in the north-east of modern Iran). Buddhism also became established in Sindh and this would have served as a second point of geographical contact with the Sassanian and later Muslim dynasties.

The second mechanism involved in this movement was trade. From the earliest times Buddhism made great headway with the mercantile community in India (witness the great cave monasteries lining the trading routes of western India), and this very likely involved contact with traders from other countries. Branches of the ancient silk route passed through Bactria and Gandhāra *en route* to the Mediterranean Sea, and would have carried Buddhist traders far westwards (as they also did eastwards). It is also known that as early as the 2nd century BCE Indian traders, from western and southern India, and doubtless Sindh too, were regularly visiting ports in the Gulf and Arabia, and these contacts probably explain the frequency of names in the region which contain elements such as *but*, and also *hind* (Indian), and *bahār* (from the Sanskrit *vihāra*, i.e. a Buddhist monastery). It certainly explains the conversion of the Maldive Islands to Buddhism in the 6th century.[190]

Although Zoroastrianism was the dominant religious force in the area, Buddhism did make headway there, as demonstrated by the coins of Peroz, son of Ardashir I (226–41CE), which present him as honouring the Zoroastrian and Buddhist faiths.[191] However, there is also evidence that Buddhism met with resistance, for in the 3rd century a Zoroastrian high-priest, Kartir, recorded in inscriptions that Buddhists (and others) in the Sassanian kingdom (i.e. the pre-Muslim Persian dynasty) were being suppressed. Al-Bīrūnī, writing in the 11th century, claims that prior to this suppression, 'Khurasan, Persis, Irak, Mosul, and the country up to the frontier of Syria' were Buddhist,[192] and that the resultant retreat of Buddhists eastwards explains their concentration in the area of Balkh.

Concrete evidence for the presence of Buddhism in Persia is slim. Rock-cut cave complexes at Chehelkhaneh and Haidari on the Gulf have been tentatively identified as Buddhist monasteries, built in the same style that is ubiquitous in both India and Central Asia to serve the local trading community. Unfortunately no explicit evidence survives to substantiate this identification. Persian tradition describes a powerful dynastic family of the 8th and 9th centuries, originating in Balkh, and with the name Barmak. Arab authors recognized this as the hereditary title of the 'high priest' of a temple in that city known as the Nawbahār. In fact *barmak* is derived from the Sanskrit term *pramukha*, literally 'chief', the term for the head of a Buddhist monastery. This interpretation is confirmed by the name Nawbahār itself, which is a corruption of the Sanskrit for *nava-vihāra*, 'new monastery'. The diffusion of the name Nawbahār to sites in Persia, the greatest concentration in north-eastern Iran, and spreading both west and south from there, has led to speculation that the *nava-vihāra* of Balkh (a known site, mentioned independently by Chinese pilgrims) had been the centre of a western-oriented Buddhist sect, overseen by the Barmakid family and acting as their power-base, albeit shrinking, in negotiations with the ruling Abbasid dynasty based in Baghdad.[193] It seems likely that the Persian Nawbahār system had been effectively suppressed by the time of the Islamic conquest of the area, such that specifically Buddhist associations with these sites were not known to them. Even so, the theory has also been advanced that the Nawbahār monasteries of Persia served as the model for the Islamic *madrasa*, on the grounds that they retained their function as centres of learning after their specifically Buddhist function was removed or suppressed.[194] (This theory is circumstantially supported by the reputation of such monasteries as Nālandā in India as centres of both secular and religious learning.) The Buddhists of Sindh, which was sporadically ruled by Buddhist kings until the 7th century, appear to have been able to negotiate a stable and friendly *modus vivendi* with their Muslim conquerors, and again this may have been through some connection with the *nava-vihāra* in Balkh – there being sites of the same name there. We should not assume that Buddhism disappeared from Persia as a result of religious persecution, for there is evidence that Muslim rulers showed tolerance towards other religious groups.[195]

The second wave of movement westwards was powered by the Mongol conquests of the early 13th century which led to the establishment of the Mongol Īlkhānid dynasty in Persia from 1256 onwards. The Mongol Khāns were Buddhists, of a Tantric character, and patronized Buddhism in their kingdom for the remainder of the century, until Ghazan Khān was converted to Islam in 1295. This brief period of patronage witnessed an enthusiastic programme of temple building, in Maragheh the capital in north-eastern Persia, and elsewhere, but was curtailed by Ghazan's order that all Buddhist temples be destroyed or converted to use as mosques. Possible physical evidence for this are two further sets of rock-cut caves, at Rasatkhāneh and Varjuvi, both sites near the old Mongol capital of Maragheh. Both conform to the well-known pattern of Buddhist cave complexes, but have had frescoes removed and have been converted for use as mosques. Later attempts by Buddhists to convert Uldjaitu Khān (1305–16) to Buddhism are witness to the survival of Buddhism in Persia after this date, although it appears to have disappeared by the mid-14th century.[196] The presence to this day of stūpa-type buildings ornamented with flags in Dhagestan in the Caucasus may also reflect Mongol influence of this period.

NOTES

WHERE A NOTE REFERS TO A TEXT *not* in the bibliography referring to its own chapter, the reference is preceded by a letter or number indicating the section of the bibliography in which that work is listed. Hence, (D) Williams 1989 indicates that the reference is to the work published by Williams in 1989 and listed in the general section (D). Numbers in this position correspond to chapter numbers.

Technical terms are usually quoted in Sanskrit in preference to Pāli, unless direct reference is being made to a Pāli source. All references to the Pāli Canon are to the editions of the Pali Text Society. Where reference is made to a complete sutta, only the number of the sutta is given. Where reference is made to a passage from a sutta, then volume and page numbers are given for the Pāli text (the standard practice). In the English translations published by the Pali Text Society, these numbers are usually to be found at the head of the page, on the inner margin.

Abbreviations used in the notes:

AK.	*Abhidharmakośa*
AN.	*Aṅguttara-Nikāya*
Aṣṭa.	*Aṣṭasāhasrikā-prajñāpāramitā Sūtra*
Dh.	*Dhammapada*
DN.	*Dīgha-Nikāya*
J.	*Jātaka*
MN.	*Majjhima-Nikāya*
Mv.	*Mahāvastu*
SN.	*Samyutta-Nikāya*
Sn.	*Sutta Nipāta*
Ud.	*Udāna*
V.	*Vinaya* (V.i *Mahāvagga*; V.ii *Cūlavagga*)

PREFACE

1 (18) Chappell 1980 and Nattier 1991

CHAPTER 1: THE ANCIENT INDIAN CONTEXT

2 Renfrew 1990
3 (2) Carrithers, pp.26–7
4 DN.1 and 2

CHAPTER 2: THE BUDDHA

5 Gombrich 1992
6 MN.26
7 MN.4, 19, and 36
8 DN.16
9 Sn.vv.405–24
10 MN.8
11 MN.36
12 V.i.1–5 and *Nidānakathā*, Rhys Davids, pp.199ff.
13 MN.67
14 (D) Lamotte, 1988, pp.19–20 and (1) Ling, 1973, p.100
15 DN.ii.156

CHAPTER 3: THE BUDDHA'S TEACHING

16 MN.26
17 V.i.6.17 and SN.v.420
18 V.i.6.36
19 (D) Sangharakshita 1993, pp.143ff. and (1) Gombrich, 1988, p.59
20 AN.iii.415
21 SN.ii.10
22 R. Gombrich, Jordan Lecture, Seminar 1, November 1994 (forthcoming)
23 Dh.273–9
24 V.i.6.42

CHAPTER 4: THE PATH TO AWAKENING

25 Sangharakshita 1989
26 MN.i.351; i.38; SN.v.115–21; AN.i.193–6
27 See for example Vajirañāna, 1962, for a classic Theravādin account of these two forms of meditation.

CHAPTER 5: THE EARLY SAṄGHA

28 Dh.vv.190–2
29 V.i.4; J.i.80–1
30 V.i.16–17

31 V.i.11.1
32 MN.128
33 Gombrich 1991, p.35
34 ibid. and (1) Gombrich, 1988, p.109
35 Dutt 1962, p.67
36 DN.ii.49
37 MN.iii.9–10
38 DN.ii.154
39 DN.ii.73–80
40 MN.56
41 MN.ii.8–9
42 Sn.976–1149
43 (17) Gombrich 1994
44 V.x.1–6
45 Sn.136; MN.ii.147ff.
46 DN.31
47 V.vi.4; SN.x.8
48 (1) Gombrich, 1988, pp.73–4, summarizing MN.iii.261
49 AN.iv.211
50 Ud.v.6; V.v.13.8
51 Sn.1142–4 tr. Hare

Chapter 6: The Councils

52 V.ii.189ff.
53 (8) Cousins 1990
54 (D) Lamotte 1988, p.172

Chapter 7: Developments in the Saṅgha

55 V.i.27; also (B) Warren, pp.393–401
56 V.ii.1
57 (B) Warren, pp.405–10
58 (D) Lamotte, 1988, pp.499ff.
59 Bareau 1962 and Schopen 1989 (JPTS)
60 Strong 1977 and 1979
61 (8) Bechert 1982
62 Huntington 1990

Chapter 8: The Buddhist Schools

63 Bechert 1981
64 Frauwallner 1956
65 (9) See *śaikṣya* rules in *Vinaya Piṭaka*, Prebish 1975
66 DN.iii.59f.
67 (3/4) Brough 1980

68 See (D) Williams 1989, pp.16ff.
69 V.i.6.8
70 DN.ii.102–18
71 MN.i.171
72 Mv.i.161–72
73 DN.iii.230
74 (9) *Kathāvatthu* 'Points of Controversy', pp.323f.
75 Mv.i.63–157
76 *Lokānuvartana Sūtra,* Harrison 1982
77 Compare the two versions of the *Mahāgovinda Sūtra;* DN.ii.251–2 and Mv.iii.224.
78 Thich Thien Chau 1984
79 AN.i.22; see also SN.iii.25
80 (7) Scott 1985
81 This discussion can only be fully understood in the context provided by Chapter 10.
82 AK.1136–48
83 AK.693
84 Khantipālo 1970
85 AK.810–16
86 AK.211–12

Chapter 9: The Tripiṭaka

87 (D) Lamotte 1988, p.150
88 ibid.
89 Frauwallner 1956, p.65
90 SN.i.190
91 Frauwallner 1956, p.154
92 See Thich Minh Chau 1991 and (1) MacQueen 1988.
93 (D) Lamotte 1988, pp.143ff.
94 Thich Minh Chau 1991
95 *Ekottarāgama,* Thich Huyen Vi
96 DN.ii.123 for the Pāli version, which is less complete.
97 DN.5 and 24
98 Ud.v.5

Chapter 10: The Abhidharma

99 Gethin 1992 and Jaini 1959, pp.40ff.
100 DN.ii.120
101 DN.33
102 (8) Harrison 1982
103 Sastri, pp.20 and 298

CHAPTER 11: ORIGINS OF THE MAHĀYĀNA

104 Gombrich 1992
105 (12) Lancaster 1968 and (12) Rawlinson 1972
106 (14) Kalupahana, 1991, p.24
107 (D) Williams 1989, pp.26ff.
108 Schopen 1979
109 (12) Aṣṭa., Conze 1973, p.87
110 (D) Hardy, p.97
111 (10) e.g. Gethin 1992, p.165–6
112 Harrison 1992; (12) Harrison 1978
113 (D) Williams 1989, p.218
114 (7) Schopen 1985
115 Schopen 1975; (12) Aṣṭa., Conze 1973, pp.105 and 116; *Saddharma-puṇḍarīka Sūtra*, ch.16
116 (C) Chattopadhyaya, p.99

CHAPTER 12: THE MAHĀYĀNA SŪTRAS

117 *The Drama of Cosmic Enlightenment*, Sangharakshita 1993
118 See Chapters 14, 15, and 16
119 Kṣitigarbha *Sūtra of the Past Vows of Earth Store Bodhisattva*, Heng Ching, 1974, a modern Chinese commentary; Lopez, 1988, Indian and Tibetan commentaries on the *Heart Sūtra*; Sangharakshita, 1993 and 1993, two modern Western commentaries; (15) *Abhisamayālaṅkārāloka*, Conze, 1954, a Yogācāra commentary on the *Aṣṭasāhasrikāprajñāpāramitā Sūtra*.
120 Harrison 1978
121 *Śikṣāsamuccaya*, Bendall and Rouse, p.17
122 Conze 1978
123 Nattier 1992
124 Aṣṭa., Conze 1973, p.139
125 (14) *Suhṛllekhā* v.121, Lozang Jamspal et al., p.66
126 *Bodhicaryāvatāra* 5.98; *Śikṣāsamuccaya*, Bendall and Rouse, p.263–4
127 (D) Nakamura, p.194
128 Pedersen 1980

CHAPTER 13: THE NEW SPIRITUAL IDEAL

129 *Bodhicaryāvatāra*, 3.22–7
130 *Bodhicittavivaraṇa* v.2, (14) Lindtner, 1987, p.187
131 See *Bodhicaryāvatāra*, Crosby and Skilton, introduction to chs.2 and 3
132 In the second chapter of his *Bodhicittotpāda-sūtra-śāstra* (untranslated). Sanskrit text in 'Fa Fu T'i Ching Lun, Bodhicittotpāda-sūtra-śastra of Vasubandhu', Bhadanta Santi Bhiksu, *Visva-Bharati Annals* 2 (1949), pp.185–243
133 See *Bodhicaryāvatāra*, Crosby and Skilton, introduction to ch.8.

134 (12) Lamotte, ch.XLII
135 Mv.i.76ff.

CHAPTER 14: THE MADHYAMAKA

136 *Mūla-madhyamaka-kārikā*, 24.18
137 Warder 1973

CHAPTER 15: THE YOGĀCĀRA

138 Frauwallner 1951
139 (12) Aṣṭa., Conze 1973, p.150
140 *Sāndhinirmocana Sūtra*, Lamotte, p.207
141 ibid., p.211
142 *Trisvabhāvanirdeśa* vv.27–30
143 Sponberg 1983
144 (21) Demiéville 1954
145 (D) Williams 1989, pp.179ff.
146 Schopen 1990
147 (C) I-tsing, Takakusu, pp.167–85

CHAPTER 16: THE TATHĀGATAGARBHA DOCTRINE

148 *Nidānakathā*, Rhys Davids, p.206–7; V.i.5
149 (D) Williams 1989, p.96f.
150 Nakamura in (D) Kitagawa and Cummings 1989, p.235
151 Quoted in (D) Williams 1989, p.97
152 Wayman 1978
153 (D) Williams 1989, p.101
154 ibid., pp.99–100

CHAPTER 17: THE TANTRA AND VAJRAYĀNA BUDDHISM

155 (C) *Dharmasvāmin*, Roerich 1959
156 Katz 1980
157 See Kvaerne's introduction to *Caryāgīti*
158 Sanderson (forthcoming)
159 ibid.
160 ibid.
161 See (13) *Sādhanas*

CHAPTER 18: THE END OF BUDDHISM IN INDIA

162 (D) Warder, 1980, p.506
163 (C) *Dharmasvāmin*, Roerich, pp.90ff.
164 Ritti 1989
165 (1) Gombrich 1988, p.142

CHAPTER 19: SRI LANKA

166 ibid.

167 Lance Cousins, unpublished seminar paper, 'Aspects of Esoteric Southern Buddhism, part 2, March 1993', p.5

168 See Holt 1991

169 Gombrich 1988, p.168

CHAPTER 20: SOUTH-EAST ASIA

170 Burma: Stargardt 1990

171 Burma: Strong 1992

172 See works of Bizot, under 'Tantric or Esoteric Theravāda'.

CHAPTER 21: CENTRAL ASIA AND KASHMIR

173 Private communication, Dr L. Newby, Oriental Institute, Oxford

174 (28) Ball 1989, p.5

CHAPTER 22: CHINA

175 Harrison 1993

176 Zürcher 1991

177 Zürcher 1982

CHAPTER 25: TIBET

178 Samuel 1993

179 Hookham 1991

180 Ruegg 1963 and Wilson 1991

CHAPTER 27: NEPAL

181 See Gellner 1990 and 1992

182 See Mitra 1882

CHAPTER 28: PERSIA

183 Summarized from Rhys Davids

184 Jahn 1956, pp.121ff.

185 Schopen 1982

186 Gimaret 1969

187 Melikian-Chirvani 1974, pp.5ff.

188 ibid., pp.10ff.

189 Ball 1989, p.1

190 Summarized from Ball 1989

191 Barthold 1933, p.30

192 Quoted in Ball 1989, p.4

193 Bulliet 1976
194 ibid., p.145 n.48
195 Barthold 1933
196 Jahn 1956, p.83

Bibliography

THIS BIBLIOGRAPHY DIRECTS THE READER towards further reading, and shows sources for my own work. After several general sections, it is organized around the chapter headings of this book, but it should be understood that many books cited will overlap in the range of their coverage. Books in the general section will probably have something interesting to say about the subject of almost every individual chapter here. The purpose of the chapter bibliographies is to provide the student with a basis for further serious study, in which the subject of the chapter can be pursued at greater length and in greater depth than is possible here. There will be omissions, regrettable but inevitable. I have included articles from academic journals where these seemed of especial interest or importance to the subject-matter of the chapter. Inclusion in this bibliography should not be taken to imply either that I agree with every thesis put forward in each item, or that such theses are consistent with, or represented in, this book.

The first sections of this bibliography, which are not specific to any particular chapter, are identified by letter – A, B, C, or D – for ease of reference. Almost every Buddhist text that I mention has been published in translation, and I have wherever possible included bibliographical details of these translations at the beginning of each chapter bibliography on the assumption that they are of primary importance to the student. Details of translations of suttas from the Pāli Canon will be found in the bibliography for the chapter on the Tripiṭaka; likewise, translations of Mahāyāna sūtras will usually be listed in that for the chapter 'The Mahāyāna Sūtras'. The bibliographical details provided are from the editions to hand at the time of writing, and do not necessarily show first editions or subsequent reprints or editions.

All the books mentioned below contain bibliographies which will be of use to the reader. In addition to this, I should point out that several excellent thematic bibliographies of Buddhism have been published. Frank Reynolds's *Guide to the Buddhist Religion* is the most up-to-date single-volume bibliography of Buddhism. I would also recommend the bibliographies in:

The World of Buddhism by Bechert and Gombrich (D),
The Buddhist Religion by Robinson and Johnson (D),
Historical Dictionary of Buddhism by Charles Prebish (A),
A History of Indian Buddhism, by Akira Hirakawa (D).

Prebish's *Historical Dictionary* and Warder's *Indian Buddhism* contain bibliographies of published Buddhist scriptures. Also very useful in the same vein is Peter Pfandt's *Mahāyāna Texts Translated into Western Languages: A Bibliographical Guide*, Bonn 1986. There is no single comprehensive bibliography of Buddhist sūtras in translation. The translations of the Pāli Tipiṭaka published by the Pali Text Society are largely representative of the Tripiṭakas of the early schools.

A

Readers will find a wealth of information on most aspects of the Buddhist tradition in articles in the following:

Encyclopaedia of Religion and Ethics, ed. Hastings, 13 vols., Edinburgh, London and New York 1908

Historical Dictionary of Buddhism, by Charles Prebish, Metuchen and London 1993

Encyclopaedia of Buddhism, ed. G.P. Malalasekara, Colombo 1961 *et sqq*. (not yet complete)

The Encyclopedia of Religion, ed. M. Eliade, 16 vols., New York and London 1987

The following are individual volumes giving general coverage:

B

Compilations of scriptural texts

Beyer S, *The Buddhist Experience: Sources and Interpretations*, Encino California 1974

Burtt E.A, *The Teachings of the Compassionate Buddha*, New York 1955

Conze E, *Buddhist Scriptures*, Harmondsworth 1959

Conze E, *Buddhist Texts Through the Ages*, New York 1964

Goddard D, *A Buddhist Bible*, Boston 1970

Lopez D.S, *Buddhism in Practice*, Princeton 1995

Theodore de Bary W, *The Buddhist Tradition in India, China and Japan*, New York 1972

Warren H.C, *Buddhism in Translations*, New York 1963 (reprint)

Woodward F.L, *Some Sayings of the Buddha*, According to the Pali Canon, London 1974

C
PRIMARY SOURCES FOR THE HISTORY OF BUDDHISM IN INDIA

Bu-ston, *History of Buddhism in India by Bu-ston*, tr. E. Obermiller, Heidelberg 1931
Dharmasvāmin, *Biography of Dharmasvāmin*, tr. G. Roerich, Patna 1959
Fa-hsien, *A Record of Buddhistic Kingdoms*, tr. J. Legge, Oxford 1886 (reprinted New York 1965)
Hsüan-tsang, *Si-yu-ki, Buddhist records of the western world*, 2 vols., Oxford 1884 (reprinted Delhi 1969)
I-tsing, *A Record of the Buddhist Religion as practised in India and the Malay Archipelago*, tr. J. Takakusu, Oxford 1896
Tāranātha, *Tāranātha's History of Buddhism in India*, tr. Lama Chimpa and A. Chattopadhyaya, Simla 1970 (reprinted Delhi 1990)

D
GENERAL SURVEYS OF BUDDHISM

Bapat P.V, *2500 Years of Buddhism*, Delhi 1956 (reprinted 1971)
Bechert H. and Gombrich R, *The World of Buddhism*, London 1984
Collins Davies C, *An Historical Atlas of the Indian Peninsula*, 2nd ed., Madras 1959
Conze E, *Buddhism: Its Essence and Development*, New York 1959
Conze E, *A Short History of Buddhism*, London 1980
Gombrich R, 'The History of Early Buddhism: Major Advances Since 1950', from *Indological studies and South Asia bibliography: A conference 1986*, ed. A. Das, Calcutta 1988, pp.12–30
Hardy F, ed. *The World's Religions: The Religions of Asia*, London 1990 (contains a number of useful essays on Buddhism by different authors)
Hirakawa A, *A History of Indian Buddhism: From Śākyamuni to early Mahāyāna*, tr. P. Groner, Honolulu 1990
Kalupahana J, *History of Buddhist Philosophy: Continuities and Discontinuities*, Honolulu 1992
Kitagawa J.M, Cummings M.D, *Buddhism and Asian History, Religion History and Culture, Readings from the Encyclopedia of Religion*, New York and London 1989
Lamotte E, *History of Indian Buddhism: from the origins to the Śaka era*, English tr. S. Webb-Boin, Louvain 1988
Nakamura H, *Indian Buddhism: A survey with bibliographical notes*, Delhi 1987
Prebish C, *Buddhism: A Modern Perspective*, Pennsylvania State UP 1975
Reynolds F, *Guide to the Buddhist Religion*, Boston 1981
Robinson R.H. and Johnson W.L, *The Buddhist Religion*, 3rd ed., Belmont California 1982
Sangharakshita *The Three Jewels*, Glasgow 1991
Sangharakshita *A Survey of Buddhism*, 7th ed., Glasgow 1993

Schumann H.W, *Der Mahāyāna-Buddhismus, Die zweite Drehung des Dharma-Rades*, München 1990
Snellgrove D, *Indo-Tibetan Buddhism: Indian Buddhists and their Tibetan successors*, London 1987
Takeuchi Yoshinori, ed. *Buddhist Spirituality: Indian, Southeast Asian, Tibetan, and Early Chinese*, New York 1993, London 1994
Thomas E, *History of Buddhist Thought*, 2nd ed., London 1951
Warder A, *Indian Buddhism*, 2nd (revised) ed., Delhi 1980
Williams P, *Mahāyāna Buddhism: The doctrinal foundations*, London and New York 1989
Zürcher E, *Buddhism: Its Origin and Spread in Words, Maps, and Pictures*, London 1962

1 The Ancient Indian Context

Ṛg Veda
—O'Flaherty W.D, *The Rig Veda*, Harmondsworth 1981
Upaniṣad
—Hume R.E, *The Thirteen Principal Upanishads*, New Delhi 1985 (reprint)
—Zaehner R.C, *Hindu Scriptures*, London 1966

Basham A.L, *History and Doctrines of the Ājīvikas*, London 1951
Basham A.L, *The Wonder That Was India*, London 1954 (many reprints)
Basham A.L, 'The Background to the Rise of Buddhism', in *Studies in the History of Buddhism*, ed. A.K. Narain, Delhi 1980, pp.13–31
Collins S, *Selfless Persons*, Cambridge 1982 (ch.1)
Gombrich R, *Theravāda Buddhism*, London 1988 (chs.1–3)
Hardy F, 'Vedic religion' and 'The Renouncer Traditions', from *The World's Religions: The Religions of Asia*, ed. F. Hardy, London 1990, pp.43–71
Hopkins T.J, *The Hindu Religious Tradition*, 2nd ed., Belmont California 1982
Horner I.B, 'Gotama and the Other Sects', JAOS 1946, pp.283–89
Kosambi D.D, *The Culture and Civilisation of Ancient India in Historical Outline*, New Delhi 1970
Ling T, *The Buddha: Buddhist Civilisation in India and Ceylon*, Harmondsworth 1973, Chs.3–5
MacQueen G, 'The Doctrines of the Six Heretics According to the Śramanyaphala Sūtra', IIJ 27 (1984), pp.291–307
MacQueen G, *A Study of the Śrāmaṇyaphala-Sūtra*, Wiesbaden 1988
Renfrew C, *Archaeology and Language*, 2nd (revised) ed., Harmondsworth 1990
Warder A.K, 'On the Relationships between Early Buddhism and Other Contemporary Systems', BSOAS (1956) pp.43–63
Warder A.K, 'The Pali Canon and Its Commentaries as an Historical Record', from *Historians of India, Pakistan and Ceylon*, ed. Philips, London 1961

2 The Buddha

Mahāvastu
—Jones J.J, *The Mahāvastu,* 3 vols., London 1949 1952 1956
Buddhacarita
—Johnston E.H, *Aśvaghoṣa's Buddhacarita or Acts of the Buddha,* Delhi 1984 enlarged ed.
Lalitavistara
—Bays G, *The Voice of the Buddha,* 2 vols., Berkeley California 1983
Nidānakathā
—Rhys Davids T.W, *Buddhist Birth Stories,* Varanasi and Delhi 1973 (reprint)
Abhiniṣkramaṇa Sūtra
—Beal S, *The Romantic Legend of Śākya Buddha: A Translation of the Chinese Version of the Abhiniṣkramaṇasūtra,* Delhi 1985 (reprint)
Jātakas
—Cowell E.B et al., *The Jātaka or Stories of the Buddha's Former Births,* 3 vols., London 1981 (reprint)

Bechert H, 'The Date of the Buddha Reconsidered', *Indologica Taurinensia,* Vol X (1982), Torino pp.29–36
Carrithers M, *The Buddha,* Oxford 1983
Gombrich R, 'Dating the Buddha : A Red Herring Revealed', from *The Dating of the Historical Buddha Part 2,* ed. H. Bechert, Göttingen 1992, pp.237–59
Karetsky P.E, *The Life of the Buddha: Ancient Scriptural and Pictorial Traditions,* New York and London 1992
Ñānamoli *The Life of the Buddha as it appears in the Pali canon,* Kandy 1972
Reynolds F, 'The Many Lives of the Buddha – A Study of Sacred Biography and Theravāda Tradition', from *The Biographical Process: Essays in History and Psychology of Religion,* ed. F. Reynolds and D. Capps, The Hague 1976, pp.37–61
Sangharakshita *The Three Jewels,* Glasgow 1991
Sangharakshita *Who is the Buddha?,* Glasgow 1994
Schumann H.W, *The Historical Buddha,* tr. M. O'C. Walshe, Harmondsworth 1989
Thomas E.J, 'Theravādin and Sarvāstivādin Dates of the Nirvāṇa', from *B.C. Law Volume,* Calcutta 1945, pp.18–22
Thomas E.J, *The Life of the Buddha as Legend and History,* 6th ed., London 1960
Waley A, 'Did the Buddha die of eating pork? With a note on Buddha's image', *Mélanges Chinois et Bouddhiques,* 1 (1931–2), pp.343–54

3 The Teaching and 4 The Path

The bibliography for these two chapters could be the most extensive of all, since they cover subjects addressed in some degree by almost every writer who writes on the subject of Buddhism. The titles offered below should be seen as supplementing those from the section above entitled 'General Surveys'.

Bhagavad Gītā
—Edgerton F, *The Bhagavad Gītā translated from the Sanskrit*, Cambridge, Mass. 1974

Aronson H.B, 'Equanimity in Theravāda Buddhism', from *Studies Pali and Buddhism*, ed. A.K. Narain, Delhi 1979, pp.1–18
Aronson H.B, 'Buddhist and Non-Buddhist Approaches to the Sublime Attitudes (Brahma-Vihara)', *Buddhist studies in honour of Hammalava Saddhatissa*, ed. G. Dhammapāla et al., Nugegoda, Sri Lanka 1984, pp.16–24
Aronson H.B, *Love and Sympathy in Theravāda Buddhism*, Delhi 1980
Bronkhorst J, *The Two Traditions of Meditation in Ancient India*, Stuttgart 1986
Brough J, 'Sakāya Niruttiyā: Cauld kale het', from *The Language of the Earliest Buddhist Traditions*, ed. H. Bechert, Göttingen (1980), pp.35–42
Conze E, *Buddhist Meditation*, London 1956
Conze E, *Buddhist Thought in India*, London 1962
Cousins L, 'Buddhist Jhāna: Its nature and attainment according to Pali sources', *Religion* 3 (1973), pp.115–31
Dharmasiri G, *A Buddhist Critique of the Christian Concept of God*, 2nd ed., The Buddhist Research Society, Singapore (no date)
Dharmasiri G, *The Fundamentals of Buddhist Ethics*, Singapore 1986
Gunaratana H, *The Path of Serenity and Insight*, Delhi 1985
Keown D, *The Nature of Buddhist Ethics*, Basingstoke 1992
King W.L, *In the Hope of Nibbana: Theravada Buddhist Ethics*, La Salle Illinois 1964
King W.L, *Theravāda Meditation, The Buddhist Transformation of Yoga*, London 1980
Norman K.R, 'The dialects in which the Buddha preached', from *The Language of the Earliest Buddhist Traditions*, ed. H. Bechert, Göttingen (1980), pp.61–77
Nyanaponika Thera *The Heart of Buddhist Meditation*, London 1975
Piyadassi Thera, *The Seven Factors of Enlightenment* (Wheel Series), Kandy 1960
Prasad C.S, 'Meat-eating and the rule of Tikoṭiparisuddha', from *Studies in Pali and Buddhism*, ed. A.K. Narain Delhi 1979, pp.289–95
Rahula W, *What the Buddha Taught*, London 1959
Ross Reat N, 'Some Fundamental Concepts of Buddhist Psychology', *Religion* 17 (1987) 15–28
Ross Reat N, *The Origins of Indian Psychology*, Berkeley 1990
Ruegg D.S, 'Ahiṁsa and vegetarianism in the history of Buddhism', from ed. S. Balasooriya et al., *Buddhist Studies in Honour of Walpola Rahula*, London 1980
Saddhatissa H, *Buddhist Ethics: The Path to Nirvana*, London 1970

Sangharakshita *The Ten Pillars of Buddhism*, 3rd ed., Glasgow 1989. A study of the *daśakuśalakarmapatha*.
Schmithausen L, 'On the Problem of the relation of Spiritual Practice and Philosophical Theory in Buddhism', from *German Scholars on India*, ed. Cultural Department of the Embassy of the Federal Republic of Germany, New Delhi, Varanasi 1973, pp.235–50
Soma Thera *The Way of Mindfulness*, Kandy 1981
Stoler Miller B, 'On cultivating the Immeasurable Change Heart: the Buddhist Brahma Vihara formula', JIP 7 (1979), pp.209–21
Tachibana S, *The Ethics of Buddhism*, Oxford 1926
Vajirañāna P, *Buddhist Meditation in Theory and Practice*, Colombo 1962
Vetter T, *The ideas and meditative practices of early Buddhism*, Leiden 1988

5 The Early Saṅgha

Aramaki N, 'The Development of the Term "Pātimokkha" in Early Buddhism', from *Premier Colloque Etienne Lamotte*, Louvain-la-Neuve 1993
Carter J.R, 'The Notion of Refuge (sarana) in the Theravāda Buddhist Tradition', from *Studies in Pali and Buddhism*, ed. A.K. Narain, Delhi 1979, pp.41–52
Dutt S, *Buddhist Monks and Monasteries*, London 1962
Gokhale B.G, 'Theravāda Buddhism in Western India', JAOS 92 (1972), pp.230–36
Gombrich R, '*Pātimokkha*: purgative', from *Studies in Buddhism and culture in honour of Professor Dr Egaku Mayeda on his sixty-fifth birthday*, ed. Tokyo Committee of the Felicitation Volume for Professor Dr Egaku Mayeda, Tokyo 1991, pp.31–8
Kloppenborg R, 'The Earliest Buddhist Ritual of Ordination', from *Selected Studies on Ritual in the Indian Religion – Essays to D.J. Hoens*, ed. R. Kloppenborg, Leiden 1983, pp.158–68

6 The Councils

Some material relevant to this section appears in the bibliography for Chapter 8.

Bareau A, *Les premiers conciles bouddhiques*, Paris 1955
Buddhadatta 'The Buddhist Sects', *University of Ceylon Review*, i pp.68–81
Buddhadatta 'The Early Buddhist Councils and the Various Buddhist Sects' *University of Ceylon Review*, iv pp.34–48
Prebish C, 'A Review of Scholarship on the Buddhist Councils', *Journal of Asian Studies* 33.2 (1974), pp.239–54
Tsukamoto K, 'Mahākāśyapa's Precedence to Ānanda in the Rājagṛha Council', IBK xi (1963), pp.824–17 (53–60)

7 Developments in the Saṅgha

Aśokāvadāna
—Strong J.S, *The Legend of King Aśoka: A Study and Translation of the Aśokāvadāna*, Delhi 1989
Mahāvibhāṣā
—see de La Vallée Poussin 1930 and 1931–2 under Sarvāstivādin, in bibliography to Chapter 10
Milindapañha
—Rhys Davids T.W, *The Questions of King Milinda*, 2 vols., New York 1963
—Horner I.B, *Milinda's Questions*, 2 vols., London 1963 and 1964
Suhṛllekhā
—see bibliography to Chapter 14
Vaṁsa
—see bibliography to Chapter 19
Yogācārabhūmi
—see Demiéville in bibliography for Chapter 21
Aśokan inscriptions
—Nikam N.A. and McKeon R, *The Edicts of Aśoka*, Chicago 1959
Aśvaghoṣa
—Johnston E.H, *Aśvaghoṣa's Buddhacarita or Acts of the Buddha*, Delhi 1984 enlarged ed.
—Conze E, *Buddhist Scriptures*, Harmondsworth 1959, pp.103–16 (a partial translation of Aśvaghoṣa's *Saundarananda-kāvya*)
Mātṛceṭa
—Shackleton-Bailey D.R, '*Varṇārhavarṇa-stotra*', BSOAS 13 (1949–51), pp.671–701 and 947–1003
—Shackleton-Bailey D.R, *The Śatapañcāśatka of Mātṛceṭa*, Cambridge 1951
—Thomas F.W, 'Mātṛceṭa and the *Mahārāja-kaniṣka-lekha*', *Indian Antiquary* 32 (1903), pp.345–60
—Python P, *Vinaya Viniścaya Upāli Paripṛcchā*, Paris 1973, appendice II (a translation of Mātṛceṭa's *Sugatapañcatriṁśat-stotra*, 'hymn of praise to the Sugatas in 35 verses')

Basham A.L. 'Asoka and Buddhism – A Re-examination', JIABS 5 (1982), pp.131–43
Bareau A, 'La Construction et le Culte Des Stupa d'Apres les Vinayapitaka', BEFEO L(ii) (1962), pp.229–74
Dutt S, *Buddhist Monks and Monasteries of India*, London 1962
Gokhale B.G. 'Theravāda Buddhism in Western India' JAOS 92 (1972), pp.230–36
Huntington S.L, 'Early Buddhist Art and the Theory of Aniconism', *Art Journal*, 1990, pp.401–8
Przyluski J, *The Legend of Emperor Aśoka in Indian and Chinese Texts*, Calcutta 1967

Schopen G, 'Two Problems in the History of Indian Buddhism: The Layman/Monk Distinction and the Doctrines of the Transference of Merit', *Studien zur Indologie und Iranistik* 10 (1985), pp.9–47
Schopen G, 'Burial "ad sanctos" and the physical presence of the Buddha in early Indian Buddhism', *Religion* 17 (1987), pp.193–225
Schopen G, 'On the Buddha and His Bones: The Conception of a Relic in the Inscriptions of Nāgārjunakoṇḍa', JAOS 108 (1988), pp.527–37
Schopen G, 'A verse from the Bhadracarīpraṇidhāna in a 10th Century Inscription found at Nālandā' JIABS 12 (1989), pp.149–57
Schopen G, 'The Stupa Cult and the Extant Pali Vinaya', JPTS (1989) 13 pp.83–100
Scott D.A, 'Ashokan Missionary Expansion of Buddhism among the Greeks (in NW India, Bactria, and the Levant)', *Religion* 15 (1985), pp.131–41
Seneviratna A, *King Aśoka and Buddhism: Historical and Literary Studies,* Kandy (forthcoming 1990)
Strong J, 'Gandhakuṭi: The Perfumed Chamber of the Buddha', *History of Religions* 16 (1977), pp.390–406
Strong J, 'The Transforming Gift: an analysis of devotional acts of offering in Buddhist Avadana literature', *History of Religions,* 18 (1979), pp.221–37
Subramanian K.S, *Buddhist Remains in South India and Early Andhra History 225 A.D. to 610 A.D.,* New Delhi 1981 (reprint)

8 The Buddhist Schools

Abhidharmakośa
—see bibliography to Chapter 10
Lokānuvartana Sūtra
—Harrison P, 'Sanskrit Fragments of a Lokottaravādin Tradition', from *Indological and Buddhist Studies,* ed. L.A. Hercus et al., Canberra 1982, pp.211–34 (partial translation)
Mahāvastu
—see bibliography to Chapter 2
Vibhāṣa
—see bibliography to Chapter 10 (under Sarvāstivādin)
Visuddhimagga
—see bibliography to Chapter 20

Bareau A, *Les sectes bouddhiques du petit véhicule,* Saigon 1955
Banerjee A.C, *Sarvāstivāda Literature,* Calcutta 1957
Bechert H, 'Studies on the Origin of Early Buddhist Schools, Their Language and Literature', from *Indology in India and Germany, Co-ordination and Co-operation,* ed. H. von Stietencron, Tübingen 1981
Bechert H, 'The Importance of Asoka's So-Called Schism Edict', in *Indological and Buddhist Studies,* ed. L.A. Hercus et al., Canberra 1982, pp.61–8
Cousins L, 'The "Five Points" and the Origins of the Buddhist Schools', from *Buddhist Forum: Seminar papers 1987–8,* ed. T. Skorupski, London 1990

Frauwallner E, *The Earliest Vinaya and the Beginnings of Buddhist Literature*, Rome 1956
Gupta R, '"Twelve-Membered Dependent Origination" An Attempted Reappraisal', JIP 5 (1977), pp.163–86
Jaini P.S, 'The Sautrāntika Theory of Bīja', BSOAS XXII (1959), pp.236–49
Kajiyama Y, 'Realism of the Sarvastivāda School', pp.114–19, fr. *Buddhist Thought and Asian Civilisation*, ed. L. Kawamura and K. Scott, pp.114–31
Khantipālo, *The Wheel of Birth and Death*, Wheel Series no.147–49, Kandy (no date)
Mitchell D.W, 'Analysis in Theravāda Buddhism', *Philosophy East and West* (1971) pp.23–31
Nattier J. and Prebish C, 'Mahāsaṁghika Origins: The Beginnings of Buddhist Sectarianism', *History of Religions* 16 (1977), pp.237–72
Thich Thien Chau 'The Literature of the Pudgalavādins', JIABS 7 (1984), pp.7–15
Wang B, 'Buddhist Nikāyas through Ancient Chinese Eyes', from *Buddhist Studies Present and Future (IABS 10th International Conference 1991)*, pp.65–72

9 THE TRIPIṬAKA

Since there are only piecemeal translations of the Chinese *Āgama* into English, the texts of what might be called the scriptural mainstream are only available from the Pāli recension, published by the Pali Text Society.

Vinaya Piṭaka
—Horner I.B, *The Book of the Discipline*, 6 vols., London (various dates)
—Rhys Davids T.W, Oldenberg H, *Vinaya Texts*, Delhi 1965 (*Pātimokkha, Mahāvagga* and *Culavagga* only)
—Prebish C, *Buddhist Monastic Discipline: The Sanskrit Prātimokṣa Sūtras of the Mahāsaṁghikas and Mūlasarvāstivādins*, Pennsylvania 1975

Sutta Piṭaka
—*Dīgha Nikāya*
—Rhys Davids T.W. and C.A.F, *Dialogues of the Buddha*, 3 vols., London 1899, 1910, 1921 (reprinted)
—*Majjhima Nikāya*
—Horner I.B, *Middle Length Sayings*, 3 vols., London 1954, 1957, 1959
—*Aṅguttara Nikāya*
—Woodward F.L. and Hare E.M, *The Book of the Gradual Sayings*, 5 vols., London 1932,–33,–34,–35,–36
—Thich Huyen-Vi 'L'Ekottarāgama traduit de la chinoise par Thich Huyen-Vi', *Buddhist Studies Review*, vol.1 (1984) *et sqq.* (from vol.10, 1993 onwards, in English translation)

—*Saṁyutta Nikāya*
—Rhys Davids C.A.F. and Woodward F.L, *The Book of the Kindred Sayings*, 5 vols., London 1917,–22,–24,–27,–30
—*Khuddhaka Nikāya*
—*Dhammapada*
—Nārada Thera, *The Dhammapada*, London 1954
—Carter J.R. and Palihawadana M, *The Dhammapada*, New York and Oxford 1987
—*Udāna*
—Woodward F.L, *Minor Anthologies vol.II*, London 1935 (reprinted)
—*Itivuttaka*
—ibid.
—*Suttanipāta*
—Norman K.R, *The Group of Discourses*, Oxford 1992
—Saddhatissa H, *The Sutta-nipāta*, London 1985
—*Theragāthā and Therīgāthā*
—Norman K.R, *Elders' Verses*, 2 vols., London 1969 and 1971
—Rhys Davids C.A.F, *Psalms of the Early Buddhists*, 2 vols., London 1909 and 1937
—Murcott S, *The First Buddhist Women, Translation and commentary on the Therīgāthā*, Berkeley 1991
—*Jātaka*
—Cowell E.B. et al. *The Jātaka or Stories of the Buddha's Former Births*, 3 vols., London 1981 (reprint)
—*Buddhavaṁsa*
—Horner I.B, *Minor Anthologies, vol.III*, London 1975
—*Cariyāpiṭaka*
—ibid.

Abhidharma Piṭaka
—See bibliography to Chapter 10

Bareau A, 'La composition et les étapes de la formation progressive du Mahāparinirvāṇasūtra ancien', BEFEO (66) 1979, pp.45–103
Bechert H, 'The Writing Down Of The Tripiṭaka In Pali', WZKS 36 (1992), pp.45–53
Collins S, 'On the Very Idea of the Pali Canon', JPTS XV (1990), pp.89–126
Collins S, 'Notes on Some Oral Aspects of Pali Literature', IIJ 35 (1992), pp.121–35
Cousins L, 'Pali Oral Literature', from *Buddhist Studies: Ancient and Modern*, ed. P. Denwood and A. Piatigorsky, London 1983, pp.1–11
Frauwallner E, *The Earliest Vinaya and the Beginnings of Buddhist Literature*, Rome 1956
Galloway B, 'Thus Have I Heard: At One Time…', IIJ 34 (1991), pp.87–104
Lamotte E, 'The Assessment of Textual Authenticity in Buddhism', *Buddhist Studies Review* 1.1 (1983–4) 4–15

Lamotte E, 'The Assessment of Textual Interpretation in Buddhism', *Buddhist Studies Review*, 2.1 (1985) pp.4–24

Levi S, 'Sur la Récitation Primitive des Textes Bouddhiques', *Journal Asiatiques*, 1915, pp.401–47

Link A.E, 'The Earliest Account of the Compilation of the Tripiṭaka I + II', JAOS 81 (1961), pp.87–103 and 281–99

Manné J, 'Categories of Sutta in the Pali Nikāyas and their Implications for Our Appreciation of the Buddhist Teaching and Literature', JPTS xv (1990), pp.29–87

Norman K.R, *Pali Literature: including the canonical literature in Prakrit and Sanskrit of all the Hīnayāna schools*, Wiesbaden 1983

Prebish C, 'Theories Concerning the Skandhaka: An Appraisal', *Journal of Asian Studies*, 32.4. (1973), pp.669–78

Prebish C, 'The Pratimoksa Puzzle: Fact versus Fantasy', JAOS 94 (1974), pp.168–76

Prebish C, 'Vinaya and Pratimoksa: The Foundation of Buddhist Ethics', from *Studies in the History of Buddhism*, ed. A.K. Narain, Delhi 1980, pp.223–64

Sangharakshita *The Eternal Legacy: An Introduction to the Canonical Literature of Buddhism*, London 1985

Strong J, 'The Buddhist Avadānists and the Elder Upagupta', *Mélanges Chinois et Bouddhiques* 22 (1985), pp.862–81

Thich Minh Chau *The Chinese Madhyama Āgama and the Pāli Majjhima Nikāya: a comparative study*, Delhi 1991

Thomas E.J, *The History of Buddhist Thought*, 2nd ed., London 1951

Wijayaratna M, *Buddhist Monastic Life: according to the texts of the Theravāda tradition*, Cambridge 1990

10 The Abhidharma

Abhidhamma Piṭaka

Theravādin

Dhammasaṅgaṇī

—Rhys Davids C.A.F. *Buddhist Psychological Ethics*, London 1974 3rd ed.

Vibhaṅga

—Thittila U, *The Book of Analysis*, London 1969

Dhātukathā

—Narada U, *Discourse on Elements*, London 1962

Puggalapaññatti

—Law B.C, *A Designation of Human Types*, London 1922

Kathāvatthu

—Aung S.Z. and Rhys Davids C.A.F. *Points of Controversy*, London 1915

Paṭṭhāna

—Narada U, *Conditional Relations*, 2 vols., London 1969 and 1981 (partial translation only, with commentary)

Yamaka
—(no translation)

Sarvāstivādin
A summary of the seven books of the Sarvāstivādin Abhidharma is given in L. de La Vallée Poussin's Introduction to his translation of the *Abhidharmakośa*, pp.1–53. Sarvāstivādin Abhidharma literature surviving in Chinese is surveyed in Takakusu 1904–5.

—de La Vallée Poussin L, 'Documents d'Abhidharma: Textes relatifs au Nirvāṇa' BEFEO 30 (1930), pp.1–28 and 247–98
—de La Vallée Poussin L, 'Documents d'Abhidharma – traduits et annotés', *Mélanges Chinois et Bouddhiques*, 1 (1931–2), pp.65–109
(These two works contain translations of passages from various texts, including the *Vibhāṣā*.)
—Hurvitz L, 'Path to Salvation in Jñāna-Prasthāna' in *Studies in Indo-Asian Art and Culture*, ed. L. Chandra and P. Ratnam, New Delhi 1977, pp.77–102 (small section of the *Jñānaprasthāna*)

Abhidharmakośa
—de La Vallée Poussin L, *Abhidharmakośabhāṣyam*, English translation by L.M. Pruden, Berkeley California 1988, 4 vols.
Satyasiddhiśāstra
—Sastri N.A, *Satyasiddhiśāstra of Harivarman*, vol.2 (English translation), Baroda 1978

Bareau A, 'Les sectes bouddhiques du Petit Véhicule et leurs Abhidharmapiṭaka' BEFEO 50 (1952), pp.1–11
Gethin R, 'The 5 Khandas: Their treatment in the Nikayas and early Abhidhamma', JIP 14 (1986), pp.35–53
Gethin R, 'The Mātikās: Memorization, Mindfulness, and the List', in *In the Mirror of Memory: Reflections on Mindfulness and Remembrance in Indian and Tibetan Buddhism*, Albany 1992, pp.149–72
Govinda, Lama *The Psychological Attitude of Early Buddhist Philosophy*, London 1961
Guenther H.V, *Philosophy and Psychology in the Abhidharma*, 2nd ed., Berkeley 1974
Jaini P.S, *Abhidharmadīpa with Vibhāṣāprabhāvṛtti*, Patna 1959 (a lengthy and important introduction)
Nyanatiloka *Guide Through the Abhidhamma-Piṭaka*, 3rd ed., Kandy 1971
Potter K.H, Buswell R, Jaini P.S, and Ross Reat N, *Encyclopaedia of Indian Philosophies – vol.VII: Abhidharma Buddhism to 150 A.D.*, Delhi (forthcoming)
Pruden L.M, 'The Abhidharma: The Origins, Growth and Development of a Literary Tradition', introductory essay to *Abhidharmakoṣabhāṣyam*, tr. L. de La Vallée Poussin, vol.1

Stcherbatsky T, *The Central Conception of Buddhism and the Meaning of the Word 'Dharma'*, 4th ed., Delhi 1970
Takakusu J, 'On the Abhidharma Literature of the Sarvāstivādins', JPTS 14 (1904–5), pp.67–146
Warder A.K, 'Dharmas and Data', JIP 1 (1971) 272–95
Watanabe F, *Philosophy and its Development in the Nikāyas and Abhidhamma*, Delhi 1983

11 Origins of the Mahāyāna

Tārānātha, *History of Buddhism in India*, tr. L. Chimpa and D. Chattopadhyaya, Simla 1970

Ajitasena Sūtra
—Dutt N, *Gilgit Manuscripts vol. 1*, Srinagar 1939, pp.73–90 (summary)
Ugradattaparipṛcchā Sūtra
—Schuster N.J, 'The Ugraparipṛcchā, the Mahāratnakūṭasūtra and Early Mahāyāna Buddhism' (Ph.D thesis), University of Toronto 1976

For translations of the other sūtras mentioned in this chapter see bibliography to Chapter 12

Bechert H, 'Notes on the Formation of Buddhist Sects and the Origins of the Mahāyāna', in *German Scholars on India, contributions to Indian studies*, ed. Cultural Department of the Embassy of the Federal Republic of Germany, New Delhi, Varanasi 1973, pp.6–18
Beyer S, 'Notes on the Vision Quest in Early Mahāyāna', *Prajñāpāramitā and Related Systems*, ed. Lewis Lancaster, Berkeley 1977, pp.329–40
Gombrich R, 'How the Mahāyāna Began', from *The Buddhist Forum: Seminar papers 1987–8*, ed. T. Skorupski, London 1990, pp.21–30
Gombrich R, 'A momentous effect of translation: The "vehicles of Buddhism"', from *Apodosis: Essays presented to Dr W.W. Cruickshank to mark his 80th birthday*, London 1992, pp.34–46
Hardy F, 'Mahāyāna Buddhism and Buddhist Philosophy' from *The World's Religions: The Religions of Asia*, ed. F. Hardy, London 1990, pp.627–37
Harrison P, 'Who gets to Ride in the Great Vehicle? Self-Image and Identity Among the Followers of the Early Mahāyāna', JIABS 10 (1987), pp.67–89
Harrison P, 'Commemoration and Identification in Buddhānusmṛti', from *In the Mirror of Memory, Reflections on Mindfulness and Memory in Indian and Tibetan Buddhism*, ed. J. Gyatso, Albany 1992
Hirakawa A, 'The Rise of Mahāyāna Buddhism and its Relationship to the Worship of Stupas', *Memoirs of the Research Dept. of The Toyo Bunko (The Oriental Library)* no.22 (1963), pp.57–106
Kent S.A, 'A Sectarian Interpretation of the Rise of Mahāyāna', *Religion* 12 (1982), pp.311–32
Lamotte E, 'Sur la formation du Mahāyāna', from *Asiatica, Festschrift Friedrich Weller*, Leipzig 1954, pp.377–96

Pande S, 'Conceptual Background of the Development of Bhakti in Mahāyāna Buddhism', *Buddhist Studies* 6 (1979), pp.74–85
Rawlinson A, 'Visions and Symbols in the Mahāyāna', from *Studies in the History of Buddhism*, ed. A.K. Narain, Delhi 1980, pp.191–214
Rawlinson A, 'The Problem of the Origin of the Mahāyāna', from *Traditions in Contact and Change*, ed. P. Slater and D. Wiebe (1983), pp.163–70 and 693–99
Ross Reat N, 'The Śālistamba Sūtra and the Origins of Mahāyāna Buddhism', from *Buddhist Studies Present and Future (IABS 10th International Conference 1991)*, pp.137–43
Rowell T, 'The Background and Early Use of the Buddhaksetra Concept' (in 3 parts) *The Eastern Buddhist*, I and II 6 (1935), pp.199–246 and 379–431; III 7 (1936), pp.131–76
Schopen G, 'The Phrase "sa pṛthivīpradeśaś caityabhūto bhavet" in the Vajracchedikā: Notes on the Cult of the Book in Mahāyāna', IIJ 17 (1975), pp.147–81
Schopen G, 'Mahāyāna in Indian Inscriptions', IIJ 21 (1979), pp.1–19
Schopen G, 'The Inscription on the Kusan Image of Amitabha and the Character of early Mahāyāna in India', JIABS 10 (1987), pp.99–137
Schopen G, 'On Monks, Nuns and "Vulgar" Practices: The Introduction of the Image Cult into Indian Buddhism', *Artibus Asiae* 49 (1988–9), pp.153–68
Schopen G, 'An Old Inscription from Amarāvatī and the Cult of the Local Monastic Dead in Indian Buddhist Monasteries', JIABS 14 (1991) pp.281–329
Schopen G, 'On Avoiding Ghosts and Social Censure: Monastic Funerals in the Mūlasarvāstivāda-Vinaya', JIP 20 (1992), pp.1–39
Shizutani M, 'Mahāyāna Inscriptions in the Gupta Period', IBK 19 (1962), pp.358–55 (47–50)
Warder A.K, '"Original" Buddhism and Mahāyāna', *Pubblicazioni di 'Indologica Taurinensia' Callana di Letture diretta da Oscar Botto* XVI, Torino (1983), pp.5–43
Yoshimura S, 'The People of the Early Mahāyānistic Order', IBK xiv (1966), pp.968–62 (29–35)

12 The Mahāyāna Sūtras

Akṣobhyavyūha Sūtra
—Dantine J, *La Splendeur de l'Inébranlable (Akṣobhyavyūha)*, Louvain-la-Neuve 1983
Avataṁsaka Sūtra
—Cleary T, *The Flower Ornament Scripture: a translation of the Avatamsaka Sutra*, 3 vols., Boston 1984, 1986, and 1987

Bhaiṣajyaguru
—Birnbaum R, *The Healing Buddha*, Boston 1989, revised ed. (contains translations from the Chinese of four sūtras on Bhaiṣajyaguru)
Brahmajāla Sūtra
—Groot J.J.M, *Le code du Mahāyāna en Chine*, Amsterdam 1893
Daśabhūmika Sūtra
—Honda M, 'Annotated Translation of the Daśabhūmika-sūtra (revised by Johannes Rahder)', in *Studies in South, East, and Central Asia*, ed. D. Sinor, New Delhi 1968, pp.115–276
Gaṇḍavyūha Sūtra
—Cleary T, *Entry into the Realm of Reality: The text: A translation of the Gandavyūha, the final book of the Avatamsaka Sutra*, Boston 1989
Kāraṇḍa-vyūha Sūtra
—Thomas E.J, *The Perfection of Wisdom*, London 1952, pp.72–8 (ch.1 only)
Kāśyapa-parivarta Sūtra
—(see ch.16 of Chang's translation of the *Mahāratnakūṭa Sūtra*)
Kṣitigarbha
—Heng Ching *Sūtra of the Past Vows of Earth Store Bodhisattva*, New York 1974
Mahāratnakūṭa Sūtra
—Chang G.C.C, *A Treasury of Mahāyāna Sūtras: Selections from the Mahāratnakūṭa Sūtra*, Pennsylvania and London 1983 (contains 22 of the 49 sūtras in this collection)
—Regamey K, *The Bhadramāyākāravyākaraṇa*, Delhi 1990 (Sūtra 21 of the *Mahāratnakūṭa Sūtra*)
Mahāsaṁnipāta Sūtra
—Only one sūtra from this collection has been translated into English in full (see *Akṣayamatinirdeśa Sūtra* below), although several are quoted in part in Śāntideva's *Śikṣāsamuccaya* (see below)
Maitreyavyākaraṇa
—Conze E, *Buddhist Scriptures*, Harmondsworth 1959 (partial translation pp.238–42)
Mañjuśrī-buddhakṣetra-guṇa-vyūha
—see ch.10 of Chang's translation of the *Mahāratnakūṭa Sūtra*
Prajñāpāramitā Sūtras
—Conze E, *The Perfection of Wisdom in Eight Thousand Lines and its Verse Summary*, San Francisco 1973 (*Aṣṭasāhasrikā-prajñāpāramitā Sūtra and Ratnaguṇasaṁcayagāthā*)
—Conze E, *The Short Prajñāpāramitā Texts*, London 1973 (containing 21 short *prajñāpāramitā* texts, including the *Vajracchedikā-prajñāpāramitā Sūtra* and the *Heart Sūtra*)
—Conze E, *The Large Sūtra on Perfect Wisdom*, Delhi 1979 (the *Prajñāpāramitā Sūtra* in 18,000 lines)
Pratyutpanna Sūtra
—Harrison P, *The Samādhi of Direct Encounter with the Buddhas of the Present*, Tokyo 1990

Saddharma-puṇḍarīka Sūtra
—Hurvitz L, *Scripture of the Lotus Blossom of the Fine Dharma: Translated form the Chinese of Kumārajīva*, New York 1976
—Kern H, *Saddharmapuṇḍarīka or the Lotus of the True Law*, New York 1963 (reprint) (the only translation from the original Sanskrit to date, but not reliable)
—Watson B, *The Lotus Sūtra*, New York 1993 (the latest translation from the Chinese)
Saddharmasmṛtyupasthāna Sūtra
—Lin L, *L'Aide-mémoire de la Vraie Loi*, Paris 1949
Śālistamba Sūtra
—Ross Reat N, *The Śālistambha Sūtra*, Delhi (forthcoming 1991)
Samādhirāja Sūtra
—Cüppers C, *The IXth Chapter of the Samādhirāja Sūtra – A text critical contribution to the study of Mahāyāna sūtras*, Stuttgart 1990
—Gomez L. and Silk J, *Studies in the Literature of the Great Vehicle – Three Mahāyāna Buddhist Texts*, Ann Arbor (chs.1–4)
—Regamey K, *Three Chapters of the Samādhirāja Sūtra*, New Delhi 1990 (chs.8, 19, and 22)
Sukhāvatīvyūha Sūtras
—Müller M, 'The Larger Sukhāvatī-Vyūha' and 'The Smaller Sukhāvatī-Vyūha' in *Buddhist Mahāyāna Texts*, ed. E.B. Cowell et al., Delhi 1965
—see ch.18 of Chang's translation of the *Mahāratnakūṭa Sūtra*
Śūraṅgama-samādhi Sūtra
—Lamotte E, *La Concentration de la Marche Héroïque (Śūraṁgamasamādhisūtra), Mélanges Chinois et Bouddhiques*, XIII (1965)
Suvarṇa-prabhāsa Sūtra
—Emmerick R.E, *The Sūtra of Golden Light: Being a Translation of the Suvarṇaprabhāsottamasūtra*, Oxford 1990 2nd (revised) ed.
Triskandha Sūtra
—Beresford B.C, *Mahāyāna Purification: The Confession Sūtra with commentary by Ārya Nāgārjuna*, Dharamsala 1980
Upāli-paripṛcchā Sūtra
—Python P, *Vinaya-viniścaya-Upāli-paripṛcchā: Enquête d'Upāli pour une exégèse de la discipline*, Paris 1973
—see ch.15 of Chang's translation of the *Mahāratnakūṭa Sūtra*
Vimalakīrti-nirdeśa Sūtra
—Lamotte E, *The Teaching of Vimalakīrti (Vimalakīrtinirdeśa)*, English tr. S. Boin, London 1976
—Thurman R.A.F, *The Holy Teaching of Vimalakīrti: A Mahāyāna Scripture*, Pennsylvania and London 1976

Mahāyāna Sūtras and texts not mentioned in the chapter
Akṣayamatinirdeśa Sūtra
—Braarvig J, *The Tradition of Imperishability in Buddhist Thought*, 2 vols., Oslo 1993 (Part 12 of the *Mahāsaṁnipāta Sūtra*)
Karuṇāpuṇḍarīka Sūtra
—Yamada I, *The Karuṇāpuṇḍarīka Sūtra*, 2 vols., London 1968 (summary only)
Rāṣṭrapālaparipṛcchā Sūtra
—Ensink J, *The Questions of Rāṣṭrapāla*, Zwolle 1952
Śikṣāsamuccaya
—Bendall C. and Rowse W.H.D, *Śikṣā-samuccaya: A Compendium of Buddhist Doctrine*, 2nd ed., Delhi 1971 (consists largely of quotations from Mahāyāna sūtras)

Conze E, *The Prajñāpāramitā Literature*, 2nd (revised) ed., Tokyo 1978
Davidson R.M, 'An Introduction to the Standards of Scriptural Authenticity in Indian Buddhism', appendix from *Chinese Buddhist Apocrypha*, ed. R. Buswell, Honolulu 1990, pp.291–325
de Breet J, 'The Concept Upāyakauśalya in the Aṣṭasāhasrikā Prajñāpāramitā', WZKS 36 (1992), pp.203–15
Eracle J, *La doctrine bouddhique de la Terre Pure*, Paris 1973
Fuss M, *Buddhavacana and Dei Verbum: A Phenomenological and Theological Comparison of Scriptural Inspiration in the Saddharmapuṇḍarīka Sūtra and in the Christian Tradition*, Leiden 1991
Hamlin E, 'Magical Upāya in the Vimalakīrtinirdeśa-sūtra', JIABS 11 (1988), pp.89–121
Harrison P, 'Buddhānusmṛti in the Pratyutpanna Sūtra', JIP 6 (1978), pp.35–57
Lamotte E, *Le Traité de la grande vertu de sagesse de Nāgārjuna*, Louvain, I 1944 (chs.1–15); II 1949 (chs.16–30); III 1970 (chs.31–42); IV 1976 (chs.42–8); V 1980 (chs.20 and 49–52)
Lancaster L, 'An Analysis of the Aṣṭasāhasrikā-prajñāpāramitā Sūtra from the Chinese translations' (Ph.D. thesis), University of Wisconsin 1968
Lopez D.S, *The Heart Sūtra Explained: Indian and Tibetan Commentaries*, Albany 1988
MacQueen G, 'Inspired Speech in Early Mahāyāna', I *Religion* 11 (1981), pp.303–19; II *Religion* 12 (1982), pp.49–65
McDermott J, 'Scripture as the Word of the Buddha', *Numen* XXXI, pp.22–39
Nattier J, 'The Heart Sūtra: A Chinese Apocryphal Text?', JIABS 15 (1992), pp.153–223
Pedersen P, 'Notes on the Ratnakūṭa Collection', JIABS 3 (1980), pp.60–6
Pye M, *Skilful Means: A concept in Mahāyāna Buddhism*, London 1978
Rawlinson A, 'Studies in the Lotus Sūtra (Saddharmapuṇḍarīka Sūtra)', 2 vols. (Ph.D. thesis), Lancaster 1972
Rawlinson A, 'Spiritual Practice in the Saddharmapuṇḍarīka Sūtra', *Wege zur Ganzheit, Festschrift Lama Anagarika Govinda*, Almora 1973, pp.110–43

Rawlinson A, 'The Position of the Aṣṭasāhasrikā-prajñāpāramitā Sūtra in the Development of Early Mahāyāna', from *Prajñāpāramitā and Related Systems*, ed. Lewis Lancaster, Berkeley 1977, pp.3–34
Sangharakshita *The Drama of Cosmic Enlightenment: Parables, Myths, and Symbols of the White Lotus Sutra*, Glasgow 1993
Sangharakshita *Wisdom Beyond Words: Sense and Non-Sense in the Buddhist Prajñāpāramitā Tradition*, Glasgow 1993
Schopen G, 'Sukhavati as a Generalised Religious Goal in Sanskrit Mahāyāna Sūtra Literature', IIJ 19 (1977), pp.177–210
Snellgrove D, 'Note on the Adhyāsayasaṁcodana Sūtra', BSOAS XXI (1958), pp.620–23

13 The Bodhisattva

Bodhicaryāvatāra
—Batchelor S, *A Guide to the Bodhisattva's Way of Life*, Dharamsala, 1979 (translated from the Tibetan translation)
—Crosby K. and Skilton A, *The Bodhicaryāvatāra*, Oxford 1996 (translated, with introduction and full annotation, from the Sanskrit original)
Bhadracarīpraṇidhānagāthā
—Izumi H, 'The Hymn of the Life and Vows of Samantabhadra, with the Sanskrit Text: Bhadracarīpraṇidhāna', *Eastern Buddhist* 5 (1929–31), pp.226–47
—Asmussen J.P, *The Khotanese Bhadracaryādeśanā*, København 1961
—see *Gaṇḍavyūha Sūtra* in bibliography to Chapter 12
Daśabhūmika Sūtra
—see bibliography to Chapter 12
Pāramitāsamāsa
—Meadows C, *Āryaśūra's Compendium of the Perfections: Text, translation and analysis of the Pāramitāsamāsa*, Bonn 1986
Sādhanas
—Beresford B. et al., *Āryaśūra's Aspiration and A Meditation on Compassion*, Dharamsala 1979 (contains an Avalokiteśvara *sādhana*, pp.65–107)
—Khetsun Sangpo and Hopkins J, *Tantric Practice in Nying-ma*, London 1982 (contains a Vajrasattva *sādhana*, pp.141–53)
—Mañjuśrī Institute, *Mañjuśrī Sādhana*, Cumbria 1983
—Willson M, *In Praise of Tārā: Songs to the Saviouress*, London 1986 (contains Tārā *sādhanas*, pp.329–50)

Basham A.L, 'The Evolution of the Concept of the Bodhisattva', from *The Bodhisattva Doctrine in Buddhism*, ed. L. Kawamura, Waterloo 1981, pp.19–59
Blofeld J, *Compassion Yoga: The Mystical Cult of Kuan Yin*, London 1977
Dayal H, *The Bodhisattva Doctrine in Buddhist Sanskrit Literature*, London 1932 (reprinted Delhi 1978)

Gomez L, 'The Bodhisattva as Wonder-worker', from *Prajñāpāramitā and Related Systems*, ed. Lewis Lancaster, Berkeley 1977, pp.221–61

Lamotte E, 'Mañjuśrī', *T'oung Pao* 48 (1960), pp.1–96

Landow J. and Weber A, *Images of Enlightenment, Tibetan Art in Practice*, Ithaca NY 1993

Lethcoe N.R, 'The Bodhisattva Ideal in the Aṣṭasāhasrikā and Pañcaviṁśati-prajñāpāramitā Sūtras', from *Prajñāpāramitā and Related Systems*, ed. Lewis Lancaster, Berkeley 1977, pp.263–80

Schumann H.W, *Buddhistische Bilderwelt, Ein ikonographisches Handbuch des Mahāyāna- und Tantrayāna-Buddhismus*, München 1986

Schuster N.J, 'The Bodhisattva Figure in the Ugraparipṛcchā', from *New Paths in Buddhist Research*, ed. A.K. Warder, Durham NC 1985, pp.26–55

Sinha B.M, 'Metamorphosis of Avalokiteśvara: from the Saddharmapuṇḍarīka to the Kāraṇḍavyūha', from *Buddhist Studies Present and Future (IABS 10th International Conference 1991)*, pp.168–80

Sponberg A, *Maitreya the Future Buddha*, ed. A. Sponberg and H. Hardacre, Cambridge 1988

Vessantara, *Meeting the Buddhas: a Guide to Buddhas, Bodhisattvas, and Tantric Deities*, Glasgow 1993

14 The Madhyamaka

Bodhicaryāvatāra

—see bibliography to Chapter 13

Catuḥśataka

—Bhattacarya V, 'The Catuḥśataka of Āryadeva, with Extracts from the Commentary of Candrakīrti. Reconstructed from the Tibetan Version with an English Tr. Chapter VII', in *Proceedings and Transactions of the Fourth Oriental Conference, Allahabad University, November 5, 6, and 7, 1926*, vol.2, Allahabad 1928, pp.831–71

—Vaidya P.L, *Études sur Āryadeva et son Catuśataka, chapitres VIII–XVI*, Paris 1923

Mūlamadhyamakakārikā

—Inada K.K, *Nāgārjuna, A Translation of His Mūlamadhyamaka-kārikā with an Introductory essay*, Tokyo 1970

—Kalupahana D.J, *Mūlamadhyamakakārikā of Nāgārjuna: The Philosophy of the Middle Way*, Delhi 1991

Suhṛllekhā

—Lozang Jamspal, Ngawang Samten Chopel, and P. Santina, *Nāgārjuna's Letter to King Gautamīputra*, Delhi 1978

Tattvasaṁgraha

—Jha G, *The Tattvasaṁgraha of Śāntarakṣita: with the commentary of Kamalaśīla*, 2 vols., Vadodara (India) 1991 (reprint)

Vigrahavyāvartanī
—Johnston E.H, and Kunst A, 'The Vigrahavyāvartanī of Nāgārjuna with the Author's Commentary', *Mélanges Chinois et Bouddhiques* ix (1948–51), pp.99–151

Gomez L, 'Proto-Mādhyamika in the Pali-Canon', *Philosophy East and West* 26 (1976), pp.137–65
Katz N, 'An Appraisal of the Svatantrika-Prasangika Debates', *Philosophy East and West* 26 (1976), pp.253–67
Lindtner C, *Nagarjuniana: Studies in the writings and philosophy of Nāgārjuna*, Delhi 1987
Lopez D.S, *A Study of Svātantrika*, Ithaca NY 1987
Ruegg D.S, 'The Uses of the Four Positions of the Catuṣkoṭi and the Problem of the Description of Reality in Mahāyāna Buddhism', JIP 5 (1977), pp.1–71
Ruegg D.S, *The Literature of the Madhyamaka School of Philosophy in India*, Wiesbaden 1981
Ruegg D.S, 'Towards a Chronology of the Madhyamaka School', from *Indological and Buddhist Studies*, ed. L.A. Hercus et al., Canberra 1982, pp.505–30
Warder A.K, 'Is Nāgārjuna a Mahāyānist?' from *The Problem of Two Truths in Buddhism and Vedanta*, ed. M. Sprung, Dordrecht 1973

15 The Yogācāra

Abhidharmakośa
—see bibliography to Chapter 10
Abhidharmasamuccaya
—Rahula W, *Le Compendium de la super-doctrine (Philosophie) (Abhidharmasamuccaya) d'Asaṅga*, Paris 1971
Abhisamayālaṁkāra
—Conze E, *Abhisamayālaṁkāra: Introduction and Translation from the Original Text with Sanskrit-Tibetan Index*, Rome 1954
Daśabhūmika Sūtra
—see bibliography to Chapter 12
Laṅkāvatāra Sūtra
—Suzuki D.T, *The Lankavatara Sutra: A Mahayana Text*, London 1932
Madhyāntavibhāga
—Stcherbatsky T, *Madhyānta-Vibhaṅga: Discourse on Discrimination between Middle and Extremes Ascribed to Bodhisattva Maitreya*, Calcutta 1970 (reprint) chs.1–5
Mahāyānasaṁgraha
—Griffiths P. et al., *The Realm of Awakening: A Translation and Study of the Tenth Chapter of Asaṅga's Mahāyānasaṁgraha*, New York 1989
—Lamotte E, *La Somme de Grand Véhicule d'Asaṅga (Mahāyānasaṁgraha)*, 2 vols., Paris 1938–9

Mahāyānasūtrālaṁkāra
—Lévi S, *Asaṅga: Mahāyānasūtrālaṁkāra. Exposé de la Doctrine du Grand Véhicule selon le Système Yogācāra*, 2 vols., Paris 1907–11
Pramāṇasamuccaya
—Hattori M, *Dignāga: On Perception, Being the Pratyakṣaparicchedа of Dignāga's Pramāṇasamuccaya*, Cambridge Mass. 1968, ch.1
—Hayes R, 'Diṅnāga's Views on Reasoning (Svārtānumāna)', JIP 8 (1980), pp.247–60, part of ch.2
Pramāṇavārttika
—Mookerjee S. and Nagasaki H, *The Pramāṇavarttikam of Dharmakīrti*, Patna 1964, ch.1
Pratyutpanna Sūtra
—see bibliography to Chapter 12
Saṁdhinirmocana Sūtra
—Lamotte E, *Saṁdhinirmocana Sūtra: L'Explication des mystères*, Paris 1935
Triṁśikā
—Anacker S, *Seven Works of Vasubandhu*, Delhi 1984
Viṁśatikā
—ibid.
Trisvabhāva Nirdeśa
—ibid.
—Tola F. and Dragonetti C, 'The Trisvabhāvakārikā of Vasubandhu', JIP 11 (1983), pp.225–66
Yogācārabhūmi
—Demiéville P, 'Le chapitre de la Bodhisattvabhūmi sur la Perfection du Dhyāna', in *Choix d'études bouddhiques*, Leiden 1973, pp.304–19, part 1, section 15 (part)
—Wayman A, *Analysis of the Śrāvakabhūmi Manuscript*, Berkeley 1961, part 1, section 13 (part)
—Willis J.D, *On Knowing Reality: The Tattvārtha Chapter of Asaṅga's Bodhisattvabhūmi*, New York 1979, part 1, section 15 (part)

Frauwallner E, *On the Date of the Buddhist Master of the Law Vasubandhu*, Rome 1951

Gadjin Nagao 'On the Theory of Buddha-Body (Buddha-kāya)', *The Eastern Buddhist* n.s. 6 (1973), pp.25–53

Harrison P, 'Is the *Dharma-kāya* the Real "Phantom Body" of the Buddha?', JIABS 15 (1992) pp.44–93

Keenan J.P, 'Original Purity and the Focus of Early Yogācāra', JIABS 5 (1982), pp.7–18

McDermott A, 'Asaṅga's Defense of Ālayavijñāna', JIP 2 (1973), pp.167–74

Olson R.F, 'Candrakīrti's critique of *Vijñānavāda*', *Philosophy East and West* 25 (1975), pp.405–11

Powers J, *The Yogācāra School of Buddhism: A Bibliography*, Metuchen NJ and London 1991

Powers J, *Hermeneutics and Tradition in the Sandhinirmocana Sūtra*, Leiden 1993
Schopen G, 'The Buddha as an Owner of Property and Permanent Resident in Medieval Indian Monasteries', JIP 18 (1990), pp.181–217
Schmithausen L, *Ālayavijñāna, On the Origin and the Early Development of a Central Concept of Yogācāra Philosophy*, Tokyo 1987
Sponberg A, 'The Trisvabhāva Doctrine in India and China – A Study of Three Exegetical Models', *Ryūkoku Daigaku Bukkyo Bunka Kenkyūjo kiyo* xxl (1983), pp.97–119
Suzuki D.T, *Studies in the Lankavatara Sutra*, London 1930
de La Vallée Poussin L, 'Le petit traité de Vasubandhu-Nāgārjuna sur les trois natures', *Mélanges Chinois et Bouddhiques*, i (1931–2), pp.147–61

16 The Tathāgatagarbha Doctrine

Awakening of Faith in the Mahāyāna
—Hakeda Y, *The Awakening of Faith*, New York 1967
Mahāparinirvāṇa Sūtra
—Yamomoto K, *The Mahāyāna Mahāparinirvāṇa-Sūtra*, 3 vols., Ube City 1974
Mahāyānasūtralaṁkāra
—see bibliography to Chapter 15
Ratnagotravibhāga
—Holmes K. and Holmes K, tr. *The Changeless Nature (the mahāyānottaratantraśāstra)*, 2nd ed., Eskdalemuir 1985
—Takasaki J, *A Study on the Ratnagotravibhāga (Uttaratantra)*, Rome 1966
Śrīmālādevī-siṁhanāda Sūtra
—Wayman A. and Wayman H, *The Lion's Roar of Queen Śrīmālā: A Buddhist Scripture on the Tathāgatagarbha Theory*, New York and London 1974
Tathāgatagarbha Sūtra
—(no translation)

Brown B.E, *The Buddha-nature: A Study of the Tathāgatagarbha and Ālayavijñāna*, Delhi 1990
Liebenthal W, 'New Light on the Mahāyānaśraddhotpāda-śāstra', *T'oung Pao*, 46 (1958), pp.155–216
Ruegg D.S, *La Théorie du Tathāgatagarbha et du Gotra*, Paris 1969
Takasaki J, 'Tathāgatagarbha and the Community of Bodhisattvas', from *Kalyāṇa Mitta – volume in honour of Prof. H. Nakamura*, Delhi 1991, pp.247–55
Wayman A, 'The Mahāsaṁghika and the Tathāgatagarbha', JIABS 1 (1978), pp.35–50

17 The Tantra and Vajrayāna Buddhism

Aparimitāyurjñānahṛdayadhāraṇī
—Walleser M, *Aparimitāyur-jñāna-nāma-mahāyāna-sūtram*, Heidelberg 1916

Āryamañjuśrīmūlakalpa
—Lalou M, *Iconographie des Étoffes Paintes dans le Mañjuśrīmūlakalpa*, Paris 1930
—Macdonald A, *Le maṇḍala du Mañjuśrīmūlakalpa*, Paris 1962
Caṇḍamahāroṣaṇa Tantra
—George C.S, *The Caṇḍamahāroṣaṇatantra*, New Haven 1974
Caryāgīti
—Kvaerne P, *An Anthology of Buddhist Tantric Songs*, 2nd ed., Bangkok 1986
Dohakośa
—Guenther H.V, *The Royal Song of Saraha*, Berkeley 1973
Guhyasamāja Tantra
—Fremantle F, 'Chapter Seven of the Guhyasamāja Tantra', in *Indo-Tibetan Studies*, ed. T. Skorupski, Tring 1990, pp.101–14
—Wayman A, *Yoga of the Guhyasamājatantra: The Arcane Lore of Forty Verses*, New York 1980
Hevajra Tantra
—Snellgrove D, *The Hevajra Tantra: A Critical Study*, 2 vols., London 1959
Kālacakra Tantra
—Sopa G.L, Jackson R, Newman J, *The Wheel of Time: The Kālachakra in Context*, Madison, Wisconsin 1985
—Dalai Lama, Hopkins J, *The Kālachakra Tantra. Rite of Initiation for the Stage of Generation*, London 1985
—Dhargyey G.N, *A Commentary on the Kālachakra Tantra*, Dharamsala 1985
Mahāmegha Sūtra
—Bendall C, 'The Mahāmegha Sūtra' JRAS (1880), pp.286–311
Mahāvairocanābhisaṁbodhi Tantra
—Yamamoto C, *Mahāvairocana-Sūtra. Translated into English from the Chinese version of Śubhākarasiṁha and I-hsing (A.D. 725)*, New Delhi 1990
Mañjuśrīnāmasaṁgīti
—Davidson R.M, 'The Litany of Names of Mañjuśrī - Text and Translation of Mañjuśrīnāmasaṁgīti', *Mélanges Chinois et Bouddhiques* 20 (1981), pp.1–69
—Wayman A, *Chanting the Names of Mañjuśrī*, Boston, Mass. 1985
Mettā Sutta
—see *Sutta Nipāta* in bibliography to Chapter 9
parittā
—Lokuliyana L, *Catubhāṇavārapāli, The Text of the Four Recitals, or The Great Book of Protections, Sinhala – Maha Pirit Pota*, pub. Mrs H.H. Gunasekera Trust, Colombo (no date)
—Piyadassi Thera *The Book of Protection*, Kandy 1981
Sādhanamālā
—(no translation)
Saṁvarodaya Tantra
—Tsuda S, *The Saṁvarodaya Tantra (Selected Chapters)*, Tokyo 1974

Sarvadurgatipariśodhana Tantra
—Skorupski T, *The Sarvadurgatipariśodhana Tantra. Elimination of All Evil Destinies*, Delhi 1983
Sarvatathāgatatattvasaṁgraha Tantra
—Chandra L. and Snellgrove D, *Sarvatathāgatatattvasaṁgraha: a facsimile reproduction of a tenth century Sanskrit manuscript from Nepal*, New Delhi 1981 (contains a useful Introduction)

Other primary sources

Dowman K, *Masters of Mahāmudra. Songs and Histories of the Eighty-Four Buddhist Siddhas*, Albany 1985
Guenther H.V, *The Life and Teaching of Nāropa*, Oxford 1963
Lessing F.D. and Wayman A, *Fundamentals of the Buddhist Tantras*, The Hague 1968
Robinson J.B, *Buddha's Lions: The Lives of the Eighty-Four Siddhas*, Berkeley California 1980
Wayman A, *The Buddhist Tantras: Light on Indo-Tibetan Esotericism*, New York 1973

Beyer S, *The Cult of Tārā*, California 1973
Gombrich R, 'Who was Aṅgulimāla?', Jordan Lecture at the School of Oriental and African Studies, 16 November 1994 (forthcoming)
Huntington J, 'Note on a Chinese Text Demonstrating the Earliness of Tantra', JIABS 10 (1987), pp.88–98
Katz N, 'Indrabhūti's rDo rJe Theg pa'i rTsa ba dang yan 'Lag gi lTung ba'i bShags pa: A Tantric Confessional Text', from *Tibetan Studies in Honour of Hugh Richardson*, ed. M. Aris and Aung San Suu Kyi, Warminster 1980, pp.169–76
Matsunaga Y, 'A History of Tantric Buddhism in India (with reference to Chinese Translations)', in *Buddhist Thought and Asian Civilisation*, ed. L. Kawamura and K. Scott, Emeryville California 1977, pp.167–81
Newman J, 'Buddhist Sanskrit in the Kālacakra Tantra', JIABS 11 (1988), pp.123–40
Samuel G, *Civilized Shamans: Buddhism in Tibetan Societies*, Washington and London 1993
Sanderson A, 'Vajrayāna: Origin and Function', in *Buddhism Into the Year 2000*, ed. Mettanando Bhikkhu et al., Dhammakāya Foundation, Bangkok (in press)
Skilling P, 'The Rakṣā Literature of the Śrāvakayāna', JPTS XVI (1992), pp.109–82
Snellgrove D, *Indo-Tibetan Buddhism: Indian Buddhists and Their Tibetan Successors*, London 1987
bSod nams rgya mtsho, *The Ngor Maṇḍalas of Tibet*, plates, Tokyo 1989
Tucci G, *The Theory and Practice of the Maṇḍala*, London 1969

Wayman A, 'The 21 Praises of Tara, a syncretism of Saivism and Buddhism', from *Buddhist Insight; Essays by Alex Wayman*, ed. G. Elder, Delhi 1984, pp.441–51

18 The End of Buddhism in India

Vajrasūcī
—'The Vajrasuci of Asvaghosa', *Visva-Bharati Annals* 2 (1949), pp.123–84
Alberuni
—Sachau, E.C, *Alberuni's India – an account of the religion, philosophy, geography, chronology, astronomy, customs, laws and astrology of India, about A.D.1030*, London 1910

Roerich G, *Biography of Dharmasvāmin. A Tibetan Monk Pilgrim*, Patna 1959
Chappell D.W, 'Early Forebodings of the Death of Buddhism', *Numen* 27 (1980), pp.122–53
Nattier J, *Once Upon a Future Time, Studies in a Buddhist Prophecy of Decline*, Berkeley 1991
Ritti S, 'Buddhism in Kannada Inscriptions', from *Ratna Chandrikā*, ed. D. Handa and A. Agrawal, New Delhi 1989, pp.315–21
Waley A, 'New Light on Buddhism in Medieval India', *Mélanges Chinois et Bouddhiques* 1 (1931–2), pp.355–76
Yocum G.E, 'Buddhism Through Hindu Eyes: Saivas and Buddhists in Medieval Tamilnad', from *Traditions in Contact and Change*, ed. P. Slater and D. Wiebe, pp.143–62 and 690–3

19 Sri Lanka

Buddhāpadāna
—Mellick-Cutler S, 'A Critical Edition, with translation, of Selected Portions of the Pāli Apadāna' (D.Phil. thesis), Oxford 1993
Cūlavaṁsa
—Geiger W, *Cūlavaṁsa, being the more recent part of the Mahāvaṁsa*, tr. C. Mabel Rickmers, Colombo 1953
Dīpavaṁsa
—Oldenberg H, *Dīpavaṁsa*, London 1897
Mahāvaṁsa
—Geiger W, *Mahāvaṁsa, The Great Chronicle of Ceylon*, Colombo 1950
Vimuttimagga
—Ehara N.R.M, Soma Thera, Kheminda Thera, *The Path of Freedom by Arahant Upatissa*, Colombo 1961
Visuddhimagga
—Ñyāṇamoli, *The Path of Purification (Visuddhimagga)*, Boulder and London 1976

Commentaries
The commentaries as a whole are still not translated, but portions of them are available in the following:

—Bhikkhu Bodhi *The Discourse on the All-Embracing Net of Views*, Kandy 1989 (commentary by Buddhaghosa and sub-commentary by Dhammapāla on the *Brahmajāla Sutta*)
—Bhikkhu Bodhi *The Discourse on the Root of Existence*, Kandy 1980 (same for the *Mūlaparyāya Sutta*)
—Bhikkhu Bodhi *The Great Discourse on Causation*, Kandy 1984 (same for the *Mahānidāna Sutta*)
—Burlingame E.W, *Buddhist Legends*, 3 vols., Harvard 1921 (reprinted Oxford 1990) (stories edited from the *Dhammapada* commentary by Buddhaghosa)
—Carter J.R. and Palihawadana M, *The Dhammapada*, New York 1987 (contains the philological content of the *Dhammapada* commentary)

Adikaram E.W, *Early History of Buddhism in Ceylon*, Migoda 1946
Bechert H, 'Theravāda Buddhist Sangha: Some General Observations on Historical and Political Factors in its Development', *Journal of Asian Studies* 29 (1970), pp.761–78
Bechert H, 'Mahāyāna Literature in Sri Lanka: The Early Phase', from *Prajñāpāramitā and Related Systems*, ed. Lewis Lancaster, Berkeley 1977, pp.361–7
Bechert H, 'On the Identification of Buddhist Schools in Early Sri Lanka', from *Indology and Law: Studies in Honour of Prof. J. Duncan M. Derrett*, ed. G. Santheimer and P.K. Aithal, Wiesbaden 1982, pp.60–76
Bechert H, 'Buddha-field and Transfer of Merit in a Theravāda Source', IIJ 35 (1992), pp.95–108
Buddhadatta 'The Second Great Commentator, Ācariya-Dhammapāla', *University of Ceylon Review*, iii pp.49–57
Gombrich R, 'Merit Transference in Sinhalese Buddhism: a case study of the interaction between doctrine and practice', *History of Religions* 11 (1971), pp.203–19
Gombrich R, *Precept and Practice, Traditional Buddhism in the rural highlands of Ceylon*, Oxford 1971
Gombrich R, *Theravāda Buddhism*, London 1988, later chapters
Holt J.C, *Buddha in the Crown: Avalokiteśvara in the Buddhist Traditions of Sri Lanka*, Oxford 1991
Malalasekera G.P, *The Pāli Literature of Ceylon*, Colombo 1928
Norman K.R, 'The Role of Pali in Early Sinhalese Buddhism', in *Buddhism in Ceylon and studies on religious syncretism in Buddhist countries*, ed. H. Bechert, Göttingen 1978, pp.28–47
Paranavitana S, 'Bodhisattva Avalokitesvara in Ceylon', in *B.C. Law Volume* 2, Calcutta 1946, pp.15–18
Rahula W, *History of Buddhism in Ceylon*, 2nd ed., Colombo 1966

Schopen G, 'The Text on the "Dhāraṇī Stones from Abhayagiriya": A Minor Contribution to the Study of Mahāyāna Literature in Ceylon', JIABS 5 (1982), pp.100–08

Smith B.L, 'Kingship, the Sangha, and the Process of Legitimation in Anurādhapura Ceylon: an Interpretive Essay', from *Buddhism in Ceylon and studies on religious syncretism in Buddhist countries*, ed. H. Bechert, Göttingen 1978, pp.100–26

Smith B.L, *Religion and the Legitimation of Power in Sri Lanka*, Chambersburg 1978

20 South-east Asia

Coedes G, *The Making of South East Asia*, London 1966

Coedes G, *The Indianized States of Southeast Asia*, Honolulu 1968

Lester R, *Theravāda Buddhism in Southeast Asia*, Ann Arbor, Mich. 1972

Smith B.L, ed. *Religion and the Legitimation of Power in Thailand, Laos and Burma*, Chambersburg 1978

Tantric or Esoteric Theravāda

Bizot F, *Le figuier à cinq branches, Recherches sur le bouddhisme khmer I*, PEFEO, vol.CVII, Paris 1976

Bizot F, 'La grotte de la naissance', *Recherches sur le bouddhisme khmer II*, BEFEO, vol.LXVII, Paris, pp.222–73

Bizot F, *Le don de soi-même, Recherches sur le bouddhisme khmer III*, PEFEO, vol.CXXX, Paris 1981

Bizot F, *Les traditions de la pabbajjā en Asie du Sud-Est, Recherches sur le bouddhisme khmer IV*, Göttingen 1988

Coedes G, 'Dhammakāya', *Adyar Library Bulletin* 20 (1956), pp.254ff.

Reynolds F, 'The Several Bodies of Buddha: Reflections on a neglected aspect of the Theravāda tradition', *History of Religions* 16 (1977), pp.374–89

Rhys Davids T.W, *Yogāvacara's Manual*, London 1896 (rep. 1981)

Skilling P, 'The Rakṣā Literature of the Śrāvakayāna', JPTS XVI (1992), pp.109–82

Burma

Lokapaññatti

—Denis E, *La Lokapaññatti et les idées cosmologiques du bouddhisme ancien*, three volumes, Lille 1977

Saddanīti

—Smith H, *Saddanīti*, Lund 1928–66

Ray N, *Sanskrit Buddhism in Burma*, Amsterdam 1936

Ray N, *An Introduction to the Study of Theravāda Buddhism in Burma*, Calcutta 1946

Ray N, *Theravāda Buddhism in Burma*, Calcutta 1956
Spiro M.E, *Burmese Supernaturalism*, New Jersey 1967
Spiro M.E, *Buddhism and Society, A great tradition and its Burmese vicissitudes*, New York 1970
Stargardt J, *The Ancient Pyu of Burma*, Cambridge 1990
Strong J, *The Legend and Cult of Upagupta: Sanskrit Buddhism in North India and Southeast Asia*, Princeton 1992

CAMBODIA

(see works of F. Bizot under 'Tantric Theravāda' above.)
Pym C, *The Ancient Civilisation of Angkor*, New York 1968

THAILAND

Prince Dhani Nivat, *A History of Buddhism in Siam*, Bangkok 1965
Tambiah S.J, *Buddhism and the Spirit Cults in North-east Thailand*, Cambridge 1975
Tambiah S.J, *World Conqueror and World Renouncer*, Cambridge 1976
Yoneo Ishii *Sangha, State and Society: Thai Buddhism in History*, tr. P. Hawkes, Kyoto 1986

VIETNAM

Thich Thien-An, *Buddhism and Zen in Vietnam in relation to the development of Buddhism in Asia*, Rutland, Vt. 1975

21 CENTRAL ASIA AND KASHMIR

Saṅgharakṣa
—Demiéville P, 'La Yogācārabhūmi de Saṅgharakṣa', BEFEO XLIV (1954), pp.339–436

Texts from Central Asia in translation
—Emmerick R.E, *The Khotanese Śūraṅgama-Samādhisūtra*, London 1970
—Emmerick R.E, *The Book of Zambasta, A Khotanese poem on Buddhism*, London 1968
—MacKenzie D.N, *The Sūtra of the Causes and Effects of Actions in Sogdian*, London

Bagchi P.C, *India and Central Asia*, Calcutta 1955
Bechert H, 'The Importance of Central Asian Manuscript Finds for Sanskrit Philology', *Journal of the Bihar Research Society* 63–4 (1977–8), pp.755–62
Gaulier S, Jera-Bezard R, Maillard M, *Buddhism in Afghanistan and Central Asia*, 2 vols., Leiden 1976
von Hinüber O, 'Buddhism in Gilgit Between India and Central Asia', from *The Countries of South Asia: Boundaries, Extensions and Inter-relations*, ed. P. Gaeffke and D.A. Utz, Philadelphia 1988, pp.40–8

Jera-Bezard R. and Maillard M, *Buddhism in Afghanistan and Central Asia*, 2 vols., Leiden 1976
Khosla S, *History of Buddhism in Kashmir*, New Delhi 1972
Litvinsky B.A, *Outline History of Buddhism in Central Asia*, Moscow 1968
Nadou J, *Buddhists of Kaśmīr*, Delhi 1980 (reprint)
Petech L, 'The Silk Road, Turfan and Tun-Huang in the first millenium A.D.', from *Turfan and Tun-Huang, The Texts*, ed. A. Cadonna, Florence 1992
Puri B.N, *Buddhism in Central Asia*, Delhi 1987
Saha K, *Buddhism and Buddhist Literature in Central Asia*, Calcutta 1970
Scott D.A, 'The Iranian Face of Buddhism', *East and West* 40 (1990), pp.43–77
Also see the article on Central Asia in the *Encyclopaedia of Buddhism*

22 China

Awakening of Faith in the Mahāyāna
—see bibliography for Chapter 16
Essay on the Golden Lion
—Theodore de Bary W, *Sources of Chinese Tradition*, 2 vols., New York and London 1960 vol.1 pp.329–33
kung-an (koan)
—Lu K'uan Yü (Charles Luk) *Ch'an and Zen Teaching (Second Series)*, London 1961 (part II, The Stories of the Founders of the Five Ch'an Sects)
—Reps P, *Zen Flesh, Zen Bones*, Harmondsworth 1971 (The Gateless Gate, a translation of Ekai's *Mumonkan*, a collection of *kung an*)
—Katsuki Sekuda *Two Zen Classics, Mumonkan and Hekiganroku*, (place of publication unknown) 1977 (two collections of *kung an*)
Platform Sūtra
—Yampolsky P, *The Platform Sūtra of the Sixth Patriarch*, New York 1967
—Wong Mou-Lam *The Sūtra of Wei Lang (or Hui Neng)*, London 1957
Śūraṅgama Sūtra
—Upasāka Lu K'uan Yü, 'The Śūraṅgama Sūtra (Leng Yen Ching)' London 1966
The Sūtra in 42 Sections
—Blofeld J, *The Sūtra of 42 Sections*, revised ed., London 1977

Buswell R.E, *Chinese Buddhist Apocrypha*, Honolulu 1990
Campany R.F, 'Notes on the Devotional Uses and Symbolic Functions of Sūtra Texts as Depicted in Early Chinese Buddhist Miracle Tales and Hagiographies', JIABS 14 (1991), pp.28–72
Chang G.C, *The Buddhist Teaching of Totality: The Philosophy of Hwa-yen Buddhism*, Pennsylvania State UP 1971
Ch'en K, *Buddhism in China, A Historical Survey*, Princeton 1964
Ch'en K, *The Chinese Transformation of Buddhism*, Princeton 1973
de Bary T, *Sources of Chinese Tradition*, New York 1960
Dumoulin H, *A History of Zen Buddhism*, Boston 1969

Harrison P, 'The Earliest Chinese Translations of Mahāyāna Buddhist Sūtras' *Buddhist Studies Review* 10 (1993), pp.135ff.
Tsukamoto Z, *History of Early Chinese Buddhism. From Its Introduction to the Death of Hui-Yuan*, tr. from Japanese by L. Hurvitz, 2 vols., Hawaii 1986
Weinstein S, *Buddhism under the T'ang*, Cambridge 1987
Wright A, *Buddhism in Chinese History*, Stanford California 1959
Zürcher E, *The Buddhist Conquest of China: The Spread and Adaptation of Buddhism in Early Medieval China*, 2 vols., Leiden 1959
Zürcher E, 'Perspectives in the Study of Chinese Buddhism', JRAS (1982), pp.161–76
Zürcher E, 'A New Look at the Earliest Chinese Buddhist Texts', from *From Benares to Beijing, Essays on Buddhism and Chinese Religion*, ed. Koichi Shinohara and G. Schopen, Oakville New York and London 1991, pp.277–304

23 Korea

Buswell R, *The Korean Approach to Zen: Collected Works of Chi-nul*, Honolulu 1983
Clark C.A, *Religions of Old Korea*, New York 1932
Lee P.H, *Lives of Eminent Korean Monks*, Cambridge, Mass. 1969
Soeng Sunim, *Korean Zen – Tradition and Teachers*, Seoul 1987

24 Japan

Seventeen Article Constitution
—Theodore de Bary W, *Sources of Japanese Tradition*, New York 1958, pp.49–53
Dōgen
—Reihō Masunaga *A Primer of Soto Zen, A Translation of Dogen's Shobogenzo Zuimonki*, London 1972
Eisai
—(see Theodore de Bary)
Hakuin
—Yampolsky P, *The Zen Master Hakuin: Selected Writings*, New York 1971
Hōnen
—(see Theodore de Bary)
Kukai
—Yoshito Hakeda *Kukai: Major Works*, New York 1972
Nichiren
—Murano S, *Rissho Ankoku Ron, or Establish the law and save our country*, Tokyo 1977
Shinran
—Suzuki D.T, *The Kyogyoshinsho*, Kyoto 1973
—Ueda Yoshifumi *The True Teaching, Practice and Realization of the Pure Land Way: A Translation of Shinran's Kyogyoshinsho*, 4 vols., Kyoto 1983–7

de Bary W.T, *Sources of the Japanese Tradition*, New York 1958
Dumoulin H, *A History of Zen Buddhism*, Boston 1969
Hanayama S, *A History of Japanese Buddhism*, Tokyo 1966
Matsunaga D. and A, *The Foundation of Japanese Buddhism*, 2 vols., Los Angeles 1974 and 1976
Taiko Yamasaki *Shingon, Japanese Esoteric Buddhism*, Boston and London 1988

25 Tibet

Bar do thos grol
—Evans-Wentz W.Y, *The Tibetan Book of the Dead*, Oxford 1960
—Fremantle F. and Chögyam Trungpa, *The Tibetan Book of the Dead*, Boulder 1975
—Thurman R.A, *The Tibetan Book of the Dead*, London 1994
Bhāvanākrama
—Tucci G, *Minor Buddhist Texts II: First Bhāvanākrama of Kamalaśīla, Sanskrit and Tibetan Texts with Introduction and English Summary*, Rome 1985
Bodhipathapradīpa
—Sherburne R. (S.J.) tr. *A Lamp for the Path and Commentary (by Atīśa)*, London 1983

Mi la ras pa
—Mi la ras pa, *The Hundred Thousand Songs of Milarepa*, 2 vols., tr. G.C.C. Chang, Boulder 1977
—Evans-Wentz W.Y, *Tibet's Great Yogi Milarepa, a Biography from the Tibetan*, 2nd ed., Oxford 1951
—Lhalungpa L, *The Life of Milarepa*, London 1987
sGam po pa, *The Jewel Ornament of Liberation*, tr. H.V. Guenther, Boston and London 1986
kLong chen rab 'byams pa, *Kindly Bent to Ease Us*, 3 vols., tr. H.V. Guenther, Emeryville 1975–6
Tsang Nyon Heruka, *The Life of Marpa the Translator*, tr. The Nālandā Translation Committee, Boulder 1982
Tsong kha pa, *Calming the Mind and Discerning the Real, Buddhist Meditation and the Middle View*, tr. A. Wayman (from the *lam rim chen mo*), New York 1978
Yeshes Tsogyal, *The Life and Liberation of Padmasambhava*, tr. K. Douglas and G. Bays, Emeryville California 1978

Broido M, 'The Jo-nang-Pas on Madhyamaka: A Sketch', *Tibet Journal* 14, 1989, pp.86–90
Chattopadhyaya A, *Atīśa and Tibet*, Calcutta 1967
Demiéville P, *Le Concile de Lhasa*, Paris 1952
'Gos lo-tsa-ba, *The Blue Annals*, tr. G. Roerich, Delhi 1976 (a 15th century history of Buddhism in Tibet)

Hookham S.K, *The Buddha Within; Tathāgatagarbha Doctrine According to the Shentong Interpretation of the Ratnagotravibhāga*, Albany 1991
Kvaerne P, 'Aspects of the Origin of the Buddhist Tradition in Tibet', in *Numen*, 19 (1972), pp.22–40
Ruegg D.S, 'The Jo Nang Pas: A School of Buddhist Ontologists According to the grub mtha' sel gyi me lon', JAOS 83 (1963), pp.73–91
Samuel G, *Civilized Shamans: Buddhism in Tibetan Societies*, Washington and London 1993
Snellgrove D, *Indo-Tibetan Buddhism: Indian Buddhists and Their Tibetan Successors*, Boston 1987
Tucci G, *The Religions of Tibet*, Berkeley California 1972
Wilson J.B, 'Pudgalavāda in Tibet? Assertions of Substantially Existent Selves in the Writings of Tsong-kha-pa and His Followers', JIABS 14 (1991), pp.155–80

26 Mongolia

Hessig W, *The Religions of Mongolia*, Los Angeles 1979
Siklós B, 'Buddhism in Mongolia' from *The World's Religions: The Religions of Asia*, ed. F. Hardy, London 1990, pp.279–85

27 Nepal

Allen M.R, 'Buddhism without Monks: the Vajrayana Religion of the Newars of the Kathmandu Valley', *South Asia* 2 (1973), pp.1–14
Gellner D, 'Hodgson's Blind Alley? On the So-Called Schools of Nepalese Buddhism', JIABS 12 (1989), pp.7–19
Gellner D, 'Monk, Householder, and Priest: What the Three Yānas Mean to Newar Buddhists', from *Buddhist Forum: Seminar papers 1987–8*, ed. T. Skorupski, London 1990, pp.115–32
Gellner D, 'The Perfection of Wisdom' – A Text and Its Uses in Kwā Bahā, Lalitpur, from *Change and Continuity in the Nepalese Culture of the Kathmandu Valley*, ed. S. Lienhard, Turin CESMEO 1992
Gellner D, *Monk, Householder, and Tantric Priest: Newar Buddhism and its Hierarchy of Ritual*, Cambridge 1992
Locke J, *Karuṇamaya: The Cult of Avalokiteśvara-Matsyendranāth in the Valley of Nepal*, Kathmandu 1980
Mitra R, *The Sanskrit Buddhist Literature of Nepal*, New Delhi 1981 (reprint, originally published 1882)
Shaha R, *Ancient and Medieval Nepal*, New Delhi 1992

28 Persia

Ball W, 'How Far did Buddhism Spread West?', *Al Rafidan* X (1989), pp.1–11

Barthold W, 'Der Iranisches Buddhismus und Sein Verhältnis zum Islam', from *Oriental Studies in Honour of C.E. Pavry*, ed. J.D.C. Pavry, London 1933, pp.29–31

Bulliet R.W, 'Naw Bahār and the Survival of Iranian Buddhism', *Iran: Journal of Persian Studies* 14 (1976), pp.140–5

Gimaret D, 'Bouddha et les Bouddhistes dans la Tradition Musulmane', *Journal Asiatique* 257 (1969), pp.272–316

Jahn K, 'Kamālashrī-Rashīd Al-Dīn's "Life and Teaching of the Buddha", A source for the Buddhism of the Mongol Period', *Central Asiatic Journal* 11 (1956), pp.81–128

Lanman C.R, *A Sanskrit Reader, Text and Vocabulary and Notes*, Cambridge Mass. 1884 (reprinted 1967), pp.310–15

Melikian-Chirvani A.S, 'L'Évocation Litteraire du Bouddhisme dans l'Iran Musulman', *Le Monde Iranian et l'Islam* II (1974), pp.1–72

Melikian-Chirvani A.S, 'Recherches sur l'Architecture de l'Iran Bouddhique', *Le Monde Iranian et l'Islam* III (1975), pp.1–61 (with 12 plates)

Rhys Davids T.W, *Buddhist Birth-Stories*, London 1880 (reprinted Varanasi 1973) pp.xxvii–xxxix

Schopen G, 'Hīnayāna Texts in a 14th Century Persian Chronicle', in *Central Asiatic Journal* 26 (1982), pp.226–35

Stern S.M. and Walzer S, *Three Unknown Buddhist Stories in an Arabic Version*, Oxford 1971

Abbreviations

BEFEO	*Bulletin d'École Française d'Extrême-Orient*
BSOAS	*Bulletin of the School of Oriental and African Studies*
IBK	*Indogaku Bukkyogaku Kenkyū*
IIJ	*Indo-Iranian Journal*
JAOS	*Journal of the American Oriental Society*
JIABS	*Journal of the International Association of Buddhist Studies*
JIP	*Journal of Indian Philosophy*
JPTS	*Journal of the Pali Text Society*
JRAS	*Journal of the Royal Asiatic Society*
PEFEO	*Publications d'École Française d'Extrême-Orient*
WZKS	*Wiener Zeitschrift für die Kunde Südasiens*

Index

The Windhorse symbolizes the energy of the enlightened mind carrying the Three Jewels – the Buddha, the Dharma, and the Sangha – to all sentient beings.

Buddhism is one of the fastest growing spiritual traditions in the Western world. Throughout its 2,500-year history, it has always succeeded in adapting its mode of expression to suit whatever culture it has encountered.

Windhorse Publications aims to continue this tradition as Buddhism comes to the West. Today's Westerners are heirs to the entire Buddhist tradition, free to draw instruction and inspiration from all the many schools and branches. Windhorse publishes works by authors who not only understand the Buddhist tradition but are also familiar with Western culture and the Western mind.

For orders and catalogues contact

WINDHORSE PUBLICATIONS
11 PARK ROAD
BIRMINGHAM
B13 8AB
UK

WINDHORSE PUBLICATIONS INC
14 HEARTWOOD CIRCLE
NEWMARKET
NH 03857
USA

Windhorse Publications is an arm of the Friends of the Western Buddhist Order, which has more than forty centres on four continents. Through these centres, members of the Western Buddhist Order offer regular programmes of events for the general public and for more experienced students. These include meditation classes, public talks, study on Buddhist themes and texts, and 'bodywork' classes such as t'ai chi, yoga, and massage. The FWBO also runs several retreat centres and the Karuna Trust, a fundraising charity that supports social welfare projects in the slums and villages of India.

Many FWBO centres have residential spiritual communities and ethical businesses associated with them. Arts activities are encouraged too, as is the development of strong bonds of friendship between people who share the same ideals. In this way the FWBO is developing a unique approach to Buddhism, not simply as a set of techniques, less still as an exotic cultural interest, but as a creatively directed way of life for people living in the modern world.

If you would like more information about the FWBO please write to

LONDON BUDDHIST CENTRE
51 ROMAN ROAD
LONDON
E2 0HU
UK

ARYALOKA
HEARTWOOD CIRCLE
NEWMARKET
NH 03857
USA

Also From Windhorse

SANGHARAKSHITA
A Guide to the Buddhist Path

Which Buddhist teachings really matter? How does one begin to practise them in a systematic way? Without a guide one can easily get dispirited or lost.

In this highly readable anthology a leading Western Buddhist sorts out fact from myth, essence from cultural accident, to reveal the fundamental ideals and teachings of Buddhism. The result is a reliable map of the Buddhist path that anyone can follow.

Sangharakshita is an ideal companion on the path. As founder of a major Western Buddhist movement he has helped thousands of people to make an effective contact with the richness and beauty of the Buddha's teachings.

256 pages, with illustrations
ISBN 1 899579 04 4
£12.50/$24.95

SUBHUTI
Sangharakshita: A New Voice in the Buddhist Tradition

Sangharakshita was one of the first Westerners to make the journey to the East and to don the monk's yellow robe. In India he gained unique experience in the main traditions of Buddhist teaching and practice. His involvement with the 'mass conversion' of ex-Untouchable Hindus to Buddhism exposed him to a revolutionary new experiment in social transformation. More recently he founded one of the most successful Buddhist movements in the modern world - pioneering a 'living Buddhism' that seems ideally suited to our times.

Highly respected as an outspoken writer and commentator, he has never been afraid to communicate his insights and views, even if they challenge venerated elements of Buddhist tradition.

But what are those insights and views? How have they arisen and developed? Here one of Sangharakshita's leading disciples offers an account of his evolution as a thinker and teacher.

336 pages
ISBN 0 904766 68 3
£9.99/$19.95